Matrilineal Communities, Patriarchal Realities

Matrilineal Communities, Patriarchal Realities
A Feminist Nirvana Uncovered

Kanchana N. Ruwanpura

The University of Michigan Press
Ann Arbor

Matrilineal Communities, Patriarchal Realities
A Feminist Nirvana Uncovered

Published in the United States of America by the University of Michigan Press
First published in 2006 by Zubaan, an imprint of Kali for Women
Manufactured in India

Copyright © 2006 by Kanchana N. Ruwanpura

All rights reserved

2009   2008   2007   2006   4   3   2   1

No part of this publication may be reproduced, stored in a retrieval system, or transmitted in any form or by any means, electronic, mechanical, or otherwise, without the written permission of the publisher.

Library of Congress Cataloging-in-Publication Data applied for

ISBN-13: 978-0-472-09977-1 (cloth)
ISBN-10: 0-472-09977-9 (cloth)
ISBN-13: 978-0-472-06977-4 (paper)
ISBN-10: 0-472-06977-2 (paper)

*First, I dedicate this work to my ammi and thaththi
And then equally, to the many women in Eastern
Sri Lanka who gave their time to make
this research possible*

Acknowledgements

This book was embarked upon in one location and brought to fruition in another. During this time I have traversed different spaces and places where numerous people, directly or indirectly, helped me achieve closure on this project. The mentoring, sharing of knowledge, encouragement, and friendship offered by them is noted with appreciation.

The initial research gestation began in Cambridge, England many years ago. Jane Humphries and Tony Lawson's role as politically sound feminists, political economists and methodologists was influential in ensuring that links between theory and practice were maintained throughout my work.

Even as Jane and Tony have been sound and engaged mentors, I could not have done the bulk of the research without the countless women in eastern Sri Lanka who took time to share their experiences with me. Despite the difficult and demanding conditions in which they live, the time they gave me has been fundamental to this work. Their kindness and generosity in making my year of fieldwork rewarding intellectually, socially, and emotionally is sincerely appreciated.

I would also like to mention many activists from eastern Sri Lanka who welcomed my project with enthusiasm, opening their homes, making the necessary connections with local communities and institutions and setting me up in Ampara,

Batticaloa, and Trincomalee. I should especially mention Simon Harris, Chithra Maunaguru, Maithreyai Prabakaran, P. Senthurajah, Daniel Sinnathamby and Satha Vivekanandan for facilitating my access to the unknown territory of eastern Sri Lanka. They made it possible for me to work with/through the Affected Women's Forum (AWF) and Social Welfare Organization of Ampara District (SWOAD) in Ampara, SURYA – Women's Development Center and World-University Services of Canada (WUSC) in Batticaloa, and Family Rehabilitation Center (FRC) and OXFAM in Trincomalee. I also need to thank Manjula, Krishna, Hidaya, Dhana, Logitha, Mallika, Jeevaka, Sitthi, Yamuna, and Shanthini for research assistance, sensitizing me to "cultural" issues and guiding me through their hometowns. Similarly, my thanks to Durga, Deepa, Gauthami, Jayanthi, Maithrayei, Sarojini, Thillai, Vani, Vijayalakshmi, Vasuki and the Prabakaran family for hearty meals, friendship and assistance provided at all times. The high point of my research was my time in eastern Sri Lanka, and all of them undoubtedly made this possible.

There are three Sri Lankans I need to make a special note of. During my fieldwork the guidance on touching base with persons in the NGO sector in eastern Sri Lanka was initially made possible by Malathi de Alwis (International Center for Ethnic Studies) and Kumari Jayawardena (Social Scientist Association). They have also kindly read various drafts of my work and have attempted to make sure that I remain firmly grounded in the political realities of present-day Sri Lanka and that my research captures the rich and complex nuances of our social world. Similarly, a kindly aunt, Aurasie nandi, in non-apparent ways supported my academic endeavours by talking up the importance of academic engagement with my extended family – when "good" Sri Lankan girls (we are never quite women until we get married, presumably) should be getting married rather than pursuing higher education!

Returning to revise this manuscript was possible because of my slow drift back into academia through a generous Humboldt Research Fellowship awarded by the Alexander von Humboldt

Stiftung. For this, my heartfelt gratitude to Stephan Klasen (University of Göttingen) who coaxed me, despite my many reservations, to spend time at the Ludwig Maximilians University (Munich) and take-up the prestigious fellowship offered by AvH. He created the space and precious time necessary to return to my research work, and it is his strong support, positive encouragement, and quiet enthusiasm that instilled in me the necessary confidence to publish this research. The careful mentoring offered by Stephan was immensely valuable in making my academic experience in Munich a positive one and creating a suitable context for disseminating my research.

In writing up my research over several years many people have assisted me by sharing their skills and cheerfulness. Roger Butcher and Nitinant need a special mention for their role in helping me get through the data-analysis process as painlessly as possible! Ted, Rod, Brian, Derek (N), Derek (T), Anne Ellis, Sabine Mennella, Pam Sanford, and Jan Peterson made dreary winter days in Cambridge and Munich cheery! The support from Laurie Friday, Michael J. Payne, Catherine Seville and especially Augusta McMahon (all of Newnham College) is acknowledged for smoothing out "nightmare" occasions. For coming across kindly souls in the shape and form of Dr Carol Mowat, Professor Roger Pederson, Carole Robinson, and a guardian angel, Derek Nicholson, I need to convey my many thanks. But finalizing this text was made easier with the help of Ann Newton (*Cambridge Journal of Economics*) who was a thorough and patient editor.

My financial stresses of graduate study, on which this manuscript is based, were greatly reduced by many generous funds awarded to me. The vote of confidence on the part of the American Association of University Women who awarded me an International Fellowship paved the way for many other sources of funding; the Allen, Meek and Read Trust Award (Board of Graduate Studies), the Cambridge Commonwealth Trust, the Cambridge Political Economy Society Trust, the Dorothy Leet Fellowship (International Association of University

Women), the Marion Kennedy Research Studentship, the Vivian Stewart Bursary and many GARS awards by Newnham College.

Likewise, the initial fieldwork in Sri Lanka was made possible with awards from the Bartele Frere Exhibition award (Old Schools), the Gamble Fund (Newnham College), the Smuts Memorial Fund (Board of Graduate Studies), and the Suzy Paine Travel Fund (Faculty of Economics and Politics). Additionally, travel awards from Newnham College to participate in and present my work at various conferences are also noted with thanks.

Writing and revising a manuscript has its ups and downs, during which times circles of friendships greatly matter. I was fortunat in being able to draw upon these dependable networks in more ways than one – including sharing my joys and frustrations of doing research across the miles via e-mail. Ana, Annabella, Antje, Antonis, Anushka, Ahila, Ariane, Auret, Azra, Bahar, Carola, Cedric, Christoph, Cindy, Claudio, Dave, Derek, Emma, Eileen, Eva, Farana, Fatmata, Fernando, Hedi, Aunty Indra, Geetu, Geremia, Jane, Kodi, Lalith, Laura, Lisa, Ludovica, Mara, Margarit, Margaret, Mark, Mihaela, Mirco, Muriel, Nicole, Nimanthi, Nitinant, Olga, Petra, Pumla, Paolo, Pierpaolo, Rahul, Sarasali, Tere, Terri, Thierry and Thush are remembered for their caring friendships at various moments and phases.

Equally, I have fortunately come across gentle, kind and friendly colleagues, their partners, and engaging/caring students who have created enabling surroundings. Alan, Alex, Bahar, Brad, Cerri, Charu, Chloe, Dia, Dan, David, Eric, Gary, Geoff G., George, Geoffrey, Helen, James, James-Henry, Jen, Judith, Lars, Leanne, Lee, Lisa, Lowell, Pasad, Pat, Sacra, Sandra, Sara, Scott, Sherrow, Randy, Ronny, Teresa, Thelma, and Ulla generously extended themselves at various points. These times have included supporting my teaching, research, and professional endeavours as well as the more mundane details, such as helping me furnish empty apartments, last minute proof-reading, bringing soup, food, flowers, chauffeuring me to hospital and grocery stores when in ill-health.

x *Matrilineal Communities, Patriarchal Realities*

All these people have kept me at this research process in more ways than they realize. I, however, need to make a special note of two people: Antonis, for being a near and dear friend during the past years, and Christoph: his initial encouragement and support was vital in continuing with my graduate studies and getting to this point.

My greatest debt in making me pursue and stay in a research career is due to my dedicated intellectual mentors. They have closely and kindly watched, encouraged, and actively supported my intellectual growth during its different phases. I make note of Chris Gunn, Geoff Gilbert, Bernie Lanciaux, David Ost, Anu Seth and Bill Waller (William Smith College), Manuela Tomei and David Kucera (International Labour Organization), Chuck Craypo, Esther-Mirjam Sent, and David Ruccio (University of Notre Dame). Thanks also to Chris Bramall (University of Sheffield) and David Sneath (University of Cambridge) for quietly encouraging various academic endeavours during my time at Cambridge, and Randy Albelda (University of Massachusetts-Boston), Suzanne Bergeron (University of Michigan -Dearbon), Gary Dymski (University of California-Riverside), and Steve Fleetwood (Lancaster University) for intellectual and moral support in staying firmly grounded in academia.

However, I have to especially express my immense gratitude to Anu, Chris, Bill, David R., Stephan and Randy for being mentors who went above and beyond their call of duty. They have enriched my intellectual trajectory in multiple ways and my guardian angels on earth they surely have been!

Raphael Allen at the University of Michigan Press helped to cultivate this end result for the USA readership, while Urvashi Butalia, Jaya Bhattacharji, and Preeti Gill at Zubaan Books/Kali for Women nurtured the research into book form from its early stages. Upeksha and Damayanthi provided initial inspirations for the cover page, while Jeff patiently worked on refining and redesigning it to meet the competing demands of the co-publishers and myself: undoubtedly not an easy task for him!

Their support and patience was crucial in bringing to close in what seemed like an endless process once upon a time.

Last, but not least, I am immensely indebted to my family. My thanks to malli for his crazy chats, cryptic e-mails and quiet encouragement, and a special mention of nangi for coming across the miles and putting me back to fine health and good spirits after a cycling accident. Most crucially, however, it is necessary to convey this sense of immense gratitude that I feel towards ammi and thaththi for the sacrifices they have made to help me realize my potential capabilities.

Contents

Acknowledgements   vi

One
Introduction: Unpacking A Feminist Nirvana   1

Two
Diverse Households: Literature on Female-headship   14

Three
The "Grand" and "Meta" Narratives: Situating Sri Lankan
Female-heads   29

Four
Matrilineal Muslims: Female-heads in the
Muslim Community   51

Five
Variation on a Theme: Sinhala Female-heads in Hybrid
Lineage Systems   71

Six
Matriclan Ideologies and Patriarchal Structures:
Female-headship among Tamils   95

Seven
Dutiful Daughters, Sacrificing Sons   117

Eight
Juggling Acts: Political, Economic and Social Realities   144

Nine
Nearing Limits or Pushing Boundaries?   174

Ten
Conclusion: Interested Engagement—Feminist Issues in
Development Economics   204

Appendix A
Map of Sri Lanka   213

Appendix B
Sample Questionnaire for Female-headed Households   215

Appendix C
Data Analysis: Methods, Motivations and Outcomes   226

References   232

ONE

Introduction

Unpacking A Feminist Nirvana

Introducing Sri Lanka: A Fool's Paradise?

Development economists often consider Sri Lanka to be an exemplar of human development (Sen 1981: 301–9, 1984a: 496, Anand and Kanbur 1995, Basu 1995: 373–81). Prima facie, there are very good reasons for doing so. Sri Lanka's performance in the social and human development sphere is impressive, and it has been achieved despite its low per capita income as well as the protracted and bloody ethnic conflict (Sen 1981, 1984a, 1988, UNDP 2001).[1] But it is not only Sri Lanka's human and social progress that is lauded by development economists. The country is highly regarded even among feminist economists for the relatively favourable position of its women, reflected in the egalitarian achievements in gender-based human development indices (HDIs) as well as matrilineal and bilateral inheritance patterns and property rights (Sen 1984b: 383–4, Agarwal 1990, 1996, Humphries 1993: 228, Klasen 1993: 23). What validity do these assessments have when translated into women's capabilities at the micro-level? Are they hasty conclusions that

---

[1] At one level these latest figures are problematic, as from 1983 they have not included the Northern and Eastern Provinces of Sri Lanka. However, indices for the period prior to the ethnic conflict were also impressive, and these were based on all-island figures.

need closer scrutiny? Does a detailed search reveal many paradoxes in this serendipitous island?

I use female-headship[2] as the entry point for this study. My concern is the need for caution, especially on the part of feminist economists, in reading Sri Lanka as a feminist nirvana. I use a feminist framework to examine the eastern Sri Lankan[3] experience and uncover the patriarchal ideology and institutions that continue to influence the lives and choices of local women. By focusing on changing household formations, structures and relations and the playing out of gender relations within these units, I illustrate, using case studies, how female heads of households (henceforth referred to in this book as 'female-heads'), irrespective of ethnicity, remain trapped in patriarchal community structures. Using this focal point I unravel the patriarchal assumptions underlying economic readings of the household, where the household is treated as an isolated unit without social, historical and political dimensions (Humphries 1998b: 223–4). My purpose is to include such issues as gender, ethnicity and changing household formation in eastern Sri Lanka, hitherto left out of development literature (Aturupane, Rodrigo and Perera 1997). I also advocate the need for a critical standpoint to enhance insight into social realities and complexities. My contention is that social structures in eastern Sri Lanka are embedded in patriarchal systems that manifest themselves in distinct ways for female-heads across ethnic communities. In addition, this exercise enables me to contribute towards feminist theorizing of the household. My study of female-headship in eastern Sri Lanka describes and explores specific kinds of household formation and relationships within them.

---

[2] From a feminist perspective, using "female-headship" as an analytical category may be subject to criticism. In feminist discourse, "female" refers to a biological category rather than a social one. Feminist literature in development discourse, however, uses "female-headship" as a social concept. I abide by social convention, even though this is an issue that needs to be debated in development studies.

[3] A map of Sri Lanka is attached as Appendix A.

Introduction 3

In this chapter I begin by developing a feminist analysis of the patriarchal structures and ideologies that operate within eastern Sri Lanka. I then outline the structure of the book to guide readers through the arguments I make in the subsequent chapters. This examination discloses patriarchal structures as a prominent feature of the Sri Lankan social fabric. These findings mean feminist economists need to be cautious in applauding Sri Lanka's gender-based HDI achievements and/or matrilineal communities. Uncritical optimism may place one in a fool's paradise.

Positioning Women in Gradations of Patriarchy

Present day Sri Lanka is a multi-ethnic and multi-religious society. According to the 1981 Census Sinhalese are the majority, with 74.0 per cent of the population. Tamils comprise 18.2 per cent, of which Sri Lankan Tamils make up 12.6 per cent and Tamils of recent Indian origin the remaining 5.6 per cent. Muslims form 7.4 per cent while the remaining 0.4 per cent of the population is made up, by Malays, Burghers (Eurasians) and others. According to the same census, the religious affiliations given indicate that 67.0 per cent are Buddhists, 18.0 per cent Hindus, 7.0 per cent Muslims, and 8.0 per cent Christians (Jayawardena 1992: 163).[4]

Ethnicity in Sri Lanka is not closely linked to either religion or language. Muslims and Tamils are identified as the Tamil-speaking community, but have distinct religious identities.

---

[4] An all-island census, with attempts to include the Northern and Eastern Provinces, was carried out in Sri Lanka in 2001 after a two-decade period, and was finalized in July 2001. While the preliminary rounds of the census were done in districts in the Northern and Eastern Provinces, the final count was carried out only in 18 districts (Sri Lanka has a total of 24 districts). The final census was once again not carried out in many of the districts in Northern and Eastern Provinces for security reasons – i.e. because the Liberation Tamil Tigers for Eelam (LTTE) explicitly forbade people living in the Northern and Eastern Provinces to co-operate with census reporting. For this reason, I continue to rely on the 1981 census to provide more accurate estimates of the ethnic composition in Sri Lanka.

4 Matrilineal Communities, Patriarchal Realities

Muslims practise Islam and Tamils largely identify with Hinduism. Language separates Sinhalese and Tamils, groups that also have distinct religious affiliations, with the Sinhalese being primarily Buddhist and Tamils mostly Hindus. However, some Sinhalese and Tamils are Christians. In addition, of course, there is an array of religious practices that "Sinhala-Buddhists" have adopted whose roots can be traced to the Hindu tradition, clouding distinct ethno-religious and ethno-linguistic identities even further. Nationalist discourse on ethnic formation slides through such diversity by assuming homogeneity and downplaying the inherent contradictions of class, gender, caste and other interests within each group. Moreover, recent anthropological work suggests that the roots of Sri Lanka's population, across ethnic groups, are primarily in southern India, with common kinship structures being shared by all three ethnic groups (Guneratne 2001).[5] Various historical processes have contributed to the formation of ethnic identities in the region (ibid: 22). Which aspects of identity become prominent at any historical juncture is an outcome of the prevailing social and political circumstances, indicating the fluidity of ethnic, caste, cultural, and religious constructs (ibid: 22–5).[6]

In this multi-ethnic and multi-religious country how do patriarchal interests operate? Sri Lankan women are surely not constrained by classical patriarchy, and feminists have claimed that Sri Lankan women are relatively well positioned in the South Asian region (Agarwal 1996). Matrilineal practices in eastern Sri Lanka have distracted feminists from other aspects of women's status and position. I argue that this should not preclude a feminist analysis of the patriarchal institutions and

---

[5] The system of cross-cousin marriage shared by the Sinhalese, eastern Muslims and Tamils as well as Jaffna Tamils is an important signpost of shared kinship structures throughout these communities (ibid:34).

[6] For an excellent collection of essays on the intrinsic instabilities of ethnic formation in Sri Lanka, see Jeganathan and Ismail (1995); on Sinhala people see Scott (1995). On Tamil nationalism and women, see Maunaguru (1995) and Ismail (2000); and on Muslim identity formation, see Ismail (1995) and Samaraweera (1997).

ideologies within the Sri Lankan context. I position Sri Lankan women within gradations of patriarchy by beginning with a brief overview of the main religious traditions, Buddhism, Hinduism, and Islam, and the ways in which patriarchal interests are promoted through religious practices in the Sri Lankan context of ethno-nationalism.

Buddhism, the main religion in the country, has played a crucial role in forming Sri Lankan culture. Despite claims of a "feminist paradise", it sends dual messages to women in the Sri Lankan context (Jayawardena 1986: 110, Agarwal 1990, 1996). Women are able to move out of patriarchal society by joining the clergy, and they do not face other oppressive social practices, such as *sati/suttee* (ibid: 111). But Buddhism has been construed for Sinhala nationalist ideological purposes. The Sinhala-Buddhist movements at the turn of the 20th century revived 15th century poetry, such as the *Kavyasekeraya* and *Salalihini Sandesaya*, to promote patriarchal notions of the ideal woman and mother (ibid: 113–4). Promoting ethnically-based nationalist ideology requires a particular construction of womanhood, since women are perceived as vehicles for reproducing and socializing ethnic identities (Jayawardena 1992: 162). So while Buddhism offers some freedom to women, the patriarchal structures within which Sri Lankan women live are not challenged and women's subordination remains a pervasive feature of the social structure (ibid: 178).[7] Such dual messages are also translated at this current juncture of ethnic conflict into ideals of moral motherhood and women warriors, translating ethno-nationalist patriarchal interest into everyday practices (de Alwis 1998).

Turning to the Tamil nationalist project and its impact on women, the *Thirukkual* offered paternal protection to women, but in a context of ethnic conflict and social upheaval there have been shifts and compromises (Coomaraswamy 1996: 8).

---

[7] Not only Sinhala-Buddhist ideology but also Buddhism itself sends dual messages to women, with a patriarchal notion on the role of womanhood running right through the *Sigalovadha Sutrya* – which is a verse from the Buddhist scriptures on "rightful conduct" for lay-people.

6 *Matrilineal Communities, Patriarchal Realities*

These rapid social and political changes have been incorporated in diverse ways into the Tamil nationalist identity, and are embedded now in the ideal of an armed virgin, promoted by the Liberation Tamil Tigers for Eelam (LTTE). This provides a classic example of how patriarchal ideals have been bent towards Tamil nationalist ends (ibid: 9). Controlling women's sexuality through images of purity is common parlance in Tamil nationalist discourse (ibid: 10, Maunaguru 1995: 169–72). Moreover, by reconstructing Hindu-inspired legendary and classical literature, Tamil nationalism employs notions of motherhood to elevate the nurturing role of its women as well (ibid: 161). Through ideological notions of woman and mother, Tamil-Hindu cultural ascriptions are homogenized with these multiple patriarchal positions constructed at particular junctures, leaving limited space for feminist struggles against patriarchal appropriation (ibid: 174). Consequently, gender relations are central to the Tamil nationalist project, and when I evaluate female-heads in matrilineal Tamil communities in eastern Sri Lanka I do so against a background of such issues. It is important to acknowledge the prevalence of patriarchal structures and ideologies even among matrilineal communities.

Muslim women, too, have been measured against similar gender roles as bearers and reproducers of ethnic markers based on ethno-religious conceptualizations. Early attempts at identity formation among Muslims are noted for their gender and class rigidity. Representations of women's relegation to the private sphere and domestic labour help reproduce such divisions (Ismail 1995: 76). Religion was used in the 1980s to reify these gender-based formations of Muslim identity in an increasingly ethno-nationalist Sri Lanka (ibid: 76). Against this backdrop, a cursory overview of displaced Muslim women in the East Province notes the "cultural constraints and controls by male religious leaders" which restrict the economic options available to Muslim women (Samuel 1994: 16). Although matrilineal practices are the basis for kinship formation among eastern Muslims, they alone do not negate the patriarchal ideologies that seep through social structures, controlling the interests and rights of Muslim women. The main ideological message coming from each ethno-religious background, despite individual nuances, is that women's roles must be those of the good wife and mother. Rigid and patriarchal gender images cut across ethnicity and religion. These images and their hold over women bear upon the economic survival strategies of female-headed households, sometimes leading these households to poverty and economic deprivation.

Each social, historical, political and cultural milieu, then, leads to a particular manifestation of patriarchal practices, with possible variations even within a country and, I would argue, ethnic group (Bhasin 1993: 5). Differences must be studied so as to offer more coherent explanations of patriarchal complexities. Patriarchal structures and ideologies must be traced through the many layers in which they operate, creating and reinforcing the patriarchal order at multiple levels (ibid: 9–12). I investigate the particular position of Sri Lankan women against the backdrop of religion, kinship, and ethnicity to trace the different ways in which female-heads in the Muslim, Sinhala and Tamil communities are subject to patriarchal control. A feminist emphasis on common patriarchal ideologies and structures avoids the trap of reifying stereotypical images of ethnicity, while acknowledging its power and influence.

Female-Heads: Cultural Bearers, Material Reproducers

Understanding the economics of female-headed households, I argue, requires us to note social, cultural and political conditioning, since women's economic well-being is linked to social and cultural practices that mould the decision-making process (Sen 1990, Agarwal 1997). My previous summary of ethno-nationalist discourse in Sri Lanka has suggested that the question of women's rights is resolved at the level of the communities rather than the State and, as such, communities protect patriarchal interests (Chatterjee 1989). The implications for households and family relations are varied. There is a need, therefore, for a feminist framework capable of capturing the complexity of social reality as it is applied to female-headed households.

Orthodox economic readings of the household fail because the links between structure and agency are not included. Methodological individualism cannot accommodate the combination of human agency and social structures in dynamic interaction (Humphries 1998b: 224).[8] More progressive analyses of households and family relations have been motivated by Sen (1990) and Agarwal (1997), who incorporate social structures into their analysis of economic decision-making. The "gender and cooperative conflicts" framework and its extended analysis are useful to my study of female-headship (Sen 1990, Agarwal 1997). But I argue that, for all Sen's and Agarwal's strong points, households in their framework remain bounded, unitary and homogenous. They assume a standard patriarchal household, and neglect female-headship.[9] A feminist framework must be able to explain the diversity, contradictions, and similarities across Muslims, Sinhala and Tamil female-heads, so as to understand the roles of female-heads as bearers of culture as well as reproducers of the material sphere. I now turn to the structure of the book.

Mapping Sri Lanka's Female-headed Households

Within feminist circles, the study of female-headship is receiving increasing attention (Folbre 1994, Chant 1997, Chen 1998, Wyss 1999). The earliest documented study of female-headship from a development economics perspective, however, dates back two decades (Buvinic, Youssef and von Elm 1978). This early literature contributed to a prolific body of thought on the topic,

---

[8] This general dissatisfaction extends to the discipline of economics, which often disregards the social sphere in the methods used to analyse social issues (Lawson 1997:16).

[9] Thanks here to late Dr Sue Benson (Department of Social Anthropology, University of Cambridge) for pointing out this particular caveat in respect of the cooperative conflicts models, and suggesting that I develop this particular argument in my project.

where regional studies spreading from the West Indies to Western Africa to South Asia emerged (Youssef and Hetler 1984, Saldert 1984, Visaria and Visaria 1985, Kumari 1989, Islam 1991, Hamid 1992, Lewis 1993). The next chapter picks out some of the key social and demographic themes associated with the study of female-headed households. This literature is important to this study for two reasons. First, it provides the background for discussing female-headship as an important topic within the gender and development debate, especially in South Asia. This literature recognizes the growing importance of female-headship, in contrast with the continuing neglect of such households in orthodox economic theory. In addition, it facilitates the development of a typology of female-headship, which I then use in my economic profiling of Muslim, Sinhala and Tamil female-heads.

In the next chapter, I move to the specific situation in eastern Sri Lanka.[10] While literature on the subject from a development economics perspective is growing, it excludes the Northern and Eastern Provinces. Partly this is a consequence of the general lack of statistics during the past two decades for the Northern and Eastern Provinces, where the intensity of the ethnic conflict has prevented data collection. Thus micro-level studies on female-headship from a development perspective tend to focus on 'non-conflict' areas, while studies in the conflict regions have concentrated on war widows (Weerasinghe 1987, Perera 1991, Thiruchandran 1999).

My study is different in two ways. First, I bring into the debate the prevalence and nature of female-headship across ethnicity in the east. Second, I argue that female-headship is on the rise owing to factors that go beyond the ethnic conflict, and that the dynamics between the ethnic conflict and social change explains the rise of female-headship in eastern Sri Lanka. I discuss the economic conditions of eastern Sri Lanka, and then describe the research methods used in my fieldwork. Since I am interested in linking the economic decision-making of

[10] Appendix B contains a copy of the questionnaire used in my fieldwork.

female-heads with the social, political, and cultural circumstances, I emphasize the need for crossing disciplinary boundaries and using feminist methods.

Chapters Four, Five and Six describe the economic profiles of Muslim, Sinhala and Tamil female-heads. These chapters are arranged in alphabetical order, and the same socio-economic and demographic issues are examined for all three ethnic communities. As already noted, a notable feature of eastern Sri Lanka is the existence of matrilineal inheritance patterns and kin structures (Yalman 1971, McGilvray 1982, 1989, Agarwal 1990, 1996). Recent anthropological work has identified similar cross-cousin kinship structures for the Sinhala community too (Guneratne 2001). I begin each of these chapters by describing this cultural environment, which may help explain some choices made by female-heads in each ethnic group. Despite differences in outcomes in the economic profiles of female-heads across ethnicity, the pervasive aspects of patriarchal structures are apparent even among these matrilineal communities. I contend that matrilineal communities do not indicate the death of patriarchy, and that patriarchal structures and ideologies and matrilineal communities can be strange but ultimately compatible bedfellows. Thus feminist economists ought to be more cautious in upholding Sri Lanka as a feminist nirvana and/or paradise.

I then move beyond a simple account of the economic circumstances of female-heads to look at other important issues. The first is the importance of children for female-headed households in the productive and reproductive sphere. The chapter on "Dutiful Daughters, Sacrificing Sons" (Chapter Seven) explores the theme of the supportive role of children. Here I also complicate the feminist exposé of girls as the bearers of the burden of patriarchy. I claim, contentiously, that the detrimental effects boys suffer are equally central for feminist advocacy. While I acknowledge that the long-term consequences for girls are likely to be greater than for boys, this should not preclude probing the difficult decisions female-heads make in deciding to call on the help of their children. By complicating the narrative, I stress the need to take a unified stand on children's rights, irrespective of whether they are girls or boys. I believe such a stance promotes feminist interests by demonstrating the ill-effects of patriarchal structures and ideologies on both girls and boys.

Female-heads' welfare is dependent upon many factors: the supportive role of children, networks and institutional mechanisms. A principal mechanism invariably promoting and reinforcing gender hierarchies and patriarchal structures, especially in eastern Sri Lanka, is the non-governmental organization (NGO). Though there are some progressive NGOs involved in breaking gender taboos and hierarchies, many NGOs reinforce prevailing gender structures by promoting skill training in gender-based traditional occupations. Similarly, the labour market is another institution notorious for reinforcing gender hierarchies (Humphries 1995: 55–86). The experience of female-heads in seeking employment in the formal and informal labour market in eastern Sri Lanka bears this out. Many female-heads occupy themselves largely in home-based economic activities, reflecting more than just the political, social and economic instabilities of the region. At another level, these labour market outcomes, as well as the self-employment schemes promoted by NGOs, also reflect the gender-based occupational choices available to female-heads, which are economically exploitative and insecure.

My focus is on the gender dimension to network support. Chapter Eight introduces one of the main strands in my depiction of the relationship between patriarchal structures and female-heads in matrilineal communities. Networks buttress female-headed households in important ways but they are also sites through which patriarchal interests manifest in public/private and economic/non-economic divisions are promoted and reinforced. But there are variations in the experiences of female-heads as well. Exceptions need explanation, too, since they identify the power of human agency within social structures through the possibility that female-heads have initiated change in a volatile context. The diverse dynamics of similarities and differences is analysed in this chapter so that it feeds into the last but one chapter on feminist methodology and the theorizing of female-headed households.

Many of my findings underscore the complexity of social reality, and suggest that feminist economic analysis needs to explain this complexity rather than falling into the trap of cultural relativism or ignoring cultural variations. My penultimate chapter investigates the applicability of existing theories of the household to my study on female-headship. The partial nature of current accounts emphasizes the need for a feminist economic methodology capable of analysing social relations and structures and their diverse attributes. I find the work of feminist standpoint theorists (Harding 1986, 1995, 1999, Hartsock 1987, Longino 1990, Haraway 1991) and social theorists (Althusser 1990, Bourdieu 1998, 1999, 2000 Lawson 1997, 1999) relevant for feminist economic methodology. These theorists provide a framework within which to analyse the multiple and myriad layers of social reality of women's well-being. The other key point I make in this study is also found in Chapter Nine, where the need for economic theory to shift away from its focus on bounded readings of the household is reiterated.

That chapter leads to my final chapter which aims to promote gender-sensitive development policies that recognize the multiple levels at which patriarchal structures bear upon the lives of female-heads across ethnicity. Development policies need to incorporate sensitively the nexus between gender, ethnicity and class in targeting female-headed households. This is no easy task and is fraught with many challenges and intricacies. However, the oppressive nature of gender images constraining the choices and behaviours of female-heads across ethnic communities reveals their economic vulnerability. This is just one illustration of the ideological praxis between gender, ethnicity and class having "real" consequences at ground level. Appreciating these interconnections and differences, I argue, is important for the development arena, since policies that seek to encourage gender emancipation must cut across social position and location. In other words, gender-sensitive development policies need to integrate practical gender needs as well as strategic gender needs—with the latter requiring a nuanced analysis of social reality (Moser 1989). My project on female-headship across ethnicity and class, therefore, is also carried out with the purpose of interconnecting theory and practice in the development sphere.

Such an analysis, I also argue, helps us reflect on methodological issues in the economic theory of the household, development economics and feminist issues. This exercise aids a feminist analysis that shifts from simply being a methodological perspective to one which is capable of linking theory and practice at various levels. This is critical in recognizing the complexity of social reality of female-headed households in eastern Sri Lanka. Unpacking Sri Lanka's "feminist nirvana", therefore, requires moving beyond the surface phenomena of matrilineal practices and high ratings in gender-related human development indices.

TWO
Diverse Households
Literature on Female-headship

Introducing Female-headship into Gender and Development

Household structures take many forms. Economic analysis, however, is firmly attached to the assumption of nuclear households headed by men (Becker 1965).[1] The existence of alternative household structures, which deviate from the male-breadwinner norm, was brought to attention by researchers in the development field (Buvinc, Youssef and von Elm 1978, Youssef and Hetler 1984, Chant 1997). Early research focused on Western African and West Indian countries (Buvinic, Youssef, and von Elm 1978: 6). But evidence that female-headship was widespread in countries conventionally labelled patriarchal reveals the need for further research. In India, a country which, with little contention, can be identified as structured by patriarchal relations and ideologies, it was found that 10.0 per cent of households were female-headed as early as 1960 and 1970 (Kumari 1989: 4).

---

[1] Sen (1984b) and Folbre (1986a, 1986b) are among the early feminist critiques of Becker's conceptualization of the patriarchal household, while Humphries (1998b) brings attention to the evidence highlighting the limitations of applying this theory. I provide a cursory overview of these studies in Chapter Nine.

The widespread increase in female-headship is attributed to the break-up of families owing to war and famine, changes in land-holding systems, outward migration of surplus male labour and, in more recent times, marital dissolution (Youssef and Hetler 1984: 1–5). However, the key variable determining whether or not women assume headship is increasing levels of poverty. With the spread of globalization and integration of developing countries into the capitalist system, pre-capitalist forms of productive relations have been transformed, with low-income social groups alienated from capitalist development. Marginal social groups not only face negative effects, but also witness the break-up of their families (ibid: 40–1). This leads to female-headship for two interconnected reasons. First, men evade financial responsibility for their families and desert women, forcing the latter to assume the role of economic provider (ibid: 41–2). And second, structural changes also erode kinship support structures, which may leave the primary breadwinner role to women. Increasing economic deprivation, therefore, prevents kin from providing financial aid to women, particularly among the rural poor (ibid: 1).[2]

Despite growing evidence, female-headship remains a marginal issue within development studies, and this very lack of recognition brings its own set of problems. I begin by looking at the neglect of female-headed households in development literature and then go on to examine some of the wider conceptual issues raised in earlier studies, including the investigation and identification of different types of female-heads. The demographic profile of female-heads and their access to economic resources is then explored and the concluding section here examines methodological issues on female-headship. During this exercise I weave in evidence from

---

[2] Eastern Sri Lanka provides an interesting case study because both poor economic conditions as well as the ethnic conflict have made the lives of women doubly precarious. Ethnic war-related deaths of spouses, economic deprivation and the intense volatility and transformations in the region are more likely to precipitate a rise in female-headship. In the next chapter I explore these issues in detail in the Sri Lankan context.

South Asia, excluding Sri Lanka, to show the relevance of these issues to the region and to motivate the analysis of female-headship in eastern Sri Lanka in the next chapter.[3]

Marginal Issues? Female-headship in Development

Anthropologists and feminists have investigated development literature for its ethnocentric and patriarchal assumptions, highlighting many examples of such biases in development theory, practice and policies (Kabeer 1994: 22, Escobar 1995: 13, Jackson and Pearson 1998: 1–16). From this perspective, the absence of alternative household formations in mainstream development literature is not surprising, especially since economics, the root from which development discourse springs, has been shown to have the same biases (Ferber and Nelson 1993: 1–22, Chant 1997: 7). Such narrow conceptualizations disguise the complexity of household formation, relations and resource allocations, both within and outside these structures, making women invisible (ibid: 7–8). The limited conceptualization of households also has an impact on legal institutions, which curtail women's access to productive resources, family and divorce legislation, as well as social welfare policies (ibid: 100–4).

When the untested assumption is of the patriarchal nuclear household with a male breadwinner, computing the proportion of households headed by women poses many challenges. First, there are the conceptual differences associated with definitions of "household", "family", and "head" (Youssef and Hetler 1984: 6). Even though there have been recommendations for standard international definitions on these concepts, there is diversity in the application of these terms across surveys at national, regional and case study levels.

Second, enumerating headship is likely to be distorted by patriarchal notions, where men are "supposed" to head the

---

[3] I exclude the Sri Lankan evidence in this general literature review since I leave this for Chapter Three, where I discuss Sri Lanka in light of the social, political, and economic backdrop of the Eastern Province.

household. Cultural factors and perceptions are likely to lead data collectors and statisticians to downplay the complexities of household structures if they deviate from the expected. For example, where female-headship exists in countries traditionally characterized by patriarchal figureheads, women probably cite a male relative as household head even though in reality his role may be limited (ibid: 9). These difficulties hinder cross-country comparisons, but estimates of female-headship as early as the 1970s indicated rural female-headship to be in the 15.0–25.0 per cent range: Ghana (25.5 per cent), Sudan (23.6 per cent), Honduras (18.7 per cent), and Indonesia (16.6 per cent) (ibid: 6–25). South Asian countries revealed similar levels of incidence in female-headship in the following decade (1980s): Bangladesh (17.0 per cent), India (16.6 per cent), Sri Lanka (17.8 per cent) (Buvinic and Gupta 1997: 261–2). In spite of possible underestimation of female-headship, existing evidence suggests similar proportions of female-headed households across different regions with varied cultural values.

Third, most households are located within a system of kin networks and structures, and female-headed households are no exception. Typically, households draw upon different resources from individual members to maintain a particular standard of living, since kin are tied together by interactions, rights, duties and obligations (Youssef and Hetler 1981). The absence of an older male, however, may significantly hinder the reciprocal rights due from other male kin towards female-headed households, especially for agricultural tasks and activities, because these households may not be in a position to reciprocate male labour. Moreover, changing economic conditions impose more restrictions on networks, preventing female-heads from obtaining traditional sources of support (ibid: 2). Economic restructuring has weakened the ideal reciprocal-based kin structures, which may not necessarily be captured by census and statistics, leaving female-headed households more exposed to economic vulnerability and deprivation. Cain, Khanam and Nahar (1979) take evidence from Bangladesh to underline this point, where a widow has no legal claim on her husband's property and is dependent upon the goodwill of her brothers-in-law to maintain the well-being of her household. Under these circumstances women are more susceptible to poverty, with the practice of purdah and widow seclusion limiting their access to independent income-generating avenues and exacerbating poverty (ibid: 411).

Finally, there are different developmental stages and life-cycle transformations of households that will determine headship. Where female life expectancy is higher than male life expectancy and/or where there are wide age gaps between the marital ages of partners, female-headship is more likely to take place through widowhood. This is another dimension of female-headship, where it is also a functional relationship between demography and economics and not simply the result of cultural factors (Youssef and Hetler 1984: 39). Such factors show the need to investigate the demographic characteristics of female-headed households, where households headed by older widows will have very different needs and wants from those with younger female-heads. Older widowed female-heads depend on their sons' benevolence and help. Chen and Dreze (1992) show that older widows' legal access to property and resources characterizes the benefits they can accrue from their sons (1992: 88–9).[4]

These factors show that female-headship cannot and should not be considered a marginal issue in development literature. Sensitizing development studies to feminist issues must involve reducing the levels of vulnerability women might otherwise experience, an area where the susceptibility of women in

---

[4] Bangladesh and many regions of India (but with exceptions being noted in South India) are characterized by patrilineal inheritance, patrilocal residence and patriarchal kinship structures well-known for increasing the vulnerability of female-heads (ibid: 88–9). Female-heads in eastern Sri Lanka have an advantage over their South Asian cohorts in that they reside in matrilineal communities. But the benefits female-heads in the eastern region can claim are limited because their daily lives are shaped by other forms of patriarchal realities, and these factors are explored in detail in Chapters Four, Five and Six for Muslim, Sinhala, and Tamil female-heads, respectively.

female-headed households appears high. Additionally, enhancing the capabilities of women also entails ensuring at least minimal access to their entitlement rights. Female-heads' rights are usually neglected in the patriarchal discourse that emphasizes the duties and obligations of kin, without recognizing the political, economic and social realities preventing "golden days" of help, if indeed there ever was such widespread support. The gap between reality and myth is reason enough to advocate moving female-headship from the sidelines of development studies to centre-stage, and this remains a key objective of my study. This analysis requires navigating through the conceptual definitions of female-headship used by feminists, and I now turn to this task.

Towards Logical Conceptions: Categories of Female-headed Households

Initial research on developing a coherent and comprehensive typology of female-headship was done by Youssef and Hetler (1983). I begin with their contributions in this section, then move on to look at its application in South Asian studies, before finally noting some of the shortcomings that recent feminist work has pointed out.

Youssef and Hetler (1981) categorize female-heads into *de jure* and *de facto*, a distinction that has been the basis for much of the subsequent research by others. *De jure* headship occurs when women are pushed into assuming headship because of death, divorce, or legal separation from the male partner. The law implicitly recognizes such women as possibly heading their households. The absence of an adult male here results in female-headship arising "of law", as the term *de jure* implies (ibid: 40). Traditionally, death or marital dissolution did not necessarily lead to female-headship, since the social organization of family structures led to social and economic support within a framework of absorption. Even now, whether *de jure* female-heads become the main economic providers depends on the interaction between the legal position accorded to women and their social and cultural situation, which may or may not be compounded by economic factors (ibid: 41). Studies for India show the interactions between class, caste, and gender dynamics in the positioning of female-heads. Caste structures permit "low-caste" female-heads to participate in the productive/public sphere, but female-heads from "middle-caste" households only occasionally deviate from caste and patriarchal structures since they fear losing status. For these women, such constraints, even in the face of absolute poverty, leave them economically vulnerable and dependent on community structures (Lingam 1994: 701–3).

What factors lead to *de facto* female-headship? According to Youssef and Hetler (1981) *de facto* female-headship exists where there is a temporary absence of a "real" male head (1981: 40–2). This is usually due to migration, desertion and/or civil conflict. *De facto* headship also occurs when men are present in the household but relinquish their economic responsibilities because they are alcoholic, physically disabled, underemployed and/or unemployed (ibid: 48–9). But male absenteeism need not necessarily produce a change in the household structure, especially where women have to depend on male kin for household decision-making, even where remittances are insufficient to maintain the household unit. For example, women in Pakistan have to depend on male relatives to sign remittance forms and other legal documents because of high female illiteracy (ibid: 55–65). Moreover, male migration accentuates gender roles since migration makes men more mobile and less bound to their responsibilities and routine tasks, yet retaining control over property and access to productive resources (Youssef and Hetler 1984: 42–55).

No one factor, whether male mortality, male absenteeism or male incapacity, necessarily leads to female-headship. Families can be broken up and/or folded into wider kin. But it is clear that these circumstances can give rise to women heading their own households, and recognition of the diverse origins of female-headship is important in understanding their particular problems and survival strategies. These typologies, therefore, have been constructive in developing more nuanced types of female-headship appropriate to the particular country studies, and I summarize their extension as found in studies on South Asian countries.

Youssef and Hetler's (1981) initial conceptual categories have been adopted by most studies on female-headship in South Asia (Visaria and Visaria 1985, Kumari 1989, Hamid 1995). However, the study on Bangladesh by Islam (1991) provides the most comprehensive typology. Islam's study notes the diverse circumstances leading to female-headship, ranging from widowhood to adult sons surrendering their authority and control of resources to their mothers (1991: 6–7).[5] The common denominator in these numerous situations identified by Islam is that women are the main economic earners and have control and/or authority over resources. These situations indicate that female-headship is a dynamic process, requiring appropriate gender-sensitive policies to reduce women's economic vulnerability as a result of changes in their marital or cohabitation status.

These conceptual distinctions do have their limitations. Many of these shortcomings were already noted in the original research. In Chant's work (1997) she cites three primary difficulties associated with this simplified categorization. The first is that although *de facto* female-headed households are supposedly temporary in comparison with *de jure* households, the former group may spend longer on their own than the latter (ibid: 15). The possibility of re-marriage is an option for younger *de jure* female-heads, while older *de facto* female-heads may have less potential in this regard. Second, *de facto* female-heads are often assumed to be economically better positioned than *de jure* female-heads, especially where women assume *de facto* headship because their spouses are migrants. However, the evidence seems to contradict this, with *de facto* female-heads more commonly facing greater poverty. Remittances may

---

[5] I do not detail the five categories developed by Islam here, but it is sufficient to note that her grouping is a detailed breakdown of *de jure* and *de facto* female-headship as developed by Youssef and Hetler (1981).

become increasingly sporadic over time and income may be kept low by such women's reluctance to work in agricultural activities because of gender and social constraints and status conditions (ibid: 16). Finally, *de facto* headship may be a halfway house to *de jure* headship, especially where migration results in the breakdown of marital unions because of extra-marital relationships (ibid: 17–18). We shall see these experiences played out in the life-stories of the female-heads in my survey. Feminist researchers need to be alert to these problems with the conceptualization of female-headship. Although I note these difficulties in my study, I follow the literature in using the simple distinction of *de facto* and *de jure*. Simplicity of categories aids in unravelling other complexities also pertinent to studying female-headship.

Demographic Indicators and Economic Profiles

The ability of female-heads to provide economic support and to draw upon other resources and obligations is constrained by age, marital status, and household composition (Youssef and Hetler 1984: 29–30). An example is the importance of household size and female-heads' age in determining variations in human capital assets and in linking this to the economic strategies adopted by these households. Resource pooling of human capital is a common and successful survival strategy adopted by female-heads. Households with multiple earners are economically better off, and data on the average size of the households is a useful proxy for the economic welfare of female-headed households (ibid: 30). For these reasons, obtaining survey information on household size and structure is important. Some key attributes of female-headed households are noted here, and I shall highlight the similarities and differences when I discuss my findings on the economic dimensions of female-headed households in eastern Sri Lanka.

Early studies at the international level revealed the average size of female-headed household to vary between 2.5 and 5.0 members, whereas the average size of a male-headed household ranged between 5.0 and 6.5 members (ibid: 31). Differences in household sizes do have an impact on their earning potential and may limit the number of earners. Some have argued that female-headed households require less income because of their smaller size (ibid: 31). However, a study by Standing (1980) stresses that even after correcting for size, male-headed households have incomes twice as high as female-headed households (ibid: 31–2).

How do these global patterns apply to South Asia? Evidence from Bangladesh also shows that the average size of the female-headed household is smaller than the national average. The national mean is 5 household members in all female-headed households, compared to 5.7 members in male-headed households, and the size of *de jure* female-headed households is significantly smaller, with only 3.6 members (Hamid 1995: 119). Besides the size of the household, the proportion of women in female-headed households is 54.0 per cent as opposed to 47.0 per cent in the national household average, with *de jure* households having nearly 62.0 per cent women members. Likewise, the number of children in all female-headed households (31.0 per cent) is higher than the national average (29.0 per cent) (ibid: 119). Findings in India exhibit similar characteristics, where the average size for female-headed households is smaller (4.60) relative to the size (5.89) of male-headed households (Visaria and Visaria 1985: 61).[6] Another finding linked to household size is the female labour force participation rate, which was found to be higher than for male-headed households (ibid: 78).[7] But fewer female-heads were occupied in the main economic activities of agriculture, and

---

[6] There is contradictory evidence from the all-India story at the micro-level. Data from Uttar Pradesh find nearly 76.0 per cent of female-headed households composed of 5+ members, and this is largely because these households were either joint families (52.0 per cent) or extended families (14.0 per cent) (Kumari 1989: 55).

[7] None of the studies for India reviewed by me provided the sex composition of household members, and therefore it was difficult to explore the other theoretical findings that were found to be relevant in Bangladesh.

this is partially ascribed to the limited land-rights of female-heads, suggesting the legal constraints faced by them (ibid: 64). Household size and composition, traditional markers for well-being, do provide a guide to the welfare levels of female-headed households. My research and findings for the three ethnic communities in Sri Lanka look at these variables also, with a specific focus on household size and composition.

The life-cycle stages of female-headed households are another important demographic variable, where the age structure is a significant indicator of welfare levels (Youssef and Hetler 1984: 34). Decomposing female-headed households by age groups also reflects child-dependency ratios, earning capacities and children's share of household income (ibid: 35). Two distinct characteristics were found to be pertinent for female-heads in 14 countries. These consisted of either, a) "a bell-shaped curve with a peak or plateau at or near the 35–44 year-old age group", or b) a low prevalence of younger age groups, increasing to higher levels with older age groups (ibid: 20).

Country-specific data reveal that the majority of female-heads belong to older age groups and that there are relatively low numbers of young female-heads (ibid: 21). There is supporting evidence for this from Bangladesh and India. In Bangladesh 40.0 per cent of female-heads belong to the 40–49 age group and assume headship through widowhood (Islam 1991: 21–3). Similarly, in India age-based female-headship creates a step pattern on a bar chart: with ascending age, female-headship increases (Institute of Social Studies Trust 1984: 8). Visaria and Visaria (1985) find that female-headship increases from 6.07 per cent for the under 30 age group to 12.48 per cent in the 50+ age group at the national level (1985: 56–7). Micro-level studies done in India confirm the general trends found at the national level, with the 50+ age group having the highest fraction of female-heads (Institute of Social Studies 1984: 23, Kumari 1989: 53).

Household size and the age of female-heads provide possible clues for analysing the economic options of these units. The economic and non-economic contributions from household members are crucial for female-headed households' welfare levels (Youssef and Hetler 1981: 69). There is non-economic input when there are a greater number of young adult women and girls present in the household, while the presence of young boys need not necessarily have similar implications (ibid: 74). Similarly, where female-heads have young/adult sons providing a regular income, then the economic well-being of these households is likely to be better than when there are daughters. However, it is only when female-heads have an independent source of income that there is likely to be any change in conventional gender relations and family practices (Youssef and Hetler 1984: 47).[8] The crucial distinction is that households headed by older women probably depend on their income-earning-age children, as their own age inhibits active participation in the labour market, while younger female-heads have to balance their time between childcare and income-earning activities.

The occupational choices of female-heads usually reflect their age as well as their domestic arrangements, with a fair proportion of them selecting home-based wage labour. Even where female-heads choose "other" occupations, there is a high prevalence of selecting gender-based occupations. Islam's (1991) study corroborates these points for Bangladesh. Female-heads, who gave their occupation as wage labourers (79.0 per cent), were employed as casual labourers providing domestic help to higher income households. Employment as domestic labourers is viewed as an extension of women's traditional responsibilities, and raises few eyebrows. It permits women to combine their domestic activities with an important source of income-generation (ibid: 22–4). But, those in home-based activities record meagre and irregular incomes, irregular

---

[8] Speaking of household members can also mean incorporating non-nuclear family members, and studies of the British Industrial Revolutionary period show how non-relatives were taken into female-headed households to supplement household income, obtain child support, and overcome Poor-Law discrimination (Humphries 1998a).

working hours and work insecurity (ibid: 24). Comparable conclusions were reached in studies of female-headed households in India too. The degree of participation of female-headed households in home-based economic activities is high, and this is especially the case with *de facto* households (Bhatt 1988: 9). Poor working conditions, income insecurity, and atypical forms of employment are then a trademark of the work of female-heads that does have a bearing on the long-term economic welfare and poverty conditions of female-headed households.

Rights and Resources: Some Methodological Notes

One entry point used by researchers for uncovering the methodological dynamics of female-headed households is the intra-household bargaining literature (Lewis 1993).[9] Bargaining helps uncover two aspects of the behaviour of female-heads (ibid: 20–4). First, the distinctions between female-heads and their implications for social, political, and economic factors that bear upon women's roles are examined. Second, whether female-headship leads to more assertive roles for women and/or whether in the absence of viable safety nets this status leads to a collapse of their limited yet restrictive social protections are both investigated (ibid: 23–4). The purpose in this methodological essay is to develop a distinct rights and resources discourse for female-heads, so that advocating enhancing the endowment and entitlements of female-heads is given necessary precedence in development literature and policy (ibid: 23).

The rights and resources of female-heads are based on non-economic variables as well. This is because kin structures are a

---

[9] The co-operative conflict model (Sen 1990), a particular bargaining model, is useful for analysing the methodological issues related to female-headed households. I too apply this framework in my case studies since I am interested in exploring the bargaining of the female-head within the wider kin group. However, I then proceed to argue that, for all it benefits, this framework has its limitations too (see Chapter One, page 8, footnote 9).

salient feature of female-headed households' well-being, and cultural and social resources also determine the welfare of these households (ibid: 25). A discussion of female-heads' "poverty as a process" leads to the recognition that there is a gradual deterioration in their endowments and exchange entitlements taking place (Lewis 1993: 27–33). The absence of a male reduces the entitlement levels of the household; but this loss is not simply an economic one, it is also a cultural and social process. The cultural process is the perceived status of female-headed households, which affects community-level bargaining relationships (ibid: 31–2). This point is made in Chen and Drèze's work, which shows how widows in India have to abide by a hierarchical social structure restricting their employment opportunities (1992: 85).

Community perceptions place female-heads as producers and labourers at a disadvantage, where their relative welfare is linked to social norms and patriarchal values. The absence of effective state-based social security measures means that community structures are crucial sources of support. But the nature of such community support needs also to be analysed since this will help us recognize potential complementary factors in social welfare policy. For example, where a female-head possesses rights to property and assets, her children, and especially sons, are unlikely to make her vulnerable and deprived because there is a credible threat that she may leave one child's family and join the household of another. Her bargaining power within such households is strengthened and secured (ibid: 89). Plurality of effective and legal support systems is an advantage for any woman, but especially effective for augmenting the endowment levels of female-heads.

The social resources of the community, market, and state are, therefore, vitally important for female-heads. The endowment levels of female-headed households are dependent upon cultural and social factors, and not merely on economic endowments. The main point is that these resources intersect with each other to determine the entitlement and endowment levels of female-headed households. The illustration of a resource poor, young female-head who is forced to depend heavily on child labour, with implications for the educational standards of her children, helps make the point that age and demographic structure have direct implications for the human resource base of children (Lewis 1993: 35).[10] Development policies should aim to meet both practical needs, female-heads' access to resources, and strategic needs, promoting the human capital investment in children (Moser 1989). Intervention, Lewis contends, should be based on a resource and rights discourse, which will provide the bedrock for secure, stable and engendered programmes for enhancing the endowment and entitlement levels of female-heads (Lewis 1993: 39).

This focus on female-heads highlights the complex and multi-layered realities of female-headed households, where patriarchal norms, community structures and legal-economic-social rights determine levels of well-being (Chen and Drèze 1992: 88). The need to recognize the interplay between social and cultural norms and social welfare systems is a pressing one. Defending their basic property rights within the existing legal and policy framework will be an essential first step, which can ensure that female-heads' bargaining power improves within a co-operative conflict situation. Intra-familial and intra-caste oppressions can be eradicated through a recognition of the inter-links between the dimensions that bear upon co-operative conflicts (Lingam 1994: 704). For these basic reasons it is imperative to focus on the economic, social and demographic analysis of female-headed households, and I do this by first drawing attention to the literature on the topic in Sri Lanka (Chapter Three). Then I analyse this for female-heads in eastern Sri Lanka by focusing on these demographic and economic profiles for each ethnic group in Chapters Four, Five and Six.

---

[10] The role of children in supporting households is an important issue for female-heads. My focus on children moves beyond the usual analysis to disclose the complex decision-making process female-heads go through in deciding whether to involve children in income-generating activities (Chapter Seven).

THREE

The "Grand" and "Meta" Narratives:
Situating Sri Lankan Female-heads

Female-headship in Sri Lanka: Is it Something New?

Census and other statistics on female-headship in Sri Lanka are scant. While there have been attempts in recent years to tabulate the incidence of female-headship at a national level, there is still little evidence of consistent reporting of female-headship (Department of Census and Statistics 1995). The lack of national level time-series coverage is a problem for evaluating changes in the political economic structures that lead to female-headship. Patchy data feed into the dominant view that female-headship in Sri Lanka, and particularly in the Northern and Eastern Provinces, is the outcome solely of the ethnic conflict, rather than associated changes in the social fabric. However, microlevel studies in "non-conflict" areas of Sri Lanka have drawn attention to changes in the political economy and social fabric leading to female-headship (Weerasinghe 1987, Perera 1991). How far is female-headship in the Eastern Province also the product of socio-economic change? Exposing the changes in the social fabric and the political economic structures that lead to female-headship undoubtedly means that Sri Lankan development planners can no longer complacently hold the view that female-headship, especially in the North and East, simply requires temporary relief strategies. By associating female-headship with changes in social and political-economic structures, my objective is to demonstrate the need for concerted development policies targeting female-heads.

With this goal in mind, this chapter begins with a brief review of the existing literature in the "non-conflict" areas of Sri Lanka in order to locate female-headship within the wider political economy.[1] The next section describes the eastern coastal region, with a focus on the economic and demographic character of the region. The final section summarizes my fieldwork techniques. I argue that the economy is not neatly separated from cultural, class, religious and social mores, and that these factors colour the decision-making of female-heads. I use both quantitative and qualitative data to substantiate this point. Feminist economic research increasingly makes use of a diverse source of sample techniques (Pujol 1997). My rationale for adopting these alternative research methods is laid out in this concluding section. First, however, I offer a summary of issues pertinent to female-headship in the "non-conflict" areas of Sri Lanka.

Poverty among female-heads?

Family survival depends upon the ability of household members to gain access to resources, while this in turn is usually shaped by the dynamics of gender, class, and ethnic relations. Thus women are likely to be economically disadvantaged. Some statistical indicators convey this point. Real incomes for women workers remain at two-third of those of working men for the 1969–1982 period. And the proportion of working women among the poor has only dropped from 44.0 per cent to 40.0 per cent in the same period. Further, micro studies of casual work have also pointed to consistent wage differentials favouring men (Perera 1991: 28). These facts suggest that female-heads are unlikely to evade poverty. Yet, does this hold true in Sri Lanka?

---

[1] Locating the wider social context is also pertinent to the findings of micro-level data for Ampara, Batticaloa, and Trincomalee (Chapters Four, Five, and Six), because it distinguishes specific cultural practices relevant to eastern Sri Lanka from changes in the wider social structures.

A study by the World Bank in 1995 found that poverty was, in general, higher among female-headed households (Aturupane, Rodrigo and Perera 1997: 1). A follow-up study carried out in 1997, again funded by the World Bank, came to similar conclusions (ibid: 1). The 1995 and 1997 studies of Sri Lanka covered all provinces, except in the Northern and Eastern areas. The sample size for the 1997 study was 3000 female-headed households and 1500 male-headed households. This study revealed that while the incidence of poverty among female-headed households (55.26 per cent) was not higher than for male-headed households (56.22 per cent), the depth and severity of poverty for female-heads is greater than for male-headed households. Depth of poverty was at 35.33 per cent for female-heads compared with 34.73 per cent for male-heads, and severity of poverty at 17.41 per cent for female-heads versus 17.13 per cent for male-heads (ibid: 6).[2]

Sector-based evidence from the 1997 study also reveals that the incidence of poverty for female-heads is highest in the estate sector, followed by the rural and urban sectors. However, the depth and severity of poverty is greatest in the rural sector (ibid: 8). These trends are consistent with economic developments in Sri Lanka where, despite a sound agricultural base, significant recent investment, infrastructure expansion and economic growth are urban-led. So the choice of access to resources and economic opportunities is wider in urban areas.[3] Poverty is usually linked to employment status and prospects, and since only 34.0 per cent of female-heads are employed in primary level occupations they are at high risk of poverty. Since formal sector employment for such women is limited, 30.0 per cent of 'non-working' female-heads are home-workers (ibid: 18–21).

---

[2] Head-count, poverty gap, and squared poverty gap indices are used to measure the incidence, depth, and severity of poverty, respectively. These measures are adopted because they are a popular choice in policy-oriented research studies (ibid: 5–6).

[3] This though says very little of the higher living costs and/or other constraints urban households face.

Another related issue for household income and poverty is the number of household members pooling their resources. Contrary to findings in other countries, nearly 84.0 per cent of female-heads depend upon themselves as the primary income earner (Youssef and Hetler 1981, Hamid 1992). When it comes to multiple income earners in female-headed households, 71.37 per cent depend on one other member, 18.16 per cent on two members, 7.05 per cent on three members, and 3.42 per cent on four or more members (Aturupane et al. 1997: 22–3).

Such evidence does not appear to support the thesis that female-heads are more likely to pool income from different sources. Simply focusing on the number of income earners in female-headed households, however, may give a partial picture. It is possible that these households depend on remittances and handouts from siblings and other kin that are equally essential in maintaining a basic level of household income. Certainly my empirical evidence for the Eastern Province underlines the significance of such informal income support for the economic well-being of female-heads.

Expenditure and living conditions of female-headed households are also linked to poverty. The economic welfare of households depends upon the consumption levels of these units, and the estimated average per capita income is Rs 981.00 for all female-headed household groups in the study (ibid: 28).[4] A breakdown of consumption patterns for these households reveals some noteworthy trends. A higher proportion of the household budget is spent on food, and consequently a lower proportion is spent on fuel, lighting, clothing and education with particular implications for human capital investment in the children belonging to these households (ibid: 28–29). Food expenditure patterns also indicate the possibility of nutritional deficiencies, with purchases weighted towards more starch and

---

[4] I use the average per capita figures here. But it should be noted that a breakdown of 'poor' and 'non-poor' households in the study is also provided—with Rs 495.31 and Rs 1477.72, being the respective figures for these groups (ibid: 28).

carbohydrates than protein, dairy or vitamin-rich foods (ibid: 29).[5]

The level of hygiene in home environments is usually thought to be a reflection of income levels. However, the findings in this study reveal that this relationship may not be close (ibid: 42). Many female-headed households live in dwellings built of brick (57.33 per cent) or clay (23.62 per cent), which are high quality building materials appropriate to Sri Lanka's hot and humid climate. The floors of these houses are cement (62.34 per cent) or clay (32.02 per cent), and their ceilings consist of tile (44.54 per cent) or asbestos (14.43 per cent), which are also suitable to the Sri Lankan weather. The availability of good quality housing is linked to poverty alleviation and rural development programmes, which provided assistance and/or constructed housing through village "awakening" and urban development schemes (ibid: 39–41).[6] Where the provision of facilities by the state has been low and/or non-existent there is a marked shortfall in living conditions. Specifically, water supply and electricity is poor: 47.65 per cent have access to a common well and/or tap and 56.09 per cent use kerosene oil for lighting their dwellings (ibid: 42–46).

A typical female-headed household?

The standard of living of female-heads is also linked to the demographic characteristics of their households. Age, marital status, and education levels are all important determinants of the ability of female-heads' to obtain access to economic resources. The relevance of these characteristics for

---

[5] The authors also point to how these results are not so different from those for male-headed households of similar income groups, in keeping with the observation that the incidence of poverty may not been greater for female-heads in low-income groups.

[6] Apparently, female-headed households' entitlement to such housing appears sustained. Unfortunately, the authors do not examine the discrepancy between female-heads' limited access to economic resources and sustained state entitlements. One can surmise, however, that a fair proportion of female-heads obtained housing while living with their spouses.

understanding female-headship has been shown in the previous chapter. Demographics are also pertinent to development policies since they help locate the sources of poverty and uncover the constraints on female-heads. The particularities in Sri Lanka are discussed here.

Widowhood (48.0 per cent) is the most common cause of female-headship in Sri Lanka, followed by 40.0 per cent of married women assuming headship. Aturupane et al (1997) do not discuss the reasons for the 40.0 per cent of married women assuming headship, and indeed there is no clear distinction made between *de jure* and *de facto* female-heads in the study. Since there are distinct categories of never married (4.0 per cent), divorced (1.0 per cent), separated (6.0 per cent), and other (2.0 per cent), one can surmise that the category of married female-heads encompasses women whose spouses are unemployed, disabled, suffering from ill-health, alcoholic, and/or have migrated. But it is also possible that this category encompasses women abandoned by their spouses, but who continue to claim to be married to maintain "respectability". The authors contend that "the marital bond is both popular and relatively stable" in Sri Lanka, and thus female-headship is attributed to widowhood (ibid: 11). The analysis ignores those women, a very large minority at 40.0 per cent, who assume female-headship for other reasons.

Indeed, this omission is a severe drawback that warrants critical re-thinking. The underlying premise seems to be the stability of patriarchal institutions and the belief that marital unions are both "popular and relatively stable". There are several problems here. First, the perception in question ignores micro-level studies documenting a substantial proportion of unions more likely to be based on cohabitation than on marriage (Weerasinghe 1987, Perera 1991). Second, it also overlooks feminist advocacy of the need to change the legal system to protect the rights of women in cohabiting relationships (Goonesekera 1990, 1996). Finally, it disregards the economic and social pressures increasingly placed on marital unions that lead men to shirk their patriarchal responsibilities. For example,

Perera's research (1991) emphasizes the social transformations eroding traditional male kin support, leaving the imperatives of survival increasingly to nuclear family units. Furthermore, little conclusive evidence is available that marital stability is related to the legality of the contract. Certainly, in other studies nearly 68.0 per cent of abandoned female-heads are in legal partnerships (ibid: 34).

Other research has shown abandonment to be another important cause of increased female-headship. In Perera's research, nearly 34.0 per cent of female-heads have been abandoned, and of these nearly 14.0 per cent are not legally married and consequently have no claims to support (1991: 31–5). However, death of the spouse remains the leading cause of women's assumption of headship, as 66.0 per cent of female-heads are widows. The ages of female-heads in the studies vary markedly.[7] Aturupane et al suggest that a large proportion of widows belong to middle-to-old age (41–70 years) groups, while in Perera's research 53.0 per cent of female-heads are between the age of 25–35 years (1991: 35). It appears, therefore, that women who become heads for reasons other than widowhood are on average younger. For women who have never been employed and/or have low educational attainments, widowhood at a later age does not facilitate easy entrance into the formal labour market. Similarly, younger female-heads tend to have young children who are not able to offer economic support to their households. Poverty among such groups of female-heads is likely to be high; it is no surprise that Perera's study suggests economic hardship.

The education levels in female-heads of the sample are low: 86.0 per cent of female-heads have received lower secondary education or less, with nearly 30.66 per cent having no schooling whatsoever (Aturupane et al. 1997: 15).[8] A variety of factors—

---

[7] Perera's sample size, however, is a much smaller number of 90 families located in rural, semi-urban, and city areas – once again excluding the Northern and Eastern Provinces of Sri Lanka.

[8] Weerasinghe, who did an earlier study on female-headship in two specific villages, Diyagama and Nadeegama in Sri Lanka, finds the same

poverty, ill-health, child labour, performing domestic chores, and the like – has led to gender discrimination in human capital investment in the Sri Lankan context (Weerasinghe 1987: 73). All these factors clearly thwart female-heads' ability to enter the labour market. For policy-makers the more immediate issue is the extent to which these trends can have an impact on intergenerational poverty and investment in human capital. This is an important issue since low-educational levels of women usually impinge negatively upon other development issues, such as population policy, health, nutrition, and the education of children. While Weerasinghe (1987) has not explored these issues, undoubtedly changes in household formation do disrupt children's schooling patterns and educational achievements. According to Perera's study, 48.0 per cent of children stopped schooling as a result of the termination of their parents marital and/or cohabitation unions: 44.0 per cent, 26.0 per cent, 22.0 per cent, and 8.0 per cent, had their primary, secondary, G.C.E. O/Level and G.C.E. A/Level (respectively) schooling disrupted (1991: 47–48). Despite the low educational levels of female-heads, however, their household size is no different from that of male-headed households in similar income groups. A majority of households have between 3–5 members, with 52.69 per cent of those that are female-headed belonging to this category (Aturupane et al. 1997: 17).

Aturupane et al.'s study concerns only a national-level sample, and consequently misses out on the richness that a qualitative case study on the same topic can provide. This is not to downplay the importance of national-level studies, but rather to emphasize the need for integrating case studies to obtain a more nuanced analysis of female-headship. So far, where possible, key points raised in the quantitative analysis have been clarified by a qualitative investigation of female-headship. But there remain a variety of complex issues surrounding the study of female-headship that need further exploration. Since there is a dialectical relationship between

---

where illiteracy is at 40.0 per cent and 60.0 per cent, respectively, in the two villages (1987: 72).

qualitative and quantitative issues, my research weaves together the quantitative analysis and the qualitative commentary.

Opinions that matter: self-esteem and images of female-heads

Female-heads are located in social structures and their daily lives involve social strands not usually captured through economic measurements. I shall argue that cultural perceptions influence female-heads' decision-making, which in turn determines their survival strategies.

Marriage is the most common form of union for men and women (86.0 per cent in Perera's study), but it does not preclude cohabitation by partners, with nearly 30.0 per cent–50.0 per cent in Weerasinghe's study cohabiting. But cohabitation does not imply casual alliances. Nearly 31.0 per cent of non-formal unions survived for 6–17 years. Moreover, 68.0 per cent of women abandoned by their partners were in fact in legal marriages (Perera 1991: 34). At the same time, the prevalence of non-legal unions does not necessarily imply a more accommodating attitude towards non-married women who have separated from and/or been abandoned by their spouses. In fact, such female-heads are more likely to face vilification from their community and/or kin. Weerasinghe's compilation of the life stories of female-heads points to a high proportion experiencing such ridicule, and this is vividly related by women wanting to protect their daughters from a similar fate: "I always tell my daughters what happened to me and how I faced humiliation. I want them to be married in the proper way and lead respectable lives," says Lucie, a female-head (1987: 32–6). However, as an entire group, that is whether *de facto* or *de jure*, female-heads face many difficulties as single parents. In many cases female-heads are not vociferous feminists who have dared to assume headship, but rather "victims" of patriarchal relations and structures that place them in precarious positions. However, they have held their ground, provided for their children and overcome many obstacles. Lily, another female-head, expresses her situation as follows: "My difficult days are now over. Life is a real battle. I think I have won in many respects" (ibid: 21–4).

The problems of self-worth and perception that many female-heads mention are linked to the absence of adult men in these households. An adult man is not simply an asset, he is also a source of potential social power, protection, and legitimacy at the village level. The safety and social well-being of household members is largely ensured by a male presence, and where men are absent women are more sexually vulnerable. Female-heads are aware of such personal security issues, and the following citation in Perera's study reveals the severity of the problem: " [I] kept the children in a neighbour's house each night at first, and later, kept vigil in [my] hut at night with a 'kris' knife by [my] mat" (1997: 42). Female-heads, therefore, noted that the absence of men exposed them to abuse, since their social rights and interests were no longer protected. But at the same time many women were relieved when they were separated from "drunken, wife-beating, non-earning, and philandering" spouses (Weerasinghe 1987: 7). While the physical capabilities of men may make them better "guardians" against social and sexual abuse, socialization processes and cultural perceptions have an equally important role in perpetuating practices that make women vulnerable. Low-esteem and self-worth are echoed in folk idioms and many female-heads referred to them constantly in their narratives, conveying the power of such tools in reinforcing social images of women's "inferior" status. Such narratives indicate that more than a sound welfare system is needed to facilitate the social inclusion of female-heads, since the core premises of social and patriarchal institutions pervading women's lives need to be negotiated too.[9] Focusing on case study evidence helps

---

[9] Since much of the research in these existing studies has focused on the "non-conflict" zone areas of Sri Lanka, one can safely assume that a majority of the case studies refer to Sinhala female-heads. I make this assumption because none of the studies has distinguished between the ethnic groups in Sri Lanka, and in this regard it is not too far-fetched to assume that the authors speak about Sinhala women. As my study focuses

unpack and elaborate the general 'grand' narrative of female-headship in 'non-conflict' areas of Sri Lanka. It shows that while 'economics' matter to female-heads, it is equally vital to include the institutional (including ideological) context and to look at the social and political structures within which economic decision-making takes place. My purpose is to relate to the narrative of female-heads in a particular geographic location of Sri Lanka, the East, with a distinctive history and geography. I start, therefore with a depiction of this region.

Conflict, Economics and Ethnicity in the East

Ampara, Batticaloa, and Trincomalee districts comprise the Eastern Province. Eastern Sri Lanka is unique. It is a region that is inhabited by all of Sri Lanka's three ethnic groups – Muslim, Sinhalese and Tamil – in more or less equal proportions.[10] The 1981 census reports the following breakdown for Muslims, Sinhala, and Tamils:

Table 3A: Ethnic Composition for the Eastern Province

	Ampara	Batticaloa	Trincomalee
Muslim	42.0%	24.0%	30.0%
Sinhala	38.0%	4.0%	33.0%
Tamil	20.0%	72.0%	37.0%

(Source: Department of Census and Statistics 1981)[11]

on female-heads belonging to all three ethnic groups, it is worthwhile noting possible overlaps in their experiences as well as differences – and the degree to which these distinctions can be attributed to specific patriarchal, cultural and ethnic norms.

[10] Two issues need to be noted here. First, the exact census of ethnic groups is a subject of contention, since the ongoing ethnic conflict is as much about demographics as it is about ethno-nationalist discourse. Second, the historical residence patterns of Muslims, Sinhalese and Tamils in the Eastern Province have a very different trajectory: a historical path, which is again subject to much contention and debate (for a balanced reading of Sinhala settlements in the eastern region see Hoole, Somasundaram, Sritharan and Thiranagma 1990).

The presence of all three ethnic communities is not the only distinctive feature of the eastern coastal region. Muslims and Tamils in the region follow matrilineal descent and uxorilocal marriage patterns, while the Sinhalese have a distinct household system (McGilvray 1989, Agarwal 1990, 1996). Sinhalese households are distinguishable in some measure because their settlement in the region is relatively recent: the late colonial and early post-colonial period (Hoole, Somasundaram, Sritharan and Thirangama1990). While ethnic segregation is maintained between neighbourhoods and indeed certain villages are identifiable as Muslim, Sinhala or Tamil, an infusion of the customs, social mores and practices of the other ethnic groups is likely to occur. At the same time, however, there is also an attempt to maintain the distinct practices deriving from the separate religious positions of each ethnic group. The economic strategies adopted by female-heads within each district reflect the distinctiveness of socio-cultural norms, and this is partially captured in my findings through mean incomes.[12]

The economic base of the East can be characterized as rural with primary dependence upon irrigated rice cultivation. Deep sea and lagoon fishing are other common occupations, which is a result of the ready accessibility of the eastern seaboard, with lagoons shaping the natural geographical terrain of the coastal belt. However, there is also a reliance on plantation crops, mercantile trade, and the informal economy. While these

---

[11] Though dated, I use the 1981 census for two primary reasons. First, even though the census for the past two decades at the "all-island" level was carried out in 2001, as noted in Chapter One (footnote 4) the final reports did not include Batticaloa and Trincomalee districts. This was because the state and intensity of the ethnic conflict in these regions prevented the process being finalized in an efficacious manner. Second, using the 1981 census as a point of reference is apt given that 1983 could be considered a watershed in the escalation of ethnic violence as well as ethno-nationalist discourse in Sri Lanka, that have made the use of demographic detail particularly fraught.

[12] See Appendix C for further information on a) the motivations for methods of data analysis, b) results of descriptive data, and c) ANOVA test results on mean income.

occupations are the mainstay of the people in the region, the level of economic development in each district is very different. All three districts belong to the dry zone region of Sri Lanka, and are heavily dependent upon irrigation for paddy cultivation. However, accessibility to irrigation facilities varies. And the ongoing ethnic conflict has a further negative impact on the level and quality of irrigation programmes in the region. There are no systematic data available on per capita income, gross domestic production, employment levels and the like for eastern Sri Lanka. The intensity of the conflict at different points in time during the past several years allows for only a sketchy outline of the level of economic development.

Ampara district has been the least affected by the conflict, which is probably partially attributable to its geographic location in the southernmost part of the Eastern Province. Trincomalee, after many years of severe fighting, is now facing a period of relative lull. This, however, does not hold true for Batticaloa where only a mere 25.0 per cent of landmass comes under State direction, the remaining 75.0 per cent being still occupied by the Liberation Tamil Tigers for Eelam (LTTE), with continued conflict, battle, and skirmishes taking place between the State Forces and the LTTE.[13] Consequently, Batticaloa has a low level of economic development with its infrastructure particularly battered. While a sense of economic "normalcy" has returned to Trincomalee, Ampara contains the liveliest level of economic

---

[13] Like all situations of conflict, the case of Sri Lanka is no different in being in a continuous state of flux. It should be pointed out that I summarize here my impressionistic judgements and understanding of circumstances in Sri Lanka for 1998–9 during my fieldwork in the region. When I was writing my findings (2000/1) for my Ph.D., the condition in eastern Sri Lanka changed drastically with an escalation of violence noted in both Trincomalee and Ampara. Since end 2001, and at the time of writing, a fragile cease-fire and peace has been holding in much of the country, including the North and East. This fragile cease-fire process is not to deny the continued recruitment of children, various skirmishes, suicide bombings, and killings that are taking place between the break-away faction of the LTTE (the Karuna-faction, located in Eastern Sri Lanka), northern-based LTTE and the Sri Lankan state at present (late 2004).

activity here. Following the course of events in the region it would not be far-fetched to note the relative prosperity of Ampara when compared with the poverty of Batticaloa, with Trincomalee's economic activity falling in between the other two districts. To put these impressionistic judgements of relative status in the Eastern Province in perspective, note that the region as a whole is impoverished, with high levels of unemployment and low levels of formal economic activity.[14] Given the conflict-ridden state of affairs in eastern Sri Lanka and the lack of detailed economic data, a comprehensive analysis is difficult. This limitation, however, should not devalue findings about the survival strategies and levels of economic well-being of female-heads in the region.[15]

---

[14] In making these statements, I need to make the reader aware that I do so not merely based on my own field-experience but also on the basis of personal communication from people working, usually through NGOs, in the region. Here thanks are due to Simon Harris (formerly of OXFAM), Daniel Sinnathamby (CARE), and P. Senthurajah (SWOAD) for sharing their information and understandings of the region with me. Furthermore, Batticaloa was noted as one the poorest districts in Sri Lanka even prior to the rise of hostilities in the district, with the state of conflict impoverishing the district further. Ampara, on the other hand, is noted as a district with the highest level of agricultural productivity in Sri Lanka. Chithra Maunaguru (SURIYA) gave me this information and I thank her for doing so. While there is no recent statistical data on economic indicators for eastern Sri Lanka, the Census and Statistics information from the 1981 period attest to these economic conditions. After nearly two decades of intense conflict in the region, the likelihood of economic conditions deteriorating further is probable and, therefore, is likely to continue on a downward spiral rather than lead to unexpected improvements.

[15] Indeed, a partial purpose in stating the limitations I faced in studying eastern Sri Lanka is to make the reader aware that this analysis, like any other, is partial and context-dependent (Lawson 1997). In Chapter Seven a discussion of the feminist methodology that structured my standpoint as well as of how this study contributes to the theorizing of female-headship and reinforces the building blocks of feminist methodology in economics is discussed. This exercise helps explore the social construction of economics and its contributions to the cultural production of gender (Humphries 1995: 55).

The lack of accurate official statistical economic information drives the need for a qualitative analysis of female-headship. Beside this reality, there are pressing reasons for doing qualitative research in economics and development economics. In the next section I trace some of these reasons, with a focus on calls by feminist economists for expanding methodological boundaries.

Ways of Knowing...Feminist Methods and Crossing Disciplinary Boundaries

A primary purpose of this book is to draw upon the social, cultural, and ethnic norms of Muslims, Sinhalese and Tamils in evaluating the socio-economic indicators of female-heads, so as to assess how economic decisions are shaped and influenced by these structural features of eastern Sri Lanka. This, however, is a task fraught with difficulty, because these differences do not have fixed and stable ethnic roots. By using ethnic markers I uncover the similarities as well as the differences across class and gender that inform economic decision-making to illustrate the many instances in which female-heads—having socialized gender, class, social and ethno-nationalist identities—shape economic decision-making accordingly.[16] So gender interacts with class, ethnicity and caste to structure the options available to female-heads and mould the responsiveness of female-heads to these options. My analysis seeks to uncover similarities as well as differences in the basic choices available and in the responsiveness to those choices. So while statistics are used to unravel the particular economic positions of female-heads in

---

[16] Interestingly, it also shows the many instances in which female-heads are acutely aware of the social practices that distinguish their ethnic community from others, but how these traditions perpetuate unequal gender relations within their respective communities is rarely acknowledged. (I shall, where applicable in my case studies and qualitative analysis, show the many instances of this awareness expressed by female-heads—and indeed some of the similarities of female-heads' experiences across and within class divisions. However, analysing this particular issue in depth would need a separate essay of its own.

each ethnic group, I shall argue that the socio-cultural context within which they work out survival strategies and make economic choices is also important. To appreciate these relationships, however, requires moving from orthodox survey questionnaire methods to a more varied approach to conducting research (MacDonald 1995: 175–91).

The traditional method used to gather information has been the survey/questionnaire, with the results used to indicate some general observations about female-heads in the region.[17] I aimed to interview numbers in each ethnic group roughly in proportion to their importance in the provincial population. In this way I attempt to represent the ethnic composition of each district. My total sample consisted of 298 female-headed households selected for interviewing. This number of can be broken-down into 113 Muslim, 70 Sinhala, and 115 Tamil ethnic groups for the entire region. So for example, 34 Muslim, 35 Sinhala and 30 Tamil female-heads were interviewed from Ampara in an attempt to capture the 42.0 per cent, 38.0 per cent, and 20.0 per cent demographic presence of the Muslim, Sinhala and Tamil communities respectively, in the district. A similar exercise was followed in Batticaloa and Trincomalee districts, too, although it should be noted that no Sinhala female-heads were interviewed in Batticaloa which has few, if any, Sinhala residents.[18] In Batticaloa, therefore, the questionnaire was conducted with 49 Muslim and 50 Tamil female-heads to represent the 24.0 per cent Muslim and 72.0 per cent Tamil groups. Finally in Trincomalee, the sample size was 30 Muslim, 35 Sinhala and 35 Tamil female-heads to reflect the 30.0 per cent Muslim, 33.0 per cent Sinhala and 37.0 per cent Tamil ethnic

---

[17] See Appendix B for a copy of the questionnaire.

[18] According to the 1981 Census, 4.0 per cent of the population in Batticaloa district were Sinhalese. During my time there, however, I never came across any Sinhala families – and was subsequently informed through various local sources that most Sinhala households were either forcibly removed from the area and/or had to flee because of LTTE-led terrorist activities. The only exception was Sinhala women married to Tamil and/or Muslim men, in which case these women identified themselves as Muslims or Tamils.

composition in the district. There was, however, no sophisticated means of selecting my sample. Many of the female-heads interviewed were either those who were willing and able to be interviewed or were linked to grass-roots organizations. A sample selection bias towards more involved female-heads in the community is likely, though not all organizations operate via a politicized feminist base. Most organizations are mainly concerned to reach poor women in the community, with limited grounding in feminist politics.

The fieldwork was carried out during 1998–9, at which time eastern Sri Lanka was engaged in a protracted ethnic conflict. To enter the region I needed to establish contact with non-governmental organizations (NGOs) working in each district, and I did so through the Social Scientists Association (SSA), an NGO focusing on research and advocacy on gender, ethnic, and political rights, based in Colombo. Through the project activities of NGOs in these districts, I found research assistants from each ethnic community. Together with research assistants, village locations for conducting surveys were identified—with three villages specific to each ethnic community from every district selected. The survey was conducted in a total of 24 locations, comprising 3 towns and 21 villages.[19]

In the absence of comprehensive household listings, female-headed households were selected randomly through the direction of villagers and NGOs. Then through informal

---

[19] I preserve the anonymity of these villages as well as the female-heads interviewed. This is primarily because these villages were small where everyone knows everyone else, and I do not want my case studies to be identified with specific female-heads. Moreover, I do not want the State or para-military organizations to use this information against them. This especially so because some Tamil female-heads were openly critical of their social system, and there is an intricate system of information flows that may jeopardize the safety of some households. For example, when I was in Batticaloa I was told that the LTTE knew of my presence in the area, but did not think that my study was countering the nationalist project in any direct way. Therefore, I have reservations about divulging this information, mainly because the welfare of these households is an important ethical consideration that I need to bear in mind.

discussions and word-of mouth, the purpose of the survey was explained. The enthusiasm with which it was received facilitated the subsequent work. The research assistants, some 10 young women, undertook the survey more or less simultaneously. Initial surveys by the research assistants were conducted under my supervision, with subsequent questionnaires being individually carried out by the assistants. During the one-year period in Sri Lanka, I travelled frequently between the three districts, and all the in-depth dialogues and informal discussions with female-heads and the other community members (mostly women) were carried out by me.

While questionnaires can be useful, their limitations are many. First, power hierarchies that structure the survey research setting are well known. Researchers and the research group do not always come from the same social milieu. This was the case here. Working with and through research assistants from the local community and ethnic groups did erode some of these structured social realities, but essentially I remained an outsider. While this is not necessarily a negative factor, and indeed some female-heads said that they felt freer with me precisely because of this, I was not oblivious to the power settings involved in my fieldwork. An obvious example is that during my conversations I was constantly referred to as "*miss*" by many female-heads, acknowledging the difference between our social backgrounds.[20] Sometimes these hurdles were overcome and we called each other by our first names. This happened only when there was frequent interaction, familiarity and rapport. Another example of these power structures is that some female-heads gave me information on the assumption that they might get something out of this study. This occurred even though I emphatically stated that the primary purpose of the research was academic. I did mention that I intended to disseminate my findings to NGOs in the area, but I do not know the ways in which my results will be used for development-oriented

---

[20] "*Miss*" is used for women in opposition to "*Sir*" for men in Sri Lanka to designate difference in social background.

projects. Second, survey methods oversimplify complex processes, sometimes even leading to misinformed responses. An illustration from my fieldwork serves to stress this point. A question in my survey asked if female-heads received any support from their kin and/or community. To this question one female-head responded in the negative. Talking with her, however, revealed that she did receive support from her kin in terms of using her siblings' toilet facilities, her sons sleeping on their verandahs, and so forth. When I mentioned to her that this was support too, her response to me was: "Well this isn't economic support, and anyway my siblings are there for me to rely on for such help. This kind-of support I take for granted, and didn't think that it was important to mention it on paper." Such anecdotes point both to the oversimplifications of questions as well as to the inaccurate response a researcher may get should she/he rely merely on surveys. And third, empirical questions prevent researchers from querying relational factors important to decision-making processes. For example, questioning female-heads' decisions to remarry may have a simple 'yes' or 'no' response, but this tells us nothing of the many social relationships they may have considered before making a decision one way or another. Using illustrations from my research, some limits of empirical techniques are pointed out; but anthropologists initially raised similar concerns when feminists pointed to the androcentric assumptions that are at the core of the empirical tradition (Leach 1967, Harding 1986: 24-6, 162). Feminist economists, too, have increasingly documented their reservations about relying on the questionnaire method, and have called for a broadening of the methods used in conducting research in economics (MacDonald 1995, Berik 1997, Esim 1997, Olmsted 1997, Pujol 1997, and van Stavern 1997).

As a feminist, my reservations about empirical techniques are many. This stance is not simply an outcome of my ideological commitment to broadening the feminist economics base, but also because my field experience made me more aware of the simplification and limitations of empirical methods.

Having stated my reservations, my use of these very techniques in my own research was driven by the need to establish a nuanced analysis of female-headship. A purpose of this book is to uncover the survival strategies of female-heads and, therefore, it is imperative that I begin with an economic and demographic account of female-headed households. For these very reasons quantitative data are a necessary entry point to my study, but they are used with a mindfulness of the limitations of quantitative/questionnaire-based surveys. Based on the surveys, the next three chapters (Chapters Four, Five and Six) present basic data analysis to highlight a) female-headship and its causal factors, b) the demographic attributes of female-heads, and c) the livelihood patterns and economic position of Muslim, Sinhala and Tamil female-heads.[21] Such a portrayal helps the broader aim of this study: unpacking the social, cultural, historical and political factors that influence and shape particular economic outcomes.

So while I began with collecting and analysing quantitative data, another phase of my fieldwork focused on unstructured dialogues, conversations and interviews as a means of gathering information critical for putting some flesh on the bones of the statistical account. Gender relationships have to be situated historically, socially, politically and culturally, and ethnographic studies as well as non-formal information gathering exercises are needed to capture the richness and complexity of such dynamics. Drawing upon conversations with female-heads and other women in these communities, I was able to get their impressions, thoughts and perceptions of their particular experiences. These narratives draw attention to the numerous ways in which female-heads manoeuvre structural context as well as their approach towards decision-making. Both these processes underscore the importance of social relationships and social/cultural mores in 'economic' decision-making, which, while important, are not the only use of qualitative research.

---

[21] Indeed, since I am aware of the institutional setting in determining economic outcomes, each of the subsequent chapters will begin with a discussion of the specific cultural setting applicable to each ethnic group.

Using unstructured dialogues and conversations as facets of my fieldwork has also directed my attention to the most useful quantitative results. For example, female-heads' tales of drunken spouses stress the various factors that lead to *de facto* female-headship and emphasize the need to explore their particular hardships. Olmsted (1997) makes a similar point in her work: "while qualitative results can interpret quantitative outcomes, they can also be helpful in determining which quantitative results are likely to be the most useful" (1997: 146).

Furthermore, since I am uncovering the particularities of female-headship and ethnicity, embedding economic outcomes in a social, political and life-historical context helps expand notions of economic independence and empowerment. Much of my fieldwork made me realize that speaking of women's empowerment without considering the economic, social, and political capability base of female-heads is indeed foolhardy. Younger Tamil female-heads, for example, would show a high degree of consciousness of their socio-political rights and appeared more willing to challenge gender inequalities. Yet, their economic security and independence were mostly non-existent. Similarly, middle-aged to older Muslim female-heads had more economic security because they had working children, but their readiness to question their particular social and political vulnerabilities was severly limited. Speaking of such female-heads' empowerment is indeed problematic,[22] if only because socio-political awareness does not equate with economic autonomy and/or economic security need not lead to a broadening of social and political bases. Drawing upon narratives and qualitative research, therefore, helps tease out the diversity of female-heads' experiences that is important in understanding both the political economic contexts as well as the cultural underpinnings of female-heads' decision-making processes. Indeed, economic development requires paying

---

[22] Tendencies to make such slips are notable in an essay by Rajasingham-Senanayake (1999). My particular sympathies and problems with this reading are noted in detail in Chapter Eight, page 161 and footnote 20.

attention to structures that should be re-shaped through gender sensitive policy-making, and information about these can only be acquired through qualitative research. From my sample of 298 female-heads, 30—approximately 10 from each ethnic group—were selected for in-depth dialogue. In-depth discussions often accompanied the filling in of questionnaires and this was so for many of my in-depth profiles of female-heads. However, I also came to know some female-heads better by interacting with them on a regular basis, and developing a rapport with them—with some female-heads still communicating with me by letter. I made trips to specific villages that were noted as Muslim, Sinhala or Tamil in each district, which helped ensure the ethnic variation of the profiled female-heads. There was, however, no particular procedure for selecting the female-heads who were interviewed in depth. In addition, conversations I had with women and others in the communities shaped and sharpened my perceptions of the issues of female-heads in the region. Based on these case studies, therefore, I discuss the complexities of social structures by paying explicit attention to the resources—i.e. networks and children—that female-heads draw upon in their survival strategies. While Chapters Seven and Eight cover the qualitative dimensions of female-headship, the concluding chapters (Chapters Nine and Ten) pull together these quantitative and qualitative findings to discuss the implications for feminist economic methodology and development policy.

FOUR
Matrilineal Muslims
Female-heads in the Muslim Community

Matrilineal Kin, Patriarchal Structures: Social and Gender Relations among eastern Muslims[1]

The historical roots of matrilineal and matrilocal practices in household, kin and social organization of Muslims, Sinhala and Tamils are traced to Kerala, India. Muslims initially inhabiting Sri Lanka were migrant traders who established settlements in the main ports of the country. As a trading community, their settlements were initially transient and consequently writing about Muslims as a settled community can only be traced back to the 12th century (Samaraweera 1997: 294).[2] While the position of Muslims as a trading community has undergone vicissitudes through the colonial and post-colonial period, and continues to change, the matrilineal characteristics of eastern Muslims are common knowledge (McGilvray 1989, Agarwal 1990, 1996). I begin by outlining some key characteristics of the matrilineal practices of Muslims in eastern Sri Lanka, and then proceed to present indicators of economic well-being for female-heads. Do matrilineal practices benefit female-heads' economic

---
[1] This section is based on McGilvray (1989).
[2] As pointed out by Samaweera, however, this is not to deny the presence of Muslims in Sri Lanka in an earlier period, but rather to mark them as an established Sri Lankan community by the early 12th century (1997: 294).

welfare? If so, how? Moreover, will the economic indicators shed light on economic changes, not to mention the ethnic conflict, which may transform matrilineal social and kin structures? First, however, we turn to matrilineal practices among Muslims.[3]

Muslims are a socially more uniform group as they lack the caste distinctions of Sinhalese and Tamils.[4] It is not that Muslims lack class distinctions, as they differ in their access to economic resources. In structuring kin relations there is a preference for bilateral cross-cousin marriage that tends to reduce dowry expectations between the contracting families (McGilvray 1989: 199). Cross-cousin marriage does not entail informal relations between young women and men prior to marriage, as during adolescence girls and boys are segregated and chaperoned. Daughters remain in their natal community and village, while sons marry and take up residence with their wives. Arranging respectable and secure marriages for daughters and sisters remains a primary task for kin relations, with the women's side taking the initiative in marriage negotiations. Though close cousin marriage is supposed to have the effect of reducing dowry expectations, these remain a dominant issue in marital negotiations, outweighing the educational achievements, social status and personal qualities of the young men and women.[5]

---

[3] Readers should be aware that the kin structures of Muslims in eastern Sri Lanka are very different from those of other Muslims elsewhere in the country.

[4] McGilvray infers from shared matriclan names and customs between Muslims and Tamils that these are vestiges of a caste-hierarchy among Muslims. There is also a "small group of Maulanas—a group claiming patrilineal descent from the Prophet, and an equally small group of stigmatized barbers-circumcisers" (ibid: 195). Moreover, some of these distinctions are also based on regions of origin—Arabs versus South India (This was pointed to me by Kumari Jayawardena when she read an early draft of this chapter, and I should like to thank her for this and for clarifying the issue for me).

[5] Promoting and emphasizing education in the Muslim community in Sri Lanka has been closely linked to the Muslim revivalist movement of the late 19th century, when several Muslim men advocated male and female education (Samaraweera 1997: 296–9). But there was resistance from the

While the mother's dowry property and/or house is passed on to the eldest daughter, it is the task of fathers and sons to ensure that adequate dowries are provided for all daughters/sisters. The absolute minimum for a dowry is a house or land to build a house, without which McGilvray notes that marriage is impossible (1989: 201–2). Given the emphasis of securing adequate dowries, it comes as no surprise that sons defer marriage to see their sisters securely married. In the case of female-heads, there is more likely to be pressure on the single parent and older brothers to secure the necessary dowries for their daughters/sisters. So female-heads' survival does not only concern current economic conditions, but also saving for the future to provide for their daughters' dowries. The additional stress of finding dowries was conveyed to me by several female-heads, whether Muslim, Sinhala or Tamil, who had young adult "marriageable" daughters. Here I quote the sentiments of some Muslim female-heads:

> I wanted my daughters to be educated...Unfortunately, however, the expectations of today's men are different. They are more interested in dowries, and big dowries at that, than having educated wives. I don't regret educating my daughters... but I realize this has not made giving them in marriage any easier. Dowry still remains the important variable among Muslims. The earnings of my sons, therefore, go towards both maintaining our economic well-being and setting aside monies for their sisters' dowries.
> (Kathija, a 53-year old *de jure* female-head in Batticaloa and mother of one married daughter and four unmarried daughters aged 18–28 years).

---

community to English education *per se*, with female seclusion stated as the reason for Muslim girls' education levels dropping during this period (ibid: 303). At this present juncture in eastern Sri Lanka a notable number of female-heads from the Muslim community continually stressed the need for educating their daughters. They viewed it as a way of developing their daughters' capabilities as well as "their self-worth", and indeed in certain instances they noted how their expectations differed from those of their husbands'. Such changes are of course attractive, since they can be used as the basis for actively supporting girls' education on the ground that it is a need identified by women from within the community, rather than from "outside".

Since I only had daughters, educating them was important because I wanted to earn self-respect. Even though I was only 31 years when my husband died, educating them was my only passport to improving the self-respect of the family. My daughters now earn the income for the family, have improved living conditions at home, and this has helped getting respect from the community. But I just don't have the wealth and/or property to give as dowry for my daughters. Their income goes towards maintaining the well-being of our family, but not to set aside money for their dowries.
(Shanaz, a 42-year old *de jure* female-head in Ampara and mother of seven daughters aged 18–29 years).

Once a son is married off, his responsibilities shift towards his wife and sisters-in-law, and his kin loyalties move away from his natal kin. As the patriarch grows older, the first son-in-law is required to take an active role in maintaining the economic well-being of his wife's family (ibid: 206). This has two important implications for female-heads. On the one hand, female-heads are aware that they must make great use of their sons before they are married—and this is especially so where female-heads have daughters of marriageable age. On the other hand, they are concerned to marry their older daughters to the best possible man since he will eventually play an important role in securing and maintaining the family's social and economic well-being.[6]

---

[6] I did, however, come across instances where married brothers continued to support their natal kin. One instance was Farana, a 35-year old divorced female-head, whose brother contributed to her (and her parents') family income, even though he was married and living separately. Here it is possible that, because Farana had been abandoned at the age of 21, after a year of marriage, and they also have an unmarried younger sister, the brother felt obliged to support his parents and sisters. Siththi, however, did note that their sister-in-law had to be a kindly and understanding woman to allow her husband to continue helping his natal kin. But female-heads are aware that such support is rare and/or may not be continuous. An older widowed female-head recounted the support she received from her unmarried younger brother, but this stopped when he got married, and this has been the norm. In her words, "I cannot expect him to help me any longer, as his responsibility is now towards his wife and her family."

Matrilineal inheritance patterns and kin relations do not negate the existence of patriarchal social structures and/or gender roles. Muslim women are not encouraged to go into public spaces, and gender spatial segregation is even strictly enforced within household compounds. Since women's mobility is linked in Muslim interpretation to sexual license, controlling their mobility becomes an essential component of respectability (ibid: 212). This ideal cultural norm, however, does not necessarily apply across all classes. Class distinctions do exist, with women from low-income groups seeking work as all-female weeding groups and/or selling their goods in marketplaces and bus stands. For female-heads, such cultural ascription makes interaction between economic survival and adhering to cultural norms impossible, if not difficult. The economic corollary of cultural norms that limit women's mobility in public spaces is that it greatly constrains their ability to access economic resources readily and freely. While self-employment schemes may be the only means open to some female-heads to earn an income in such circumstances, these remain potentially exploitative and insecure avenues of income-generation.

Muslim women in this region, however, do have a high degree of autonomy within the household unit. In comparison with other South Asian communities, Muslim women here do not have to deal with domineering mothers-in-law, authoritarian older brothers, patri-local isolation, and unequal rights to property (ibid: 232). Female-heads are likely to profit to some degree from matrilineal social norms and customs. This is not to say that men are marginal actors, since they are vital members of their communities. Thus, despite matrilineal structures and relations, men remain visible members of the community who play an important role in the well-being of families and households. Furthermore, matrilineal kin relations do not negate the existence of patriarchal structures, but only dampen down the more severely negative attributes of the latter. For female-heads the pertinent issue is whether the co-existence of patriarchal structures and matrilineal kin relations works for their benefit, or not. To analyse this issue I shall first present the economic evidence for Muslim female-heads in east Sri Lanka.

Female-headship: A Novelty among Muslims?

Supportive kin structures have been the hallmark of most Muslim communities, with women usually being maintained by their male relatives. Chapter Two showed that this is a fast disintegrating reality. Since there are no studies in Sri Lanka that focus particularly on Muslim female-heads, it is difficult to learn about the history of female-headship in the community. But the increasing incidence of female-headship in Sri Lanka (Chapter Three) requires us to understand possible reasons for these trends. Are female-heads most likely to be widows? If so,

Table 4A: Marital Status of Muslim Female-heads*

	Ampara	Batticaloa	Trincomalee	All Districts
Deserted	2.9%	6.1%	10.0%	6.2%
	(1)	(3)	(3)	(7)
Divorced	0.0%	10.2%	3.3%	5.3%
	(0)	(5)	(1)	(6)
Married**	17.6%	20.4%	20.0%	20.4%
	(6)	(11)	(6)	(23)
Separated	5.9%	6.1%	10.0%	7.1%
	(2)	(3)	(3)	(8)
Widowed	73.6%	57.2%	56.7%	61.1%
	(25)	(27)	(17)	(69)
Sample size	34	49	30	113

* District differences are *not* statistically significant.
** The married row consists of *de facto* female-heads supporting their families because their husbands are unemployed, suffering from a terminal illness, physically disabled, alcoholic, mentally unfit to work, and/or any other reason that precludes them from supporting the economic well-being of the household.

was the death of the spouse from natural causes or was it linked to the conflict? Do female-heads also belong to non-widow categories: are there cases of separation, abandonment and divorce? Furthermore, while there are no national-level time series data for female-headship, have any of these female-heads noted their mothers as having been similarly positioned?

Widowhood is the main source of female-headship in all three districts, with Ampara registering the highest incidence of widows in the region. A significant proportion of female-headship, however, also occurs because of desertion, separation, and/or divorce. This varies from 8.8 per cent to 23.3 per cent within the region. Interestingly, desertion, separation, and/or divorce are lowest (and widowhood highest) in Ampara, where economic conditions are healthier. This begs the question whether economic pressures are more likely to thrust men into shirking their economic and social responsibilities. Similarly, does a relatively stable economic environment keep women from more conservative social groups with their spouses, even though there may be serious shortcomings in these marital unions? Islamic norms allow women to remarry, but it is a rarity in the region. This is not simply because there are built-in mechanisms within kin structures that make marriage work (ibid: 209), but also because women are increasingly "called upon to preserve...traditional customs and to be an identifiable symbol of the community which believes itself to be under siege" (Samuel 1994: 17).[7] So while these components of *de jure* and *de facto* female-headship should be unpacked, *de facto* headship among married women hovers in the 20.0 per cent

---

[7] A primary reason for men to honour their marriages under matrilineal systems is that they usually do not own property, since their parents' inheritance is passed to their sisters, and their bachelor earnings may have been used towards dowries for their sisters (McGilvray 1989: 209). While in principle matrilineal systems are supposed to lead to a greater degree of marital stability, with built-in mechanisms for men to stay married, changing circumstances, ranging from the difference between ownership and control to ethno-nationalist thinking, may compel women to stay married.

range too, which is high. Once again Ampara has the lowest level of *de facto* headship. Significant proportions of married women do take over the economic responsibilities of sustaining their households, even among Muslim women. Since widowhood is high among female-heads, it is equally important to query the causes leading to the death of spouses. Here too there emerge patterns reflecting the economic and conflict status of the districts (see Table 4B). Widowhood because spouses

Table 4B: Reasons for Spousal Death*

	Ampara	Batticaloa	Trincomalee	All Districts
Killed (state sponsored)	0.0% (0)	0.0% (0)	0.0% (0)	0.0% (0)
Killed (paramilitary)	16.0% (4)	33.3% (9)	41.1% (7)	20.3% (14)
Killed (non-conflict related)	0.0% (0)	0.0% (0)	5.8% (1)	1.4% (1)
Missing**	8.0% (2)	18.5% (5)	6.0% (1)	20.3% (14)
Natural causes	76.0% (19)	44.4% (12)	47.7% (8)	56.5% (39)
Suicide	0.0% (0)	3.8% (1)	0.0% (0)	0.0% (0)
Sample Size	25	27	17	69

* District differences are statistically significant between Ampara and Trincomalee (sig. = 0.032), marginally significant between Ampara and Batticaloa (sig. = 0.066), but *not* between Trincomalee and Batticaloa (sig. = 0.172).
** These are men who have gone missing since the beginning of the conflict, and where female-heads suspect that it is due to their being abducted and then killed by either para-military groups and/or the State. There is, however, little way of knowing if some men used the conflict as a pretext for simply disappearing and avoiding economic responsibility for their families.

died of natural causes is highest in Ampara, while in Batticaloa and Trincomalee their deaths are closely linked to the conflict.

The tabulated presentation of the leading causes of widowhood among female-heads indicates that female-headship is not just a result of the conflict. Although such households could depend upon their kin providing an extended family network that would absorb them into their fold, this may no longer hold true in eastern Sri Lanka. Changing economic conditions as well as civil unrest have put many pressures on kin support. Sustaining such support becomes less easy, with more women having to bear the cost of the household economy. This indeed is an ironic twist. Muslim female-heads are expected to preserve traditional values when the very material circumstances and basis of "traditional values" are rapidly disappearing. Indeed, the resistance of cultural values in spite of changing economic conditions is a reality with which female-heads have to constantly grapple. They must struggle to meet their economic needs without violating acceptable cultural norms. As Rifaya, a *de facto* female-head, mentions: "Islamic culture is resistant to change, and this is so even when the material realities are changing. Islam is Islam. Just because there is no husband how long can we be inside the house? Only if we earn can we eat." So will economic realities push accepted social and cultural borders? The answer is moot because there is no necessary uni-linear relationship between the economic base and cultural norms. Clearly, however, realizing female-heads' capabilities will require addressing their economic needs, since this is one crucial dimension through which women need to be empowered. To evaluate the economic position of female-heads, I begin by looking at the reasons for *de facto* female-headship.

In a community where women have limited visibility and presence, why do significant numbers of Muslim women have to assume *de facto* headship? According to the data below (Table 4C) the unemployment of spouses—among Muslim men this is highest in Batticaloa—remains one reason; illness is another, as is alcoholism[8] which makes women take over the responsibility for decision-making in the household. To some extent matrilineal practices that give women autonomy within their households are likely to promote female-headship in such situations. There are many illustrations in the case studies, where an adult son's presence did not preclude women from identifying themselves as household heads.[9] But this need not translate to ease of access to appropriate economic resources, given the socio-cultural restrictions on women's mobility. In this context, it is important and necessary to unravel the extent to which female-heads have the ability to access resources. It is difficult to expose the problems they have in doing so through mere tabulation of data, especially where the sample size is so small that any sub-division results in very small cell sizes. Substantiating this also requires listening to the narratives of female-heads, their particular experiences as well as the multitude of income sources they depend on for augmenting the household budget. Many of these experiences will also be determined by the demographics of the household, and this is analysed in the next section.

Demographic Outcomes through Cultural Institutions?

Since the primary reason for Muslim women becoming household-heads is widowhood, this may point to an underlying cause being the significant difference in the average age of wives and husbands, a feature of other South Asian countries, evident in Sri Lanka as well. While my questionnaire did not discover

---

[8] This is another way in which reality is out of step with the ideological premise of Islam, one which does not get recognition either by development planners and/or ethno-nationalists (my thanks to Dr Jane Humphries for pointing this out to me).

[9] While many women identified themselves as female-heads, where adult sons were present decision-making within the household was not the sole prerogative of the female-head. Instead, it was a shared task in such households, though there is no way of knowing the influence of these "budding patriarchs" in shaping decisions one way, and not another!

Table 4C: Causes of *de facto* Headship*

	Ampara	Batticaloa	Trincomalee	All Districts
Alcoholic	16.7% (1)	27.3% (3)	33.3% (2)	26.1% (6)
Mentally unfit to work	0.0% (0)	9.0% (1)	16.7% (1)	8.7% (2)
Physically disabled	0.0% (0)	0.0% (0)	0.0% (0)	0.0% (0)
Terminal/Major illness	66.7% (4)	18.2% (2)	50.0% (3)	39.1% (9)
Unemployed	16.6% (1)	45.5% (5)	0.0% (0)	26.1% (6)
Sample Size	6	11	7	23

* District differences are *not* statistically significant. The significance rate are: for Ampara and Batticaloa (sig. = 0.370), Trincomalee and Batticaloa (sig. = 0.273), Ampara and Trincomalee (sig. = 0.637).

age at marriage of husbands, it inadvertently obtained this information for married *de facto* female-heads through demographic data on households. Age-difference between married partners showed notable gaps of 7–10 years. Where the marital age of female-heads is very young (13–17) assuming a wide gap between partners is not implausible. The age structure of female-heads at marriage (Table 4D) shows the relevant patterns. In all three districts between 22.3–35.3 per cent of female-heads were married at 11–15 years, with another 50.0–65.4 per cent female-heads marrying at 16–20 years.

Since nearly 75.0 per cent of the sample were married between 11–20 years of age, there is a greater probability of them becoming widowed at an earlier stage of their lifecycle. The rationale for marriage at tender ages is usually expressed as: "This is usually the norm in our community. And although legally marriage is not allowed until a girl reaches puberty, usually our male kin work together with registrars so that they

Table 4D: Age Groups of Women at Marriage

	Ampara	Batticaloa	Trincomalee	All Districts
Age: < 16 years	35.3% (12)	22.4% (11)	23.3% (7)	26.6% (30)
Age: 16–20 years	50.0% (17)	65.4% (32)	50.0% (15)	56.6% (64)
Age: 21–25 years	14.7% (5)	10.2% (5)	16.7% (5)	13.2% (15)
Age: > 26 years	0.0% (0)	2.0% (1)	10.0% (3)	3.6% (4)
Sample Size	34	49	30	113

put a false age in the marriage certificate."[10] There were yet other female-heads, who mentioned that their families were poverty-stricken and "if the man's family was not interested in

---

[10] The statement made by this female-head reflects the incongruities as well as the misconceptions about marriage laws among Muslims. The General Law, along with the Kandyan, Thesawalami and Muslim Law, governs marriage in Sri Lanka. This positions Muslim women and girls in a particularly odd situation, where the family laws applicable to them on marriage age are different from those applicable to Sinhala and Tamil women/girls (Kodikara 1999: 18). consent is required from young brides if they have reached puberty and those girls given in marriage before puberty have the right to accept or reject their marriage upon reaching puberty. Yet, there are many loopholes in Muslim law that run contrary to the interest of women and girls – namely, the bride is not expected to take part in the *nikah* (marriage) ceremony and there is no provision for her to sign the marriage register (ibid: 11–2). Consequently, girls can be given in marriage without their consent. Moreover, in the absence of proof that girls have attained puberty their minority terminates at 15 years, and so child marriages get solemnized, with courts showing unwillingness to "interfere" with customary religious practices (ibid: 17–8). Kodikara also goes on to note some of the negative outcomes for women because of young marriage ages – especially the associated health risks during pregnancy, and for education, and income generation (1999: 30–5). [My thanks to Chulani Kodikara for clarifying the legal issues on the status of Muslim women in Sri Lanka, and making me aware of the feminist legal issues involved on the topic].

a dowry then such a man was considered a godsend since this took a heavy burden off our families." Interestingly, many female-heads were fairly well aware of the legal stipulations against child marriage, but revelations of their personal experiences show how male kin connive with public authorities (usually men) to overlook legislation protecting women. So the issue here remains one where protecting "customs" is considered more important than protecting the interests of women. Such practices not only ignore women's well-being but they also spill over to their household structures with very particular implications. For female-heads, it implies assuming headship at young ages since the financial support from traditional kin structures is lacking. Table 4E below shows more detailed information on the age structures of marriage for female-headship, and it does not paint a pretty picture.

Women's age at assuming headship is usually linked to widowhood in both South Asia and other regions (Chapter Two), with headship peaking around 35–44 years. A sizable number belong to the 40–49-year age group, with it rising for the 50+ age group (Youssef and Hetler 1984). But in my data larger proportions of female-headed households are found in the younger age groups, though this varies somewhat across the regions. While in Sri Lanka a large proportion of female-headship in the Muslim community is the result of widowhood, their spouses have not died of natural causes. The role of the conflict has been to create younger female-heads, even if they are hidden in the traditional category of widowhood. The average age of women assuming headship in all three districts hovers around 34–36 years, which can be attributed to both the young age of marriage and/or the conflict thrusting them into

---

In my study then, it is no surprise that 26.6 per cent of female-heads in the sample were married between the ages of 10–15. And it should be even less of a revelation then that they assume headship owing to widowhood through natural causes, because the marriage age of their spouses is likely to be much older. Their dying through natural causes is an expected result in such a scenario (Table 4B)!

64 Matrilineal Communities, Patriarchal Realities

Table 4E: Age Structure for Women Assuming Headship

	Ampara	Batticaloa	Trincomalee	All Districts
< 20 year age group	0.0% (0)	0.0% (0)	4.2% (1)	1.1% (1)
21–25 year age group	10.7% (3)	14.7% (6)	8.3% (2)	11.8% (11)
26–30 year age group	14.3% (4)	17.1% (7)	12.5% (3)	15.1% (14)
31–35 year age group	14.3% (4)	31.6% (13)	29.2% (7)	25.8% (24)
36–40 year age group	42.8% (12)	17.1% (7)	16.6% (4)	24.7% (23)
41–45 year age group	3.6% (1)	14.6% (6)	20.8% (5)	12.9% (12)
46–50 year age group	10.7% (3)	2.4% (1)	4.2% (1)	5.4% (5)
> 50 year age group	3.7% (1)	2.5% (1)	4.2% (1)	3.2% (3)
Sample Size	28	41	24	93

female-headship at a young age.[11] With female-headship occurring at a younger age, how do these women bear the economic responsibility for their households, given the cultural restrictions on mobility in the public sphere? With deteriorating economic conditions and eroding financial support from kin, female-heads have the options of either risking poverty or breaking norms regarding their mobility. The livelihoods they choose will reflect this dilemma and their attempts to obtain a living without violating cultural norms in too flagrant a manner. What patterns are found in the livelihoods sought?

---

[11] The following chapters find patterns of younger female-heads holding true across all three ethnic groups, which makes it necessary to examine this closely for its particular ramifications on households welfare levels.

Livelihoods, Income-generation Patterns and Trends

For female-heads daily survival is critical, and this depends upon the possibilities for income generation and sources of employment. While meeting basic economic needs is a primary concern, the cultural context within which economic decisions are made also remains vital. Restrictions placed on women's mobility and cultural space are unlikely to make things easy in their ability to access economic resources. While material circumstances keep changing, there is no guarantee that the cultural milieu reflects social transformations. The cultural rhetoric may not acknowledge shifting material and social circumstances, and the discrepancies between reality and ideal norms. Islamic cultural patterns require protecting and safeguarding the interests of women kin members, and at the level of the household this gets translated into supportive kin structures. In eastern Sri Lanka, the existence of matrilineal structures must augur well for Muslim female-heads. Accessing economic resources and earning an income remains a fundamental concern of female headed-households. To analyse the economic well-being levels of Muslim female-heads, firstly the income patterns of their households for Ampara, Batticaloa and Trincomalee are presented. Next, sources of income, occupation patterns, household size, and reliance on children for income of Muslim female-headed households will be discussed to obtain a broad picture of their economic support base.

Evidence from income patterns reinforces the earlier observations of the different levels of economic development in the Ampara, Batticaloa, and Trincomalee districts. Further, the intensity of the ethnic conflict translates into economic insecurity for these families, with Batticaloa emerging as the poorest region. Batticaloa is the least developed of the districts and is characterized by the lowest income levels. It is also where the ethnic conflict has been worst and this too must have affected the poverty of the female-heads. In contrast, Ampara has economic growth and here the conflict is sporadic;

Table 4F: Income Levels and Patterns*

	Ampara	Batticaloa	Trincomalee	All Districts
Mean income	Rs 2,916.18	Rs 1,825.51	Rs 2,362.50	Rs 2,592.81
Minimum income	Rs 750.00	Rs 500.00	Rs 855.00	Rs 500.00
Maximum income	Rs 10,850.00	Rs 5,000.00	Rs 14,000.00	Rs 14,000.00
Sample Size	34	49	30	113

Income groups (in Rs)	Ampara	Batticaloa	Trincomalee	All Districts
500.00 – 1,000.00	14.7% (5)	32.7% (16)	16.7% (5)	23.2% (26)
1,100.00 – 2,000.00	35.3% (12)	36.7% (18)	30.0% (9)	34.6% (39)
2,100.00 – 3,000.00	20.6% (7)	24.5% (12)	16.6% (5)	21.3% (24)
3,100.00 – 4,000.00	5.9% (2)	4.1% (2)	6.7% (2)	5.3% (6)
4,100.00 – 5,000.00	8.8% (3)	2.0% (1)	6.7% (2)	7.1% (7)
5,100.00 – 6,000.00	8.8% (3)	0.0% (0)	10.0% (3)	3.1% (5)
> 6,100.00	5.9% (2)	0.0% (0)	13.3% (4)	5.4% (6)

* Regional differences are statistically significant for mean income (sig. = 0.002)

consequently, female-heads here have higher income trends and the highest mean income for all three districts. Ampara is the only district that has an average monthly income level above the officially designated poverty line of Rs 2,500.00 in Sri Lanka, with income levels of female-heads in Batticaloa being well below figures for other female-heads in Sri Lanka.[12]

---

[12] In addition it should be noted that the national average monthly income for female-heads is from labour earnings only (Chapter Three). For female-heads in this study the figure is the total income from all sources – including remittances and children's and State contributions.

The average size of female-headed households also varies across the regions, with household sizes mirroring the conflict and economic conditions in each district, ranging from 4.44 in Ampara to 3.59 in Trincomalee to 2.81 in Batticaloa. Conceivably, poor political, social and economic conditions in Batticaloa could be driving children away from female-headed households to other districts, where there is economic, social and political stability—relatively, speaking of course! Computing average per capita income for the three districts gives figures— at Rs 656.79 in Ampara, Rs 649.64 in Batticaloa, and Rs 658.07 in Trincomalee—below the national average reference poverty line of Rs 755.05 (Chapter Three).

Trapped at these levels of poverty, how do Muslim female-headed households survive? I hypothesize that a greater proportion of Muslim female-heads will be relegated to the informal sector, where economic insecurity and vulnerability is greatest but where seeking a livelihood is compatible with patriarchal religious and cultural norms. Economic insecurity may also imply many other things to Muslim female-heads in Batticaloa, ranging from the reduced likelihood of receiving financial support from kin to their willingness to press the boundaries of their cultural space. Also, where economic deprivation is greater do kin structures themselves get transformed? Decoding the gaps in kin structures will help show that kinship is not a fixed property; this is suggested by variations in household size where these are all female-headed Muslim households with roughly similar age distributions. We also need to evaluate the economic and cultural factors that help prop up such institutions.[13]

---

[13] Uncovering the economic "roots" of cultural institutions is not the purpose of this project. It is rather to evaluate the cultural and economic dynamics in order to show their over-determined nature. For example, some female-heads noted the need to push and question cultural restrictions in the face of economic adversity, while for others adhering to "respectable" standards (read: cultural norms) was as important as meeting their economic needs. Chapter Seven carries a detailed discussion of these issues, where anecdotal evidence helps uncover them.

Regardless of cultural prescriptions, most Muslim female-heads count themselves as providing the main source of economic support towards the household, with 55.1 per cent and 66.7 per cent of female-heads in Batticaloa and Trincomalee, respectively, identifying themselves as the main economic providers. The exception was in Ampara, with only 36.2 per cent of female-heads perceiving their role as that of chief breadwinner. Differences in the extent to which families in the three districts rely on these female-heads will be echoed in the extent to which they rely on children's own contributions, as subsequently the restrictions placed on women's mobility and limited cultural space will necessarily shape the occupations they choose. So what patterns do the responses of Muslim female-heads show? Table 4G below provides occupational data for female-heads. Significant proportions of female-heads are in home-based/self-employment work. Wage and agricultural labour also remain common occupational choices, with a significant number (26.5 per cent) of female-heads in Ampara noting that they do not work.

Despite female-heads' awareness of the need to educate their children, they rely on them to contribute to the household income. Children do play an important role, even though this may imply disrupting their education—especially when economic circumstances are dire. Table 4H (page 70) shows female-heads' reliance on children for the main source of economic support as 40.2 per cent, 40.8 per cent, and 20.0 per cent, with economic support from kin relatives accounting for a mere 23.5 per cent, 4.1 per cent, and 13.3 per cent, in Ampara, Batticaloa, and Trincomalee, respectively. An interesting point to note is that in Batticaloa, the most impoverished district, economic support from kin is lowest – a mere 4.1 per cent of female-heads getting such support—with children providing the highest incidence of economic support.[14] Obviously, severe

---

[14] This does not exclude female-heads from contributing to their household incomes, but rather points to the main source of support coming from children and/or kin with female-heads supplementing this income.

Matrilineal Muslims 69

Table 4G: Occupation Patterns of Female-heads*

Occupations	Ampara	Batticaloa	Trincomalee	All Districts
Service/Clerical/ Government worker	2.9% (2)	2.0% (1)	3.3% (1)	3.4% (4)
Wage labourer	23.5% (8)	32.7% (16)	39.9% (11)	31.0% (35)
Domestic worker	0.0% (0)	24.5% (12)	10.0% (3)	13.3% (15)
Agricultural labourer	5.9% (2)	2.0% (1)	0.0% (0)	2.7% (3)
Animal Husbandry	0.0% (0)	0.0% (0)	0.0% (0)	0.0% (0)
Small-scale farmer/ Home gardening	0.0% (0)	0.0% (0)	0.0% (0)	0.0% (0)
Home-based worker	41.2% (14)	38.8% (19)	46.8% (15)	41.6% (48)
Not employed	26.5% (9)	0.0% (0)	0.0% (0)	8.0% (9)
Sample Size	34	49	30	113

* District differences *are* statistically significant for Ampara and Batticaloa (sig. = 0.000) and Ampara and Trincomalee (sig. = 0.027) but not Batticaloa and Trincomalee (sig. = 0.615).

economic pressures added to the gravity of clashes in Batticaloa make the economic security of female-heads more fragile. Thus the statistics collected for Muslim female-heads point to the dynamics between material realities and social structures, where economic deprivation and political instability leads to deterioration in kin support.

Children's economic support towards the household plays a leading role in household welfare, but looking into gender dimensions of this economic support contradicts the conventional view that it depends only on sons. It is true that, of labouring children, sons do play the most important role in supporting their households—with 63.15 per cent, 68.0 per cent

70   Matrilineal Communities, Patriarchal Realities

Table 4H: Gender Make-up and Sources of Support

Primary Sources of Support	Ampara	Batticaloa	Trincomalee	All Districts
Children	40.2% (13)	40.8% (20)	20.0% (6)	34.5% (39)
Kin	23.5% (9)	4.1% (2)	13.3% (4)	13.3% (15)
Female-heads' own income	36.3% (12)	55.1% (27)	66.7% (20)	52.2% (59)
Sample Size	34	49	30	113
Gender of children (primary & secondary earners)				
Boys	63.15% (12)	68.0% (17)	60.8% (14)	64.2% (43)
Girls	31.5% (6)	28.0% (7)	34.8% (8)	31.3% (21)
Both	5.35% (1)	4.0% (1)	4.4% (1)	4.5% (3)
Sample Size	19	25	23	67

and 60.8 per cent of sons in Ampara, Batticaloa, and Trincomalee, respectively, supporting their households economically. But, a sizable number of daughters, however, also do the same, the figures being 31.5 per cent, 28.0 per cent and 34.8 per cent for the three districts, respectively—and this, of course, excludes domestic chores performed by daughters!

Even with Muslim female-heads relying upon a broad base for economic security, their income levels remain low and economic vulnerability is very real. This overview also shows that female-heads in Batticaloa face the greatest level of economic insecurity. Economic conditions as well as the intensity of the conflict makes their situation doubly precarious. But to treat the emergence of female-headed households as a mere consequence of the conflict is to ignore the fundamental socio-economic processes leading to social transformation in the region. I now turn to a discussion of the data and issues pertinent to Sinhala (Chapter Five) and Tamil (Chapter Six) female-heads.

FIVE
Variation on a Theme
Sinhala Female-heads in Hybrid Lineage Systems

Transitional Kinship Structures, Class and Gender Relations

A common misconception held by Sinhala people is that they are ethnically distinct from Tamils and Muslims, that they are a separate people with different roots in India (Guneratne 2001: 20). However, anthropologists have noted similarities in kinship structures across these ethnic groups as well as regional-based variations in kin rules and patterns among Sinhalese (Yalman 1971, Guneratne 2001). Aside from disparities in regionally-specific kin systems, traditional Sinhala laws of inheritance were based on bilateral transfer of property—though an important distinction for women was based on whether they were married uxorilocally (*binna*) or virilocally (*diga*) (Agarwal 1996: 122). Despite common bilateral inheritance patterns, which work favourably for propertied women, there are distinctions in kin rituals that may also shape the particular position of women in their communities. Decoding the key attributes of the kin structures for Kandyan and low-country Sinhalese[1] helps to

---

[1] The Kandyan region is located centrally in the interior of Sri Lanka, and has had a distinct social and political history (Gunasinghe 1996: 77–110). Since its location is in the hill country region of Sri Lanka, the social system of other areas in in the country are uniformly labelled as being in the low-country. Consequently, Sinhala people categorize themselves as

understand the significance of these structures for women – and female-heads in particular.[2]

While matrilineal inheritance patterns are largely absent for Sinhalese in all regions, Kandyan people exhibit kin structure characteristics more akin to matrilineal kin practices (Yalman 1971: 189–224). For low-country Sinhalese, the kin system is set at an intermediate stage between patriliny and matriliny (ibid: 281). Nevertheless, cross-cousin marriage, a key attribute of matrilineal kin structures, is common practice for Sinhalese all over Sri Lanka (Guneratne 2001: 29–34). Local patterns and variations are noteworthy since gender relations are partially patterned through kinship systems, presenting feminists with the ability to discuss the position of women vis-à-vis kin structures. Focusing on female-heads in this particular instance, the task is to understand the hybrid aspects of the low-country Sinhala kin system and the shaping of support structures for them. An amalgam of kin structures may offer women opportunities that are to not available to those living under strict patriarchal and patrilineal structures. Furthermore, Sinhala women, who are predominantly Buddhist, have less repressive social restrictions placed on them through religious structures (Jayawardena 1986: 113).[3] Altogether, then, Sinhalese female-

---

either up-country or low-country Sinhalese, which is largely a description of their geographical origins—though there are differences in the respective social systems too.

[2] Variations in kinship patterns and regional-specificity are germane to Muslims and Tamils too. The distinctive feature for low-country Sinhalese is the hybrid nature of their kin structures, which is likely to be further compounded for Sinhalese living in the Eastern Province where matrilineal systems pervade the social structure. My argument is not simply focused on the need to look at possible common attributes between the ethnic groups in eastern Sri Lanka, but also to uncover the class dynamics of kin support structures – and the ramifications for female-heads.

[3] Lack of oppressive restrictions on women in Buddhism is not to dismiss the existence of patriarchal social structures in Sri Lanka. As Jayawardena (1986) rightly articulates, "Buddhism was also instrumental in reducing the rigors of the caste system, but also some of the glaring injustices practised against women such as *sati* and the ban on widow

heads may have in place relatively "liberating" social spaces that should allow them to realize their capabilities. Narratives by female-heads and socio-economic data, however, suggest a more complicated picture, where hybrid kin/community structures convey patriarchal prejudices that adversely affect female-heads. The experiences of Sinhala female-heads in confronting patriarchal ideologies and structures are, at another level, unsurprising. Given the particular political situation in Sri Lanka, Sinhala women too are called on to preserve and nurture "Sinhala-Buddhist" culture – which, as mentioned before, is embedded in a patriarchal discourse (Chapter One). This convergence of separate dynamics, therefore, requires a closer examination of the specifics of hybrid kin relations, over-determined by class structures and ethno-nationalist discourse, that affect Sinhalese women too.

Customary bilateral and matrilineal inheritance patterns have been linked positively to the enhancement of the position and status of women, with illustrations taken from the Muslim, Sinhala and Tamil communities pressing this point (Agarwal 1990, 1996). Propertied women obviously benefit greatly where inheritance patterns favour them. But in what other ways do kin structures favour women's position and, particularly, how in the event of female-headship do these structures enable them to use this opportunity to improve their welfare? How do female-heads who have limited or no access to property and land, gain from structures that benefit propertied female-heads? Or, do ethnographers play down class distinctions that factor in female-heads from low-income levels? Equally, if there were kin and community structures that have been favourable to women in the past, do they persist or are they increasingly imbued with patriarchal values?[4] The latter, of course, is possibly

---

remarriage." But as pointed out in Chapter One, Sinhala-Buddhist revivalism did send dual messages on the position of women as good mothers and wives. So as far as the generality of women's position was concerned, patriarchal structures "gave women a subordinate role" (ibid: 113).

[4] Posing this question is appropriate in that ethnic identities are frequently expressed in terms of gender relations where women are

detrimental to female-heads. They will have more restrictions placed upon them as both sole economic providers and bearers of cultural values. In so far as economic decisions are made within the contours of cultural and social values, an increasing infusion of patriarchal values is unlikely to make life easier for female-heads. But social changes also imply opportunities that can be progressively used by female-heads to challenge restrictive practices. To explore the possibility of the latter, both the socio-economic context and the economic profiles of female-heads need to be sketched.

Like Tamils in the eastern region (Chapter Six), the Sinhalese community too primarily depends upon fishing or farming. Agriculture for the Sinhalese can be either settled paddy cultivation or *chena* (slash-and-burn) cultivation, with the former linked to rural development and settlement schemes initiated during the post-colonial period. Nuclear villages located in the interior of Ampara and Trincomalee were engaged primarily in settled paddy cultivation, though in certain instances *chena* cultivation was also the occupation of some communities. Sinhalese coastal settlements, on the other hand, have extended links to the region since deep sea fishing is linked to monsoon weather patterns, with migration between the South-West and North-East areas being commonplace in the fishing community.[5]

---

perceived as bearers of cultural values (de Alwis 2000: 53). Sinhala nationalism in Sri Lanka too has articulated the ideal role of women and womanhood (Jayawardena 1992), which interacts and transforms social structures that may formerly have benefited women. For feminist economists the essential purpose here is to uncover these dynamics as they impinge upon women's well-being—and in this project, on female-heads' levels of well-being.

[5] Sinhala settlements in eastern Sri Lanka are partly the focus of ethnic demographics in the region. Many of the Sinhala settlement schemes are perceived as attempts by the Sri Lankan (read: Sinhala) post-colonial State to change the demographic composition in the area. There is little doubt that this was a motivation for the Sri Lankan State to pursue settlement schemes in eastern Sri Lanka (Hoole et al. 1990: 340). Moreover, population pressures in urban and semi-urban areas of Sri Lanka also required rural development and regeneration—with this providing a

Another similarity linking Sinhalese and Tamils is the existence of a caste system among the two communities. Since the caste system for Sinhalese is based on a *Rajakariya* (secular ideology of kingly honour and a division of labour) system, here too notions of sexual purity and pollution are largely absent (Yalman 1971).[6] The absence of matrilineal descent systems among low-country Sinhalese however does not preclude the importance of daughters in their households: daughters provide insurance and socio-economic security for parents in old age. Consequently, maintaining good relations and ensuring the well-being of daughters, through inheritance or dowry, is commonplace among higher-income classes. For women in low-income and socially-excluded groups, dowry, where it exists, usually take the form of cash and movable wealth, and is considered a symbolic device through which social relations are cemented between kin groups. The emphasis was less on the economic dimensions to dowry transactions and more on building social relations between kin groups (ibid: 274). Since inheritance is equally divided between sons and daughters, women are relatively well positioned—and cash dowry is emphasized only in the absence of land or property for the family unit.

The presence of customs favourable to women does not negate the formulation of patriarchal ideals among low-country Sinhalese or indeed the rapid commercialization of dowries in

---

sound economic rationale for pursuing settlement policies that would change the demographic composition of eastern Sri Lanka. This aside, however, some proportion of Sinhalese would have populated the region, if simply because 450 years of colonial rule and migration of fishing communities between North-East and South-West Sri Lanka necessarily entails interaction and co-existence of the different ethnic communities in these regions.

[6] Furthermore, recent work on class composition and transformations in colonial Ceylon notes the disintegration of the caste system as a mode of labour organization (Jayawardena 2000: xi–ii). This did not, however, lead to the disappearance of the caste system as an ideology. Instead it now withdrew to the private domain, where caste became linked to the marriage patterns of women (ibid: xiii).

76 Matrilineal Communities, Patriarchal Realities

marriages (Goonasekere 1996: 314). Marriage rituals emphasize the "high" status of the groom, and hypergamous unions are commonplace. With marriage systems emulating patrilineal ideals along with hypergamous unions, social elements through which women's sexual behaviour is controlled are very much present among low-country Sinhalese (Yalman 1971: 279).[7] Additionally, colonial legislation that instituted monogamous marriages and a preference for virilocal/patrilineal residence, has been furthered through post-colonial practices that instituted patrilineal inheritance through land reform and settlement schemes (Risseeuw 1992: 48). Complex rules of inheritance and kinship systems were gradually eroded, and as Rissecuw notes:

> The woman's relatively independent position in marriage, provided by her life-long access to land and property and the right to divorce, was to shift to the position of a legal and economic dependent, with limited divorce rights, to be protected by her husband, and on his default, by the state. Her position became one, which was at best secure, but *lacked economic potential*, because even as a widow her rights to land and property were finally curtailed. (1992: 48, emphasis added).

Historical considerations have obviated any progressive legislative steps that could have promoted and protected women's rights and interests. Legislative changes that promoted patriarchal interests transformed gender relations not merely

---

[7] Contrast this with the Kandyan pattern of endogamous marriages and open (marital) unions, where there is less social compulsion on women to remain in marriages. Here women are free to enter and depart from sexual unions with men with little (or no) social stigma attached to their decisions not to remain within an unsatisfactory union (ibid: 279). [NOTE: Feminists have criticized Yalman's work for romanticizing the position and status of women in Sri Lanka. Malathi de Alwis and Kumari Jayawardena drew attention to this criticism, by highlighting cases of village practices and folklore that contravene the favourable picture painted by Yalman. A helpful example to press this feminist concern is where young women raped (usually by a man) are married-off/required to cohabit with the rapists! A Sri Lankan film, *Baddegama*, based on Leonard Woolf's book *The Village in the Jungle*, recounts a similar incident in a rural village, although the location is Southern Sri Lanka].

for women in the landed and upper-income classes, but also for working class, low-income and marginalized women. Women of these social groups had increasingly to turn to labour and trade as sources of income, where the gender division of occupations confined them in low-skill and poorly paid work (ibid: 51).

Considering the historical processes together with social customs and kinship patterns clearly shows the contradictory pulls that Sinhala female-heads may face. On the one hand, there are social customs and kin patterns that have traditionally positioned women favourably. On the other, historical and legislative reforms together with ethno-nationalist discourse curtail the possibility of women's economic independence as well as their social space. However, as Lalini—a 23-year old female-head—mentions, concerted efforts are necessary to hear the voices of female-heads and remove their economic dependency from patriarchal structures:

> When female-heads have independent access to income, land or property, and/or have parents and siblings who support them, the women do not rush to remarry. It is only when female-heads face severe economic deprivation that they remarry to avoid hardship...I am fortunate because I do get support from my parents, sibling, kin and neighbors, and feel no need to remarry. But there should be better protective mechanisms that will free us from economic dependency on kin and community—and having constantly to be concerned about adhering to "proper" behaviour. Men never worry themselves with *charithra-varitha* (proper behaviour), so why should we?
> (*Lalini, a 23-year old de facto female-head from Trincomalee whose husband was abducted by the LTTE, and a mother of two children aged 1 ½ and 6 years.*).

Lalini's incisive comments on the links between social norms, gender relations, and access to economic resources, locates the structures within which Sinhala female-heads support themselves and their households in eastern Sri Lanka. And the chapter now turns towards accounting for these facets of female-headship, first, by considering the patterns and causes of female-headship among Sinhala female-heads.

Desertion and Increasing Trends in Female-headship: Conflict-related Issues?

Tabulating and studying female-headship in Sri Lanka is relatively new, as established in Chapter Two. Yet there is incidental evidence that suggests that the female-headed household is not a recent phenomenon, with as many as 25.0 per cent of Sinhala female-heads in the region noting their own mothers as having headed such households. While female-headship may not be new for the Sinhalese, the current ethnic conflict has exacerbated an emerging pattern. Sinhala female-heads have also lost men owing to the conflict – in revenge killings and abductions by the LTTE and other para-military organizations. But, as among Tamil female-heads, there are also many instances of desertion, separation and/or divorce (Chapter Six). This common feature of Tamil and Sinhala female-headed households distinguishes them from their Muslim counterparts (Chapter Four). Analysis of the particularities of Sinhalese female-heads follows a format similar to that in the preceding chapter (Chapter Four).

Table 5A: Marital Status of Sinhala female-heads*

	Ampara	Trincomalee	All Districts
Deserted	2.9%	22.9%	12.9%
	(1)	(8)	(9)
Divorced	5.7%	0.0%	2.9%
	(2)	(0)	(2)
Married	28.6%	14.3%	21.4%
	(10)	(5)	(15)
Separated	14.3%	5.7%	10.0%
	(5)	(2)	(7)
Widowed	48.6%	57.1%	52.9%
	(17)	(20)	(37)
Sample Size	35	35	70

* District differences *are* statistically significant (sig. = 0.031)

Female-headship due to widowhood is significant—48.6 per cent in Ampara and 57.1 per cent in Trincomalee—but the apparent patterns are more complicated for the Sinhala community. A high proportion of married women assume headship—28.6 per cent and 14.3 per cent in Ampara and Trincomalee, respectively. But the numbers for desertion, separation, and divorce as factors leading to female-headship are also significant. For the category of *de jure* female-headship, i.e. widowhood and divorce, this varies between 54.3–57.1 per cent in both districts, with just Ampara noting a 5.7 per cent divorce rate. While divorce is non-existent in my sample for Trincomalee, this is negated by a higher prevalence of desertion, which is 22.9 per cent for the district. *De facto* female-headship due to desertion and separation rises to 28.6 per cent in Trincomalee, with separation accounting for 5.7 per cent. Also, *de facto* includes married women where the husband does not play the usual role as head of household. By contrast, in Ampara, desertion is only 2.9 per cent but separation is much higher, 14.3 per cent, than in Trincomalee. Stresses that pull apart marriages exist in both districts but the mechanisms through which break-ups take place are different. Greater levels of economic deprivation, as in Trincomalee, strain traditional household structures, with a greater incidence of men absconding. In Ampara, where favourable economic conditions prevail, the possibility of women initiating separation from their spouses should not be discounted, and indeed could indicate a relatively strong position for women in marital breakdown (Jackson 1998: 46). Whether female-heads separate or are deserted matters for the well-being of their households. Specifically, deserted female-heads' proclivity to poverty is likely, given the suddenness of the break-ups of their marital unions. It is not simply this factor that exposes their vulnerability, but most female-heads whose spouse abandons them live in the hope of their husband's return. An emotional inability to accept a break-up and the reality of their situation can of course hinder the economic well-being of their households too, since such female-heads are unlikely to put much effort in devising efficient survival strategies for their households.[8] In the case of separation, female-heads are aware of the crumbling nature of their unions and possibly, therefore, can take precautionary steps towards finding alternative and supplementary sources of income. A 22-year old *de facto* female-head, Gayani, recaps her separation as follows.

> I married when I was 17 years old. After the birth of my first daughter I found that my husband was involved with another woman. Whenever I confronted him, he would deny this affair. Though I had three children by Ajith, I was always aware that he was taking minimal economic responsibility for our household. I ignored it for a while. When things were getting difficult I found employment as a labourer. Since the birth of my youngest daughter, 4 months old, Ajith has separated from me. Because I took steps towards finding my own income to support my household, our separation did not jeopardize the welfare of my family. I have been fortunate to have my own family in close proximity, and my mother helps me caring for my children... Yes, it is difficult to be a young working mother, but at least I have my mother and sisters to help me.
> (*Gayani, a 22-year old* de facto *female-head from Ampara. A labourer and mother of three*).

Unravelling the dynamics of such trends is important: household structures are changing and it is well to consider these shifts since they help articulate development policies that move beyond the patriarchal household models. Furthermore, for eastern Sri Lanka it challenges the conventional wisdom that links female-headship simplistically to the ethnic conflict. Widowhood is low among the Sinhala community, closer to that experienced by Muslims than by Tamils. So there are many factors leading Sinhala women to assume headship, and they support the contention of altering household structures in

---

[8] Indeed, studies in Sri Lanka that have focused on the psycho-social dimensions of female-headship in eastern Sri Lanka reaffirm such attitudes for Tamil and Muslim female-heads who have missing spouses (Thiruchandran 1999). Comparable attitudes are also likely for Sinhalese female-heads who have been deserted, though the psycho-emotional impact of desertion is likely to be less severe than for female-heads whose spouses have been abducted by the military or State-sponsored paramilitary forces.

eastern Sri Lanka. The following table works out the different patterns for the Sinhalese community:

Table 5B: Reasons for Spousal Death*

	Ampara	Trincomalee	All Districts
Killed (State sponsored)	0.0% (0)	0.0% (0)	0.0% (0)
Killed (paramilitary)	23.6% (4)	30.0% (6)	27.0% (10)
Killed (non-conflict related)	0.0% (0)	0.0% (0)	0.0% (0)
Missing	0.0% (0)	5.0% (1)	2.7% (1)
Natural causes	58.8% (10)	60.0% (12)	59.5% (22)
Suicide	17.6% (3)	5.0% (1)	10.8% (4)
Sample size	17	20	37

*District differences are *not* statistically significant.

The number of spouses who have been killed as a result of the conflict is higher in Trincomalee, probably because the conflict here has been more intense than in Ampara. But the incidence of a husband's dying of natural causes is also higher in Trincomalee, though the difference is marginal between the two districts. While *de jure* female-headship is increased by the conflict, among Sinhalese female-heads it is not simply linked to the conflict. A fairly high rate of suicides is also notable for Ampara – markedly higher than for any of the other ethnic groups (Tables 4B and 6B).[9] Greater economic stability, as in Ampara, does not preclude other social pressures that lead to changing household structures, where women have to fend for themselves and their households.

[9] Sri Lanka is noted as having one of the highest incidence of suicides in the world (Biyanwila 1997: 141–52).

82 Matrilineal Communities, Patriarchal Realities

Having considered *de jure* Sinhala female-heads, and the absence of links between headship and the conflict, we now need to account for *de facto* female-heads.

Table 5C: Causes of *de facto* Headship*

	Ampara	Trincomalee	All Districts
Alcoholic	45.4% (5)	42.8% (3)	44.4% (8)
Mentally unfit to work	18.2% (2)	14.3% (1)	16.7% (3)
Physically disabled	0.0% (0)	28.6% (2)	11.1% (2)
Terminal/major illness	9.1% (1)	14.3% (1)	11.1% (2)
Unemployed	27.3% (3)	0.0% (0)	16.7% (3)
Sample size	11	7	18

* District differences are *not* statistically significant.

Another interesting difference emerges for Sinhalese female-heads—alcoholism is the leading factor causing women to assume headship. Alcoholism contributes to nearly half of *de facto* headship with similar figures for both Ampara (45.4 per cent) and Trincomalee (42.8 per cent). *De facto* female-heads here have alcoholic spouses who may be a drain on family resources rather than contributing to the household income. Other notable factors leading to *de facto* female-headship are unemployment (27.3 per cent in Ampara), physical disability (28.6 per cent in Trincomalee), and mental unfitness—at 18.2 per cent in Ampara and 14.3 per cent in Trincomalee. It is not possible to decode the dynamics between physical and mental disability and unemployment. Prolonged unemployment may throw men into depression and despair, rendering them unfit to seek other employment opportunities, or do mental disabilities make them unemployable? Furthermore, does the presence of intense conflict bring with it despair and depression, which leads to unemployment? Making clear-cut links is not possible. But these data suggest that household structures in eastern Sri Lanka are changing in ways that promote female-headship even among the Sinhala community. Demographic patterns for Sinhala female-heads will surely help us make more sense of the evidence, and this is the theme for the next subsection.

Demographics of Sinhala Female-heads

Ethnographic studies for Sinhalese have not noted wide age gaps in the marital ages of spouses. However, wide age gaps must exist for Sinhala marital unions too, since age-based marriage patterns indicate similar trends to those of Muslims (Chapter Four) and Tamils (Chapter Six)—with most young women married by the time they reach the age of 20 (Table 5D). Such micro-evidence for Sinhalese women suggests that there are greater similarities across ethnic divides, and accommodating attitudes towards women in the community need not always imply older marriage ages—even where the educational levels of women are higher. Even where there is an open attitude towards women, the full potential of "liberal" norms is unlikely to be reached where economic pressures are severe—and women view marriage as an escape mechanism from the poverty of their families. Here, poverty can disrupt the education of women, especially if they are the eldest sibling, and in such instances marriage at an early age is very likely. Specific to the region, however, is the possible conjunction of economic stress and patriarchal norms that prefer young marriage ages for women. Under these circumstances, the convergent practices of Muslims and Tamils permeate the Sinhala community. Indeed, when queried about their marriage at young ages, many female-heads responded with, "This is the custom in the area, where everyone, irrespective of whether we are Muslim, Sinhala or Tamil, marries at an early age." And in other instances with "My parents were very poor. Since I was the oldest in the family getting married at a young age was a means of extending financial help to my family. Also there are very limited opportunities for us to earn an independent income here, so just staying at home after a point makes little sense." So Table 5D verifies anecdotal evidence for the early marriage patterns of female-heads.

Table 5D: Age Groups of Women at Marriage

	Ampara	Trincomalee	All Districts
Age: <16 years	14.3% (5)	11.4% (4)	12.9% (9)
Age: 16–20 years	68.4% (24)	68.5% (24)	68.6% (48)
Age: 21–25 years	14.4% (5)	17.2% (6)	15.8% (11)
Age: 26–30 years	2.9% (1)	2.9% (1)	2.9% (2)
Sample size	35	35	70

While widowhood is the primary factor leading to female-headship, tabulated evidence illustrated the significance of *de facto* headship in the community (Table 5B). Since *de facto* headship is as notable as headship due to widowhood, variations in the age-cohorts of female-heads exist. The data reveal patterns similar to those for Tamil female-heads, with women assuming headship at a young age, with the average age for assuming headship at 32 years (Chapter Six). Though widowhood due to natural causes is the main factor leading to female-headship, the prevalence of conflict-related deaths and the high incidence of *de facto* headship pushes the age structure of female-heads downwards. But there are district-wise differences, since the age group of women assuming headship in Trincomalee is younger that in Ampara, which is not surprising given the higher incidence of deaths. The higher incidence of female-headship among younger women has the same implications as in the Tamil community: limitations to human capital development of their households with adverse general development consequences.

Closer analysis of district-level data, therefore, highlights the increase in female-headship due to the conflict (Table 5E). More than half the female-heads have assumed headship below 30 years of age in Trincomalee, which is obviously caused by the conflict. Yet recalling the high frequency of desertion in Trincomalee also elucidates other factors contributing to young female-headship among Sinhalese. The prevalence of a high proportion of *de facto* female-headship helps account for trends towards younger female-heads, with the Sinhalese exhibiting characteristics very different from those for female-headship in other South Asian countries.

Table 5E: Age Structure for Women Assuming Headship

	Ampara	Trincomalee	All Districts
< 21 year age group	0.0% (0)	8.6% (3)	4.3% (3)
21–25 year age group	8.6% (3)	28.6% (10)	18.6% (13)
26–30 year age group	28.7% (10)	28.6% (10)	28.6% (20)
31–35 year age group	31.6% (11)	14.1% (5)	22.9% (16)
36–40 year age group	20.1% (7)	17.2% (6)	18.7% (13)
41–45 year age group	5.8% (2)	2.9% (1)	4.2% (3)
> 50 year age group	5.8% (2)	0.0% (0)	2.8% (2)
Sample Size	35	35	70

"Liberal" Social Mores: More Survival Options?

While escaping poverty through early marriage may seem an attractive solution to poverty-ridden families, its benefits may be short-term. Where women are thrust into headship with low educational achievements, their employment opportunities become limited. The only saving grace for Sinhala female-heads is that, since there are fewer social restrictions on their seeking employment outside the domestic sphere, their ability to become daily labourers and wage workers is greater. But such options will, of course, be curtailed where young children are present—unless female-heads have the ability to draw upon their (women) kin and community to provide care. Such structures, however, do not necessarily provide unequivocal support. Various reasons restrain female-heads from undue reliance on their kin and community. The most frequently voiced disquiet was as follows: "It is unfair to depend upon others who were often not more wealthy than us", or "they have their own families and worries, can we add to their problems?" Or, when it came to depending upon kin, "my parents are too old to look after my young children, and if at all, it is I who should be caring for my parents—and not them looking after my family." Female-heads also noted that depending on networks could compromise their independence, since "depending on others means having to be on constant guard with the way we behave. We have to win others 'hearts' if we are to get their support—and this usually entails abiding by conventional conduct." On many occasions, therefore, female-heads attempted to juggle caring for their children and supporting their households through home-based income generating activities. Nevertheless, female-heads in this community frequently have varied opportunities to enter the labour market. So while "accommodating" cultural norms will not refute the reality of divergent constraints on female-heads, it certainly may ease their pressures. Both income levels and occupational patterns will show up the favourable effects of cultures "tolerant" towards their women.

Dispersion of income levels for Sinhala female-heads in both districts is low, but female-heads in Trincomalee are markedly worse-off. Even though the household size for this district is smaller, at 2.89, than for Ampara, which is 3.37, per capita

Table 5F: Income levels and Patterns*

	Ampara	Trincomalee	All Districts
Mean	Rs. 2,345.71	Rs. 1,438.86	Rs. 1,892.29
Minimum income	Rs. 1,000.00	Rs. 420.00	Rs. 420.00
Maximum income	Rs. 4,000.00	Rs. 5,000.00	Rs. 5,000.00
Sample size	35	35	70

Income group (in Rs)	Ampara	Trincomalee	All Districts
< 500.00	0.0% (0)	5.7% (2)	2.8% (2)
500.00 – 1,000.00	5.7% (2)	40.0% (14)	22.9% (16)
1,100.00 – 2,000.00	40.1% (14)	37.1% (13)	38.6% (27)
2,100.00 – 3,000.00	40.2% (14)	8.6% (3)	24.1% (17)
3,100.00 – 4,000.00	14.0% (5)	5.7% (2)	9.9% (7)
4,100.00 – 5,000.00	0.0% (0)	2.9% (1)	1.4% (1)

*District differences of mean income *are* statistically significant (sig. = 0.000)

income of these households, at Rs 497.86, falls much below the comparable national mean, at Rs 755.05. Conflict conditions and lack of economic progress seems to hit Sinhala female-heads in this district particularly hard, since their mean income is below comparable figures for Muslim and Tamil female-heads in the district (Chapters Four and Six). A partial explanation may be found in the fact that Sinhalese in this district depend for their livelihoods upon fishing and settled agriculture. The former is a livelihood option not available to women. While certain agricultural tasks are open to women, the low levels of economic activity noted in the district could also mean low labouring wages for women.[10]

A better story can be told for Sinhala female-heads in Ampara, whose per capita income—at Rs 696.06—and mean income are closer to the national averages of the same categories. With nearly 80.0 per cent of the sample falling into the middle range of low-income groups, female-heads here sustain themselves better. Indeed, only a mere 5.7 per cent of the sample falls below the Rs 1000.00 income group, and there is little evidence of female-heads risking the same level of poverty as in Trincomalee. Healthier economic conditions certainly benefit female-heads, and while this is a reason for optimism—hope should be tempered with caution. While it is possible that accommodating cultural norms enable female-heads to turn economic progress to their benefit, this should not deflect attention from the patriarchal values inherent in the capitalist system. It is quite possible, in fact, that economic progress simultaneously both facilitates and limits female-heads' abilities to be economic providers. Economic progress is enabling for female-heads if only because of the variety of opportunities that open up in such circumstances. But this does not necessarily release them from the performance of domestic chores and care-giving activities, and the limitations these responsibilities place on them could explain their lack of movement into upper income bands. Undoubtedly, however, female-heads do exploit economic conditions when there are fewer social and cultural restrictions placed upon them, since 91.4 per cent of female-heads in Ampara noted themselves as primary income providers—the largest proportion across all districts and ethnic groups.[11]

---

[10] Another explanation could be that even Tamil female-heads would have been as badly off as Sinhala female-heads had there been no grass-root level activities aimed at raising their incomes. Here, since the Sinhalese have usually not been a target group for income-generating activities sponsored by non-governmental groups, their economic situation remains quite precarious.

[11] The corresponding figure for female-heads in Trincomalee is 82.9 per cent, with 14.3 per cent noting their children and 2.9 per cent noting kin members as providing the primary source of support.

Variation on a Theme 89

Variations such as these can be further clarified by looking at the occupational patterns of Sinhala female-heads, where their visible presence in the labour market substantiates a premise of the thesis that the economic options, i.e. survival strategies, chosen by female-heads will be shaped by their socio-cultural context. Table 5G below provides the available data for the two districts.

Table 5G: Occupation Patterns of Female-heads*

Occupations	Ampara	Trincomalee	All Districts
Service/Clerical/ Government worker	8.6% (3)	5.8% (2)	7.1% (5)
Wage labourer	62.9% (22)	57.1% (20)	60.0% (42)
Domestic worker	0.0% (0)	0.0% (0)	0.0% (0)
Agricultural labourer	11.4% (4)	8.5% (3)	10.0% (7)
Animal husbandry	0.0% (0)	0.0% (0)	0.0% (0)
Small-scale farmer/ Home gardening	0.0% (0)	0.0% (0)	0.0% (0)
Home-based worker	17.1% (6)	28.6% (10)	22.9% (16)
Not employed	0.0% (0)	0.0% (0)	0.0% (0)
	35	35	70

*District differences are *not* statistically significant.

Employment patterns of Sinhala female-heads are significantly less varied than for Muslim and Tamil female-heads (Tables 4G and 6G). More remarkably, a major percentage of female-heads have noted their occupations as wage labourers, with Ampara recording a slightly larger share than

Trincomalee.[12] Female-heads in this community possibly choose labouring as their occupation not simply because they face fewer social restrictions, but also their ease of mobility is minimally hampered for security reasons—an impediment that Tamil female-heads encounter. Another advantage Sinhala female-heads possibly hold is the improbability of facing discriminatory practices in public work schemes implemented by (Sinhala) State-officials. Not facing ethnic-based discrimination in the labour market works to their benefit in finding employment as wage labourers.[13] It appears that though the average female-head is young, and therefore likely to have young children needing care, more female-heads are willing to enter the labour market. This, of course, implies the importance of kin and community support structures for care-giving activities in the households of female heads as well as their possible dependence on their own older children to provide care in their absence.[14] Female-heads in my sample recognize the implications of their reliance on networks to release them from wage labour. They perceive that, ironically, while enabling them to exercise a wide choice of employment, such reliance brings with it another set of limitations and constraints in that such networks require certain standards of behaviour if help and assistance are to be forthcoming.

Female-heads here obviously face a double-edged sword: networks are critical for households' welfare, but may be detrimental to their individual well-being,[15] and this makes

---

[12] Sole dependence on wage labour for household income does not occur, since 22.9 per cent and 17.1 per cent, in Trincomalee and Ampara, respectively, supplemented their income through self-employment as well.

[13] Ethnic-based discriminatory labour market practices, however, must be faced by every group – including the Sinhalese – since the prevailing level of ethno-nationalist discourse do have their corollary in labour market practices as well.

[14] The importance of non-financial support of children for female-heads' ability to access resources is discussed in Chapter Seven.

[15] If indeed this is a partial explanation—and it seems to be from the views echoed by female-heads—then these are rare instances in which

home-based work an obvious occupational choice. While it occurs in both districts, it is more prominent in Trincomalee, where 28.6 per cent are home-based workers. Where economic deprivation is higher, however, home-working may be even more desirable: lack of formal labour market employment and low-wages in the formal sector serve only as some examples. Furthermore, given female-heads' age structures, choosing home-based work is not surprising since they are able to combine childcare with economic activities. Hence, fewer socio-cultural restrictions does not necessarily means female-heads' entering the formal labour market, since that does not free them from childcare. Unless support networks are well in place and female-heads can rely upon them extensively, they still have to juggle between childcare and income generation. So though Sinhala female-heads may have greater opportunities to enter the formal labour market, the gender division of labour within the household may hinder their ability to take advantage of prevailing social norms.

Female-heads' eagerness to find jobs that allow them simultaneously to engage in income generation and childcare and domestic work is prevalent across all ethnic groups in eastern Sri Lanka. Nonetheless, there is a considerable difference in occupational trends for the three ethnic groups, with more Sinhala female-heads employed in the formal labour market. Construing such variations within the socio-cultural context of each ethnic group helps us to ascertain the central import of social and cultural norms in shaping economic outcomes. At the same time, the evidence also points to the pervasive presence of patriarchal values in household dynamics, where gender relations limit the openings that some social groups may offer to women. Contradictions abound, therefore, in the way social and patriarchal norms operate—and the ability of female-

---

women are able to separate their interest from that of the household. Such outcomes are more probable in communities where women feel they are "better" placed than where they face more socio-cultural restrictions.

heads to realize their potential capabilities will indeed need more than mere "accommodating" of social values.

Table 5H: Gender Make-up and Sources of Support

Sources of Support	Ampara	Trincomalee	All Districts
Children	8.6%	14.3%	11.5%
	(3)	(5)	(8)
Kin	0.0%	2.9%	1.5%
	(0)	(1)	(1)
Female-heads own income	91.4%	82.9%	87.2%
	(32)	(29)	(61)
Sample size	35	35	70
Gender of children (primary & secondary earners)			
Boys	27.8%	66.7%	47.3%
	(5)	(8)	(13)
Girls	55.6%	16.65%	36.1%
	(10)	(2)	(12)
Both Girls & Boys	16.6%	16.65%	16.6%
	(3)	(2)	(5)
Sample Size	18	12	30

The positive effects of high participation rates are low dependence on children for generating household incomes, and this observation holds for Sinhalese female-heads, with only 8.6 per cent and 14.3 per cent of children providing the primary support to their mothers in Ampara and Trincomalee, respectively. But on average, 43.5 per cent of children do supplement their households' incomes, and though this figure is much lower than for Muslim female-heads (Chapter Four), it is comparable to Tamil female-heads' (Chapter Six) experience.[16] Are there discernible trends on the gender of children providing income for the household? Clear patterns of higher dependence on boys do not emerge for both districts.

---

[16] Younger age cohorts of Sinhalese female-heads imply both small household sizes and young children.

Boys play a key role in Trincomalee in providing income to their households: 66.7 per cent are boys, with 16.65 per cent girls and 16.65 per cent both children. Similar patterns for Muslims and Tamils (for all districts) are noted in Chapters Four and Six, but trends for female-heads in Ampara in the Sinhala community are different. Here, girls have the edge over boys in their economic support for their mothers, with 55.6 per cent of girls supporting their households. This is followed by 27.8 per cent of boys and 16.6 per cent of both children providing main support towards their households. While there is a consistent gender pattern in female-heads' dependence on their children, variations are of course possible—and this is an instance of such a deviation. Daughters' non-economic support for their households is well recognized but, where socio-economic conditions permit, the probability of their economic support for households should not be discounted. A consideration of the specific dynamics of Trincomalee, however, is necessary here. Of the two districts, it is the more impoverished, and has lower labour-force participation rates for female-heads as well as a higher level of home-based work. Such circumstances facilitate several readings of this unusual trend of more girls providing economic support in the district. Firstly, of course, girls are more likely to share home-based work with their mothers – consequently, more female-heads may report their daughters as the primary income earners. Secondly, since there are less social restrictions on women's mobility, girls have more options to take over the primary role of income earners, with female-heads doing the domestic chores. Thirdly, where there are multiple sources of income flowing to households and the daughters' income constitutes the largest portion, girls will be identified as the main income earners. Finally, the lower participation rates of female-heads must place more pressure on daughters to become economically active. One or all of these factors together can act upon households to thrust daughters into roles as primary income earners, but this is still not to negate female-heads' supplementing their daughters' income from diverse sources to make their survival possible. The views of female-heads presented before serve to highlight some of the details discussed here. Primarily, they show the importance of networks for female-heads. But they also show the contradictions between social and patriarchal values that nevertheless determine their survival strategies. Sinhala female-heads may occupy more "liberal" social spaces, but this does not negate the gender division of labour within the household, nor the patriarchal values that trickle through in this as in the other ethnic communities.

Women occupy multiple positions and roles, which are structured by social relations. Sinhalese people generally pride themselves on their tolerant attitude towards women, usually citing local customs and norms that have benefited women. Early anthropological surveys have validated the veracity of such social norms and customs, and indeed at a cursory level this does hold true (Yalman 1971). However, the economic profiles of female-heads sketched above show clearly the limits of this supposedly favourable positioning of women: Most Sinhala female-heads face a level of economic deprivation similar to Muslim and Tamil female-heads and deal with it through similar options. Evidently, female-heads' ability to realize their capabilities and gain economic independence is dependent on much more than relatively "liberal" kin structures. The narratives of female-heads press the point, again and again, that community structures play a critical role in raising their welfare—and yet that at the same time they remain trapped within these structures. The very structures that support them are also the mechanism through which patriarchal values are perpetuated, with clearly defined roles and positions for women. In short, these kin structures themselves are simultaneously both supportive and oppressive. Since this is an issue for female-heads that cuts across ethnic groups, I shall return to these themes in Chapter Eight.

SIX

Matriclan Ideologies and Patriarchal Structures
Female-headship among Tamils

Caste, Gender and Matrilineal Structures

A strong caste ideology leads Tamils to hold very distinct views on the place and position of women within the household and society (Thiruchandran 1997). However, caste ideology is not uniformly applicable to all contexts; it varies and interacts with other existing social structures. Class-caste dynamics are not the only important variable for understanding the economic dimensions of household well-being. Local customs and practices also play a pivotal role in determining the socio-economic well-being of women. Economic profiling of eastern Tamil female-heads, therefore, must be understood within the context of the specific cultural and social features of the region.

Like Muslims, eastern Tamils are known for their matrilineal customs and practices.[1] In fact, the passing of matrilineal

---

[1] Given the overlap in matrilineal culture between Muslims and Tamils, this section will describe only those matrilineal practices applicable to the Tamil community i.e. only the differences that exist will be spelt out. It is for the reader to assume that all other institutional mores described for Muslims (Chapter Four) are largely applicable to Tamils as well, though some minor variations are likely to persist in practice. I, however, do not dwell on the latter. This is a task for an anthropologist rather than a feminist political economist interested in the cultural specifics of women's economic well-being.

practices to the eastern region is attributed to *Mukkuvar* Tamils, who migrated to the region, upholding and instituting a distinctive matrilineal tradition amongst all communities in the region—including among Muslims (McGilvray 1982: 87). Since the Tamils in the region are a predominantly Hindu community, an interesting question is whether the caste system overdetermines matrilineal dynamics or vice-versa. This is a particularly important issue since Hindu caste systems have been associated with symbols of purity and power, which affect women's sexuality and mobility (ibid: 40, Agarwal 1996: 139). Where matrilineal systems exist, does the interaction with caste systems push back the restrictive aspects of caste ideology?[2]

Historical, cultural, social and linguistic factors have made eastern Tamils distinct from northern Tamils. For example, although their spoken language is the same, it has dialectic variations. Furthermore, the eastern zone is also perceived as one of relative isolation, which is attributed to both geographical and historical factors (McGilvray 1982: 40). Settlements found among Tamils in the region are typically either semi-urban coastal settlements or nuclear villages situated inland. Like Muslims and Sinhalese in the region (Chapters Four and Five), Tamils are engaged in fishing or agriculture, though far fewer Tamils are engaged in trading activities. Land-holding Tamil *Mukkuvars* and *Vellalars* are also an important characteristic of the community, and are partially a spill-over from the caste system, which produces a hierarchical system for access to economic resources. The Tamil caste system is, therefore, one important difference between Tamil and Muslim communities in the region. While caste-based distinctions among Tamils are a vital social marker, there are striking ambiguities between caste and matriclan units, with caste affiliation descending

[2] Posing this question should not be taken as suggesting there is an universal answer. Rather, the anthropological evidence for eastern Sri Lanka seems to indicate that matrilineal customs and practices outweigh caste ideology, shifting the conceptual boundaries of caste and clan (Yalman 1971: 310–24, McGilvray 1982: 46). Thiruchandran (1994) similarly shows the localized nature of caste-class-customs for Jaffna Tamils in Northern Sri Lanka.

Matriclan Ideologies and Patriarchal Structures 97

strictly in the female line (ibid: 48). Maternal bonds are considered important among eastern Tamils, with the matrilineal clan reflecting substantive features of the social structures that shape the social identity of its clan members. An illustration is marriage practices cutting-across putative caste groups, with offspring of such marital unions bearing their mothers' caste rather than that of their fathers (ibid: 47–8). Usual Hindu caste notions of purity and pollution are, therefore, much less specific to eastern Sri Lanka,[3] with variations and context-linked practices being the norm among eastern Tamils. With the usual pervasive features of Hindu caste structures having few negative effects upon Tamil women—a definite boon for their economic well-being—we shall next explore the features of matrilineal inheritance patterns that benefit women's economic well-being.

Land rights are an important source of women's well-being. In South Asia women are better positioned in regions where bilateral and matrilineal practices occur than where patrilineal inheritance systems exist. Property relations are, thus, key in determining gender inequities in South Asia (Agarwal 1996). Sri Lankan women are, in this respect, fortunate in that bilateral inheritance has been the traditional system for all its three major—Muslim, Sinhala, and Tamil—ethnic communities, with matrilineal Tamil women likely to be best positioned (Agarwal 1990). Many of the characteristic features, social patterns and traditions ascribed to matrilineal Muslims are applicable to Tamil women too. Matrilocal residence patterns underlie household formations, with the provision of adequate dowries for daughters being the primary concern of households. Since dowries are the inheritance of women—usually with the oldest daughter getting a significant portion of her parent's wealth—they are well placed to negotiate over intra-household relations.[4] Eastern Tamil women are at an advantage not simply

---

[3] Another reason for the relatively fluid nature of the caste structure in eastern Sri Lanka is that orthodox caste ideology is also replaced by a secular ideology of kingly honor and division of labour (ibid: 4).

[4] Matrilineal customs does not imply the same positive consequences in all circumstances. On the one hand, for poverty-level groups bestowing

in sharing a matrilineal culture with Muslim women, but also in belonging to a community that has a more liberal attitude towards their mobility and appearances in public spaces (McGilvray 1989: 211). An open and accommodating attitude towards mobility in the public space should be an advantage for female-heads, should they seek employment that requires them to move beyond home-based and self-employment activities. There is, however, a disjunct between reality and accepted norms, since most female-heads noted that they faced many socio-cultural difficulties in accessing resources. Vasuki and Savithri, two *de facto* female-heads expressed their views as follows:

> Men are an essential part of women's lives, because they have better access to resources, are accepted by the community as leaders, and are figureheads in any community. It is difficult for women to do without men because the same opportunities are not available to us, or we have to work very hard to have access to resources that men all too easily have.
> (*Vasuki, a 44-year old de facto female-head from Batticaloa, separated several times from her husband, and mother of six children aged 11–23*).
>
> Female-heads are increasingly better accepted in society as workers, but they most certainly do not have their individual space where they can do whatever pleases them. Female-heads, in spite of some economic independence, continue to face social restrictions, which makes us more economically vulnerable. I much prefer conventional male-headed households simply because these households provided more economic security.
> (*Savithri, a 35-year old de facto head from Trincomalee and mother of four children aged 7–15. Her husband was tortured by the Sri Lankan forces, which has rendered him physically unable to work.*)

As long as patriarchal structures determine gender relations, the beneficial effects of matrilineal inheritance patterns are

---

their daughters with a dowry is either a non-issue or an immense burden. On the other hand, in spite of the existence of matrilineal practices, gender relations are also determined by patriarchal institutions. So with men being the visible agents of the social community, intra-household relations are coloured by the co-existence of patriarchal institutions and matrilineal practices.

evidently limited. Equally, matrilineal inheritance patterns are likely to benefit women from land-holding classes more than women in poverty-level groups. Where access to wealth and resources is readily available to certain classes, women from such groups are likely to benefit from matrilineal customs. In the absence of inheritable property, the relatively generous inheritance practices towards women are less valuable in practical terms in providing sustenance to female-heads. Moreover, it puts pressure on female-heads in low-income classes to find adequate dowries for their daughters. So the curious anomaly of the co-existence of matrilineal inheritance patterns and patriarchal structures implies different things for the status of female-heads, and will clearly differ according to the class position of the female-heads.[5] All this, however, is jumping ahead. First, I need to provide a profile of the economic and demographic dimensions of Tamil female-heads in eastern Sri Lanka.

---

[5] Additionally, Agarwal points to other factors that determine the position of women in matrilineal communities. Namely, a) the possible gender divergence between property ownership and control, and b) the access men have to social power bases can possibly mean concerted efforts have been made by them to consolidate their social prestige (Agarwal 1996: 150–1). Indeed in Sri Lanka, matrilineal inheritance patterns and customs were over-written during British colonial rule with the complicity of local men belonging to elite groups, since it was a means of consolidating land ownership and control by capitalist groups (Risseeuw 1988). For Tamil female-heads, this is a severe handicap where they have limited recourse to legal help should men abandon, separate and/or divorce them and take any movable property and wealth along with them, since their matrilineal inheritance has no legal recognition. (I, however, did not come across any female-heads that had experienced a similar scenario. But that does not mean that such events do not take place. More importantly, gender-sensitive policy-making will have to recognize the discrepancies that exist between local customary laws that attempt to protect the well-being of women and common laws that override such practices by perpetuating capitalist and patriarchal institutions).

The Costs of Conflict:
Young Widows and *de facto* Female-heads?

Indiscriminate killings and disappearances of young Tamil men is a harsh fact of the ethnic conflict in Sri Lanka.[6] Consequently, it is to be expected that higher proportions of Tamil female-heads are widows, who are likely to enter widowhood at a younger age than Muslim or Sinhala widows (Chapters Four and Five).[7] However, widowhood is not the only factor that leads to female-headship among Tamil women. In the Tamil community there are many instances of divorce, separation, and/or abandonment, indicating that there are other social changes that lead to female-headship. Exploring such changes is, of course, a partial purpose of this project, since my contention is that the emergence of female-headship is not linked simply to the ethnic conflict. So let me turn to what the numbers reveal.

A more varied picture emerges for Tamil women when compared to Muslims, but this has some similarity with that for Sinhala female-heads. Of the sample for the three districts, widowhood is still the leading cause of female-headship while divorced women again make up a small proportion. But overall these are not very different from Muslim women (Chapter Four).

---

[6] Two points should be noted here. Firstly, human rights violations and killings still remain a charge against the Sri Lankan State—albeit at a lower level than during the 1987–93 period (AI). Secondly, it is not simply Tamil men who have been killed, since para-military forces, i.e. the LTTE, are also guilty of human rights violations against Muslims, Sinhalese, and Tamils—with a higher incidence of men being likely targets.

[7] Widowhood, however, is simply not the only factor that thrust Tamil women into assuming headship. The torture and physical violence that some Tamil men underwent—at the hands of the Sri Lankan forces and/or the Indian Peace Keeping Force—have made them psychologically unfit, physically disabled and/or physically unable to work. While the data do not distinguish married *de facto* female-heads whose husbands underwent such traumatic events, this particular issue should be borne in mind. It is only by listening to female-heads' narratives that these subtle nuances—but harsh realities—are revealed, which would otherwise be missed by mere statistical analysis.

Matriclan Ideologies and Patriarchal Structures 101

Table 6A: Marital status of Tamil Female-heads*

	Ampara	Batticaloa	Trincomalee	All Districts
Deserted	16.7%	0.0%	5.7%	7.8%
	(5)	(0)	(2)	(7)
Divorced	6.7%	4.0%	0.0%	1.7%
	(2)	(2)	(0)	(4)
Married**	0.0%	18.0%	17.1%	28.3%
	(0)	(9)	(6)	(15)
Separated	10.0%	12.0%	8.6%	10.3%
	(3)	(6)	(3)	(12)
Widowed	66.6%	66.0%	68.6%	67.2%
	(20)	(33)	(24)	(78)
Sample size	30	50	35	116

* District differences are statistically significant between Ampara and Batticaloa (sig. = 0.016), marginally significant between Ampara and Trincomalee (sig. = 0.054), but *not* significant between Batticaloa and Trincomalee (sig. = 0.943).

** The married row consists of *de facto* female-heads supporting their families because their husbands are unemployed, suffering from a terminal illness, physically disabled, alcoholic, mentally unfit to work, and/or any other reason that precludes them from supporting the economic well-being of the household.

However, desertion and separation are notable factors pushing women into assuming headship in their households as in the Sinhala community (Chapter Five). Separation varies between a significant 8.6–12.0 per cent in the three districts, with desertion reaching a high 16.7 per cent in Ampara—and this in a district that is economically better placed than Batticaloa or Trincomalee. While separation and desertion are high in the Ampara district, there is no recorded incidence of married women noting *de facto* headship here. There are several possible explanations for this particular observation. Firstly, it could be that since Ampara has a higher level of economic progress, where women have access to resources they may feel less compulsion to stay in marriages that do not work for their benefit, and be more willing to initiate separation and/or divorce. Secondly, women's families in matrilineal communities do have a strong interest in making marriages work (ibid: 209). But the pressures on Tamil women to stay married are increasingly less. At the very least, the ethnic conflict has propelled Tamil women into an increasing awareness of their rights, of the patriarchal status quo and of exit options available to them.[8] Furthermore, the more moderate attitude towards women's mobility in public spaces in present eastern Sri Lanka could assist greater information flows through grass-root level activity (ibid: 211).[9] Rani, a female-head separated from her spouse, notes changes that are taking place as follows:

> Circumstances are changing in society that force women to stand on their own feet. This is quite different from my time and upbringing, where women were kept under men's control. Now it has come to a stage where women must fend for themselves. When there are changes in the community, we need to begin to change too. Even though

---

[8] Human and gender rights awareness activities, initiated and promoted by various NGOs activities, have done much to raise women's consciousness in these regions. But as I pointed out in the introductory chapter (Chapter One), there are many contradictions in NGO activities—especially were perpetuating gender structures through self-employment schemes is concerned. The limitations that exist to the capacity building activities of NGOs have been documented, though much work remains to be done on deconstructing the gender dynamics of NGO activities (de Alwis and Hyndmann 2000).

[9] Contradictory movements occur constantly. While some NGO activities seek to promote gender rights, as mentioned previously nationalist projects have well-defined roles on the place/role of women in their communities (Chapter One). Nationalist rhetoric moves beyond the abstract. It spills over to the "real" domain with women's behaviours and perceptions of their legitimate role in society being influenced by such views too—with many women expressing certain attitudes challenging the patriarchal status-quo as "different". Usually these "different" customs belonged to Sinhalese who were perceived as having "western" values! Moreover, NGOs in many of these regions largely tend to target Tamil women and groups. Such specific focus on just Tamils does little to reduce inter-ethnic tensions in the region, running contrary to ostensibly humanitarian efforts at building ethnic harmony among the three ethnic groups (de Alwis and Hyndman 2000).

Matriclan Ideologies and Patriarchal Structures 103

society may be resistant to accepting these changes, it is important that they recognize and accept transformations taking place in society. I certainly am doing so.
(*Rani, a 39-year old de facto female-head separated from her husband in Trincomalee and mother of two children*).

Of the *de jure* widows, is it conflict-related factors that has pushed women into assuming headship? A look at the causes of the death of husbands reveals that a considerable number of men have been killed by the conflict, with a much smaller proportion of Tamil men dying from natural causes. A detailed breakdown of reasons for husband's death is as follows:

Table 6B: Reasons for Spousal Death*

	Ampara	Batticaloa	Trincomalee	All Districts
Killed (State sponsored)	60.0% (12)	66.6% (22)	66.6% (16)	64.1% (50)
Killed (paramilitary)	10.0% (2)	6.1% (2)	8.3% (2)	7.7% (6)
Killed (non-conflict related)	0.0% (0)	0.0% (0)	0.0% (0)	0.0% (0)
Missing	0.0% (0)	3.0% (1)	4.2% (1)	2.6% (2)
Natural causes	25.0% (5)	15.2% (5)	16.7% (4)	19.0% (14)
Suicide	5.0% (1)	9.1% (3)	4.2% (1)	6.4% (5)
Sample size	20	33	24	77

* District Differences are *not* statistically significant

Natural causes for a spouse's death are proportionately highest in Ampara, where the severity of the conflict has been minimal. However, here too state-sponsored military groups have killed 60.0 per cent of Tamil men, with this being the leading cause of death in all three districts. Tabulated evidence provides unsurprising results since, as one would expect, the ethnic conflict has hit Tamil men particularly hard, with the Sri Lankan State being culpable. The economic cost of human life is downloaded onto the household economy, with female-heads having to devise strategies that cope with psychological trauma through to daily survival struggles. While describing these strategies is an objective of this research, it is equally important to understand the struggles of *de facto* female-heads too: to account for and explain other socio-economic factors that make women assume headship of their households. Why do married women assume *de facto* headship? Explanations provided by female-heads ranged from unemployed spouses to men being physically disabled. As pointed out before, however, there is little way of distinguishing—especially in the case of the Tamil community—between torture victims and those who have been affected by non-conflict related processes. Material realities and economic changes in eastern Sri Lanka prevent men from being wage earners. With the exception of Ampara, where no female-heads identified themselves as married *de facto* heads (Table 6A), the following is the evidence for Trincomalee and Batticaloa districts:

Table 6C: Causes of *de facto* Headship*

	Batticaloa	Trincomalee	All Districts
Alcoholic	11.1%	16.6%	13.9%
	(1)	(1)	(2)
Mentally unfit to work	11.1%	0.0%	5.5%
	(1)	(0)	(1)
Physically disabled	55.5%	66.7%	61.1%
	(5)	(4)	(9)
Terminal/Major illness	0.0%	0.0%	0.0%
	(0)	(0)	(0)
Unemployed	22.2%	16.7%	19.5%
	(2)	(1)	(3)
Sample size	9	6	15

* District differences are *not* statistically significant

Matriclan Ideologies and Patriarchal Structures 105

While physical disability appears as the main reason for women assuming headship while they are married, unemployment figures also are a substantial reason in the Batticaloa and Trincomalee districts. Batticaloa shows a higher incidence of unemployment (23.5 per cent), which is in keeping with the observations made before regarding the material and economic realities of the three districts (Chapter Three). Mental disabilities and alcoholism are the other two factors that keep men from providing for the economic welfare of the household. With alcoholism, whether men be employed or not, a number of female-heads noted that they had to work because "we never see the colour of our husband's earnings, and if our families are to eat then we must work and make an income!"[10] So far as female-headship among Tamils in Sri Lanka goes, the conflict is the major push factor leading to a notable—and perhaps sudden—increase in female-headship. But female-headship is not simply an aberration brought about by the conflict. Other economic circumstances lead to many social changes that also result in female-headship in eastern Sri Lanka. These need explanation, which thus far has received little attention in the analysis of female-headship in the region (Samuel 1994, Kottegoda 1996, Thiruchandran 1999).[11]

---

[10] Many female-heads noted such sentiments with annoyance and disgust with their spouses. I shall later present an anecdote of a female-head who left her husband because of alcoholism, though the separation was instigated at her mother's insistence, and the consequent emergence of complex alternative household structures. All too easily, however, policy-makers take for granted that an employed husband means a steady income to the household. This ignores the variations in proportion of household and personal expenditure patterns between men and women (Mencher 1988). And it also discounts the many instances of rampant alcoholism in rural communities that simply push women into *de facto* female-headship.

[11] Both Samuel and Kottegoda, however, focus on the key survival issues—though at a superficial level—pertinent to female-heads directly affected by the conflict. Many of the issues raised by Samuel and Kottegoda are also, however, relevant to female-heads as a group, if only because the State is yet to recognize women as primary—if not sole—earners in

Demographic Transformations of Tamilian Household Structures?

Elsewhere, trends for female-headship reveal an age structure that tilts towards older cohorts, with female-headship rising with age and peaking at/near the 35–44 year old age group (Youssef and Hetler 1984: 20). But is the concentration of female headship by age the same for all ethnic groups? It appears that among the Tamils, there are much younger female-heads, with nearly 50.0 per cent of female-heads having assumed headship at less than 30 years of age. Younger widows are clearly linked to the greater importance of ethnic conflict in creating female-heads in this ethnic group. The picture that emerges for Tamil female-heads is a bleak one, with a high proportion of young women having to bear the sole responsibility for the economic welfare of their households. From a political economic perspective, female-headship among younger groups of women cannot be favourable for human capital development nor for development *per se*. Many of these female-heads face poverty because of the suddenness with which they have had to assume headship, with the consequent lack of preparation for the role. Moreover, the relative youth of female-heads means that they have young child dependents, which bodes ill for human capital formation. With demographic trends among Tamil female-heads running contrary to evidence from other countries, Sri Lanka must target development programmes that recognize female-headship among very young women.

Age-related data for the marriage ages of Tamil female-heads reveal a pattern similar to that for Muslims and Sinhalese (Chapters Four and Five). Most Tamil women marry at a very

---

most, if not all, female-headed households (Samuel: 17). This project learns from and expands on the socio-economic issues raised by Samuel and Kottegoda, while the usefulness of Thiruchandran's study is to understand better the cultural context of Tamil and Muslim communities, and the particular psycho-social vulnerabilities female-heads in these communities face.

young age, with the average at 20–22 years.[12] Table 6D below gives the tabulated evidence for marital age groups of female-heads.

Table 6D: Age Groups of Women at Marriage

	Ampara	Batticaloa	Trincomalee	All Districts
Age: < 16 years	3.3% (1)	6.0% (3)	2.9% (1)	4.3% (5)
Age: 16–20 years	56.7% (17)	46.0% (23)	45.7% (16)	48.7% (56)
Age: 21–25 years	33.3% (9)	28.0% (14)	34.3% (12)	30.4% (35)
Age: 26–30 years	6.7% (2)	10.0% (5)	8.5% (3)	8.7% (10)
Age: 31–35 years	0.0% (0)	10.0% (5)	8.6% (3)	7.9% (8)
Sample Size	30	50	35	115

Note, however, that the proportion of female-heads married below 16 years is significantly smaller among Tamils than among Muslims and Sinhalese (Chapters Four and Five). One would expect, therefore, a higher level of education among Tamil female-heads as well as better access to resources. Interestingly, it is in the most deprived district (Batticaloa) that there is greater proportion of women married under 15 years. Though 6.0 per cent of the sample is a small number, economic pressures appear to promote marital unions at tender ages to overcome the poverty of their families.

---

[12] Anthropological evidence supports the possible existence of 5–10 year age gaps between spouses, since "greater age in marriage..works to the advantage of the man, it is felt, because he benefits from sexual relations with a strong-blooded young woman" (McGilvray 1982: 52). A notable number of female-heads have married in the 16–20 age group (Table 6D), and for 50.0 per cent–62.5 per cent of married *de facto* female-heads this age gap holds. So while my questionnaire did not obtain information for the marriage age of men, there is ethnographic as well as incidental support for 5–10 year gaps between marital spouses.

Matrilineal Communities, Patriarchal Realities

Table 6E: Age Structure for Women Assuming Headship

	Ampara	Batticaloa	Trincomalee	All Districts
< 20 year age group	3.3% (1)	4.2% (2)	2.9% (1)	3.5% (4)
21–25 year age group	10.0% (3)	22.9% (11)	14.2% (5)	15.7% (19)
26–30 year age group	46.6% (14)	25.0% (11)	31.5% (11)	34.4% (36)
31–35 year age group	20.0% (6)	27.1% (13)	28.5% (10)	25.2% (29)
36–40 year age group	10.0% (3)	14.5% (7)	11.5% (4)	12.0% (14)
41–45 year age group	0.0% (0)	4.2% (2)	11.4% (4)	5.2% (6)
46–50 year age group	6.7% (2)	0.0% (0)	0.0% (0)	2.2% (2)
> 50 year age group	3.4% (1)	2.1% (1)	0.0% (0)	1.8% (2)
Sample size	30	50	35	115

Is it just the conflict that thrust women into assuming headship at a young age? Or, do other causes of female-headship also obtain for young Tamil women? Since nearly 15.5 per cent–23.5 per cent of female-heads lose their marital partners through natural death, the age structures for women assuming headship (Table 6E) support the thesis that other factors may lead to female-headship too. This evidence must have certain implications for income levels and patterns, and is examined in the following section.

Income levels, Patterns and Generation: the Basics of Survival

Regular income and access to a steady source of income are not defining features of Tamil female-headed households. Accessing diverse sources of income-generating activities is essential to female-heads, but many barriers, usually associated with their own family formations, hamper them. Since most Tamil female-heads belong to a younger age group, the number of children in their households is small—Ampara: 2.7, Trincomalee: 2.37, Batticaloa: 3.44. When adult members are taken into account the household size becomes, 4.2, 4.82, and 3.25 for Ampara, Batticaloa, and Trincomalee respectively. The smaller number of children as well as their probable younger ages has implications for income-generating activities. All the adult members may not be able to contribute to the shared household income, since they are mostly elderly parents and/ or parents-in-law. At best, the role of elderly kin is to provide childcare so that female-heads can work. Where there is a smaller number of children, female-heads have limited human resources for income pooling, even in the future when the children reach adulthood. Furthermore, children of younger-aged female heads are likely to belong to younger age groups, imposing additional burdens on these women's ability to generate income. Caring for children is a paramount concern for female-heads, but where children belong to younger age groups their ability to earn any income for their mothers is also limited. Female-heads have not only to juggle between competing demands and needs in such circumstances, but may also have to disrupt the education of their older children.[13] Essentially, however, for younger female-heads their ability to access income beyond home-based income-generating activities is severely curtailed by the presence of young children. These concerns were expressed by most female-heads. The exception was female-heads who were educated and had access to white-collar employment, that is, teaching, administrative clerks and so on, where it was easier to reconcile their work schedule with childcare. For most female-heads, complementing productive and reproductive activities means taking up home-

---

[13] A likely consequence when there is a breakdown and/or loosening of kin support structures, which in spite of a matrilineal community, is increasingly the reality for some Tamil female-heads who have faced dislocation and disruption.

based self-employment schemes, that barely bring in a sufficient income. Jayanthi, a *de facto* female-head, mentions, "even with my husband present, I still find it difficult to look after my children and work." Most female-heads do depend upon some form of kin and/or community support for childcare.[14] Additionally, while matrilineal Tamils face moderate social and cultural restrictions on women's mobility, this is not the same as no code of conduct for the "proper" role of women. A noteworthy number of female-heads constantly repeated, "We have our needs, but we should not act against our culture. We can get respect from society, only if we look after the well-being of our families."[15] Given these different set of concerns that Tamil female-heads face, it is worth considering their income levels and patterns, before going on to discuss the sources of income available to this social group. The table below (Table 6F) charts this for us.

Income levels for Tamil female-heads in all three districts fall below the national average of poverty as well as below the national average income for female-heads (Chapter Three). Per capita income too is absolutely low for Tamil female-headed households, at Rs 559.52, Rs 452.90, and Rs 584.62 respectively for the Ampara, Batticaloa, and Trincomalee districts.

In Ampara district, the dispersion in income levels is limited, with only a 6.4 per cent of the sample earning an income below

---

[14] Where kin and/or community support does exist, then such structures may become a means of controlling female-heads "accepted" behavior patterns. So while kin support is important for the daily survival of female-headed households, they also impose constraints on female-heads through "accepted" social norms—which only perpetuate existing gender biases. This is another theme that will be picked up in more detail in the Chapter Eight.

[15] Female-heads' perceptions of their well-being, therefore, is here conceptualized in terms of their roles as mothers and repositories of traditional family values—albeit in the absence of men. As pointed out earlier, there are paradoxical movements occurring, with some female-heads more willingly challenging the status quo (see above page 103, footnote 12). Accounting for such changes is important, since they impinge upon the capabilities of female-heads.

Matriclan Ideologies and Patriarchal Structures 111

Table 6F: Income Levels and Patterns*

	Ampara	Batticaloa[16]	Trincomalee	All Districts
Mean	Rs 2,380.00	Rs 2,183.00	Rs 1,900.00	Rs 2,160.00
Minimum income	Rs 500.00	Rs 500.00	Rs 500.00	Rs 500.00
Maximum income	Rs 12,650.00	Rs 12,900.00	Rs 6,500.00	Rs 12,900.00
Sample Size	30	50	35	115

Income groups (in Rs)	Ampara	Batticaloa	Trincomalee	All Districts
500.00—1,000.00	6.4% (2)	26.0% (13)	34.3% (12)	22.2% (27)
1,100.00—2,000.00	54.7% (17)	42.0% (21)	34.3% (12)	43.7% (50)
2,100.00—3,000.00	35.4% (11)	18.0% (9)	20.0% (7)	24.5% (27)
3,100.00—4,000.00	0.0% (0)	8.0% (4)	2.8% (1)	3.6% (5)
4,100.00—5,000.00	0.0% (0)	2.0% (1)	0.0% (0)	0.7% (1)
5,100.00—6,000.00	0.0% (0)	2.0% (1)	5.7% (2)	2.6% (3)
> 6,100.00	3.5% (1)	2.0% (1)	2.9% (1)	2.8% (3)

* District differences of mean income are *not* statistically significant

Rs 1,000.00. This contrasts with Batticaloa and Trincomalee, where 26.0 per cent and 34.3 per cent of the sample fall into this income group. Both economic stability and lack of intensity of the ethnic conflict in Ampara does seem favourable for Tamil

---

[16] In my sample for Ampara and Batticaloa, there is only one family in each sample that earns an income in the Rs 12,000.00 range, also a result of there being women in the clerical/administrative/service sector. If this household is taken out of the sample, the mean income for the districts are Rs. 2,000.00 and Rs. 1,964.00, respectively with the maximum income being between Rs. 3,000.00 and Rs. 5,000.00.

female-heads, since a smaller proportion face absolute deprivation, and relative inequality is low. But their apparent inability to move to higher income levels in the Ampara district—with the exception of one female-head—should be a cause for concern for policy-makers, especially since small fractions of Tamil female-heads belong to the higher income range in Batticaloa and Trincomalee. As anticipated, however, the mean income levels in Batticaloa and Trincomalee are lower than in Ampara, and the lowest classes in these two districts have a higher ratio. This is in keeping with the economic and conflict conditions of the two districts. But economic stability and the easing of conflict conditions will not in themselves ease access to economic resources for female-heads, and income patterns for the Ampara district reveal as much. Moreover, the statistical significance of mean income highlights the particular vulnerability of Tamil female-heads vis-à-vis Muslim and Sinhala female-heads (Chapters Four and Five) in the region. Empowering female-heads with capabilities will require accounting and directing for their particular cultural, material, and social conditions, so that enhancing their income earning capacity is a real option for this social group. Occupation patterns (Table 6G) confirm their reliance on self-employment and home-based economic activities.

Tamil female-heads are occupied in a wider range of jobs than Muslims and Sinhalese. Yet home-based self-employment is the principal occupation source, which is unsurprising since Tamil women face numerous impediments—need for childcare, lack of skills, security issues that prevent ease of mobility, and the like—that prevent female-heads from exploring economic options that may provide higher wages. Chapter Eight will show that it is not for lack of exploiting different options that female-heads relegate themselves to self-employment schemes, but that their material options are constituted by social factors too. From the three districts, it is Ampara that records the lowest number of female-heads in self-employment, with wage labour and animal husbandry (poultry, cattle and goat rearing) occupations absorbing a notable number of female-heads. For

Table 6G: Occupation Patterns of Female-heads*

Occupations	Ampara	Batticaloa	Trincomalee	All Districts
Service/Clerical/ Government worker	10.0% (3)	10.0% (5)	2.9% (1)	7.6% (9)
Wage laborer	16.6% (5)	16.0% (8)	17.1% (6)	16.6% (19)
Domestic worker	6.7% (2)	8.0% (4)	5.7% (2)	6.8% (8)
Agricultural laborer	6.7% (2)	2.0% (1)	2.9% (1)	3.9% (4)
Animal husbandry	13.3% (3)	12.0% (6)	8.7% (3)	11.3% (12)
Small-scale farmer/ home gardening	10.0% (3)	2.0% (1)	5.7% (2)	5.9% (6)
Home-based worker	36.7% (11)	48.0% (24)	54.3% (19)	46.3% (54)
Not employed	0.0% (0)	2.0% (1)	2.7% (1)	1.6% (2)
Sample Size	30	50	35	115

* District differences are *not* statistically significant

female-heads in Batticaloa and Trincomalee districts, wage labour is the next significant occupation, though in two districts—Ampara and Batticaloa—a noteworthy proportion is also employed in white-collar work. Most occupations chosen by female-heads, however, are ones that can also be undertaken at home. In Ampara I came across a *de facto* female-head who was an agricultural labourer, but when her work entailed drying and pounding rice, she was also able to do the same work from home—and did so. Wage labour is an exception requiring women to leave their homes. With wage labour too, there are structural issues that also should be borne in mind when "normalcy" returns to the region: i.e. the need to ensure that wage labourers get more than simply their wages, given the volatility with wage labour conditions. A primary issue for development planners in Sri Lanka remains the unravelling of the different rationales for home-based activities as the chosen employment activity among female-heads. The answer is partially obvious: the need to engage in both productive and reproductive tasks. But the reason for engaging in these tasks can vary sharply among each ethnic group, and accounting for these rationales is equally important in breaking-down cultural prescriptions through gender-sensitive policy planning.[17]

Another related issue in considering income patterns is their source: do female-heads rely on the help of children when they are occupied in home-based economic activities? A positive response is highly probable. Dependence on children as the primary source of income among Tamil female-heads is low, and this is to be expected since children of younger female-heads will also be young. But this is neither to deny children's role in supporting home-based activities nor to dismiss them as secondary sources of income.

Approximately 55.9 per cent of female-heads for the region identified their children as providing primary or supplementary sources of income, and children supporting mothers varied in quantity and quality. Since children are important support bases for female-heads, do they tend to be girls or boys? Economic dependence on boys is greater than on girls in all three districts—54.6 per cent vs. 31.8 per cent, 42.3 per cent vs. 26.9 per cent, 40.0 per cent vs. 20.0 per cent in Ampara, Batticaloa, and Trincomalee, respectively. Nevertheless, 13.6 per cent, 30.8 per cent, and 40.0 per cent, respectively, of female-heads in the same districts depend on both children for economic support. Tamil female-heads' economic dependence on boys is similar to that of Muslim female-heads (Chapter Four) but not to that of Sinhala female-heads (Chapter Five). Depending

---

[17] The concluding chapter will discuss some of the ethnicity-specific gender norms that need to be taken into account as well as challenged through appropriate gender-sensitive policy-making. However, I do not explore the structural aspects of wage labour conditions in the region—if only because they are likely to affect other working women and men as well as female-heads.

Table 6H: Gender Make-up and Sources of Support

Sources of Support	Ampara	Batticaloa	Trincomalee	All Districts
Children	13.3% (4)	14.0% (7)	5.7% (2)	11.0% (13)
Kin	0.0% (0)	2.0% (1)	2.9% (1)	1.6% (2)
Female-heads' own income	86.7% (26)	84.0% (42)	91.4% (32)	87.4% (100)
Sample Size	30	50	35	115
Gender of children (primary & secondary earners)				
Boys	54.6% (12)	42.3% (11)	40.0% (6)	45.6% (29)
Girls	31.8% (7)	26.9% (7)	20.0% (3)	26.2% (17)
Both Girls & Boys	13.6% (3)	30.8% (8)	40.0% (6)	28.1% (17)
Sample Size	22	26	15	63

on children implies that they probably suffer from educational disruption, with real consequences for building up their capability base. Boys see their education disrupted because they are treated as an important source of income generation, while girls' role as surrogate mothers to their younger siblings means educational disruptions too. Either way, there is both an economic and a cultural rationale for the disrupted education of both sons and daughters. Vasuki and Radhika, *de facto* and *de jure* female-heads, respectively, explain their thoughts:

> Getting young daughters to work at an early age is difficult because mobility of young girls is frowned upon in my—Hindu—community. So I made the decision to remove my sons from school and get them to help me increase our wage income by their labouring in the home gardening plot.
> (*Vasuki, a 44-year old de facto female-head from Batticaloa separated several times from her husband, and mother of six children aged 11–23 years*).

After my husband's death I made every attempt to educate my children. I realize education is important for them, and though Ahila—my oldest daughter—had to stay back on the days I was ill, I was determined to see them through their education. But after I met with a motorbike accident, three years after my husband died, I did have to stop Ahila's education. She was 12 years then and I badly needed someone to care for my other children, if I was to continue working.
(Radhika, a 41-year old de jure *female-head from Batticaloa, and mother of five children aged 16–26 years*).

The lives of Tamil female-heads are harsh, particularly since their economic insecurity is aggravated by the ethnic conflict. For the latter reason they remain the most vulnerable social group. Accessing material resources depends not only on the accepted cultural and social norms, but on conditions of political security too. Specifically, they face discrimination because they are a minority community, with government bureaucrats slow to help them with compensation, etc. This latter factor is marginally less relevant to Muslim female-heads, and hardly applicable at all to the Sinhala community. Tamil female-heads encounter patriarchal institutions and ethnic-based discrimination at different levels, ranging from a gender-laden ethno-nationalist conflict to cultural proscriptions, making them sharply in need of renegotiating with the patriarchal status quo. While ethnic conflict is the primary factor leading to female-headship among Tamil women, it is worth reiterating that ordinary marital breakdowns take place in this community too. Recognizing the diversity of factors leading to female-headship is critical in assessing the social transformations taking place in eastern Sri Lanka. While the prevalence of an intense state of conflict may lead to volatility, it also hastens social transformation—which has a dynamic of its own. In my final chapter, I shall argue that these realities need to be incorporated in gender-sensitive policy-making (Chapter Ten). Ignoring these issues may lead to the misguided notion that a return to peace will remove from policy-makers the onus of having to deal with female-headship. This view is fed through the complacent view that the end of war will see a gradual reduction in the incidence of female-headship and a return to the norm of male-heads.

SEVEN

Dutiful Daughters, Sacrificing Sons[1]

Resources that Female-heads Cannot Do Without: the Value of Children

Children are an important resource for poor households and especially so for female-headed households (Buvinic, Youssef and von Elm 1978: 74, Anker 2000: 6). Children were important in the households I surveyed across ethnicity, as the preceding chapters noted (Chapters Four, Five and Six; see also Ruwanpura 2004a). The literature on female-headship not only notes the economic importance of children for these households, but also observes the particular susceptibility of girls to early working and economic demands (Panda 1997: 31–7). Unequal gender relations place less social and economic value on the human capital of girls, leading to the rapid deterioration of their capabilities. The implicit assumption here is that this is due to patriarchal structures that discriminate against girls and result in their removal from education. It is true that inequities in gender relations entail girls and boys having different socio-economic values placed on them, and that these are perpetuated through cultural, patriarchal, material and religious structures. While the interactions of these institutions usually result in girls being relatively disadvantaged, the decisions that female-heads make are layered and complex. During my fieldwork it became

[1] This chapter heading is motivated by a similarly titled paper "Moral Mothers and Stalwart Sons" by Malathi de Alwis (1998b) and Simone de Beauvoir's (2000) *Memoirs of a Dutiful Daughter*.

apparent that there was a need for a more nuanced analysis, one which recognized that female-heads make difficult choices about which children should work, and that they provided different rationales for disrupting their daughters' or sons' education.

When I began my fieldwork in eastern Sri Lanka my working hypothesis reflected the limited belief that girls in female-headed household were more likely to witness interruptions to their education. During my fieldwork, however, I quickly came to realize that it is usually the oldest child, irrespective of gender, who would see her or his education disrupted. Recognizing this particular issue made me investigate further and engage with female-heads on the motives for taking boys out of school, where this occurred, rather than girls. As pointed out in Chapters Four, Five and Six there was, however, an ethnic aspect to the decisions made by female-heads. Normally, Muslim female-heads did conform to convention by taking girls out of school at an early age to help with domestic chores and/or self-employment activities, but this was less true for the Sinhala and Tamil communities. My point in this chapter is not to argue that decisions with respect to children's well-being are based simply on ethnic differences but rather to draw attention to the complexities of the decision-making processes of female-heads and see them influenced and shaped by a convergence of material, cultural and patriarchal dynamics. A feminist analysis should move beyond the simplistic anticipation that the welfare of girls is likely to suffer in comparison with their brothers, and we need to complicate the frequently repeated simple story of gender bias. Ironically, boys should be seen to bear the brunt of patriarchy too.

Using case studies of female-heads in eastern Sri Lanka, the complexities of human capital investment decisions regarding boys and girls are examined in this chapter. Cultural, religious, social, and political norms colour decisions made by female-heads. These decisions are not based on economic considerations. The complication is that female heads provide very different rationales, influenced by patriarchal premises, for disrupting either their sons' or their daughters' education.² Accordingly, the next two sections of this chapter investigate female heads' narratives on whether to disrupt the education of their girls or boys. The subsequent section studies the connections and dynamics linking motherhood, dutiful daughters and sacrificing sons.³ Through the narratives of female-heads, this section brings together the potency of maternal ideology in the socio-economic decisions made by female-heads with respect to their daughters and sons.⁴ Finally, the concluding section links the short-term and long-term consequences faced by girls and boys of not realizing their human capabilities, particularly in female-headed households. This is partially accomplished through the retold experiences of the female-heads' own unsettled childhood and adolescent years.⁵

Patriarchal Logic and Girl-Power?

A standard feminist theme is that girls suffer disproportionately from poverty. This issue has been subject to much research in

---

² This investigation also leads to my feminist methodology chapter (Chapter Nine), which argues that social reality is embedded in structures that require analysis—even though the outcomes depend on context, are interconnected and highly differentiated.

³ My thanks to Dr. Jane Humphries for suggesting the idea, and specifically for encouraging incorporating this chapter on children.

⁴ In pursuing this exercise, I make extensive use of studies on motherhood, politics and nationalism in Sri Lanka, that provide a valuable precursor to developing similar themes in the economics of female-headed households (de Alwis 1998a and de Alwis 1998b). But motherhood as a social construct has also been subject to critique by feminist anthropologists, who have attempted to show its historical and cultural specificity (Moore 1996).

⁵ This, of course, begs the question whether emphasizing the short-run negative consequences for children as a social group helps set the stage for pressing policy planners to integrate gender-sensitive policy prescriptions. The emancipatory potential of gender mechanisms that affect both girls and boys, and consequently the alternative strategies feminists can formulate, is explored in detail in the concluding chapter (Chapter Ten).

the Sri Lankan context (CENWOR 1993). An associated assumption is that girls' education is disrupted to allow them to contribute to family labour and/or to perform domestic chores. But the decision to make girls do such work is not determined solely by poverty (Anker 2000: 28). Anecdotal evidence about decision-making by female-heads reveals that there is no single line of reasoning that dominated when the capability bases of their children were at stake. Reflection on their own economic difficulties made them critically re-evaluate the prevailing options for their daughters. Interestingly, the same themes ran across the accounts by female-heads of all ethnic groups of the factors that figure in their decision-making. Here, I begin with a discussion of those female-heads with little or no education who made the decision to educate their daughters, despite the associated economic hardships, because they viewed education as a stepping stone towards improved welfare for their daughters as well as for the household.

> Neither I not my husband had studied beyond primary education, but a key aim I have is to educate my daughters. Even though I face economic difficulties I hope to continue their education. To disrupt their education would be to hinder their ability to achieve better things. (*Savithri, a 35-year old Tamil* de facto *female-head from Trincomalee, and mother of three children.*)

> My husband is terminally ill and has been so for the past few years. Even though he is in hospital at present, when he is less severely ill we have to bring him home. Since I am working full-time as an agricultural labourer I am at home only during limited hours, and this implies that one of my three daughters has to attend to my husband's needs. However, I am resolute in my decision not to disrupt their education, because I know the limited opportunities I have in seeking wage employment are due to my own inadequate schooling. So I make sure that my daughters and I share all responsibilities in caring for my ill husband as well as the domestic chores. This way, I hope, my daughters will be able to succeed in their studies and be able to have a better future than me.
> (*Jameela, a 42-year old Muslim* de facto *female-head from Ampara, and a mother of three daughters*).

> Even when my husband was alive, there was no dispute about educating our children. I did not study beyond grade 8, but in today's

society not having educated daughters is only going to make their lives' harder. I want to make my daughter's life better than mine and for this I have to ensure that her education is uninterrupted.
(*Ramani, a 38-year old Sinhala de jure female-head from Trincomalee, and a mother of two children—where the daughter is at school while the son is the main income earner for the household*).

These women's limited education combined with their experiences of economic hardship coloured the decisions they made to struggle to continue to send their daughters to school. They also show an ability to link their economic vulnerability to their limited education which, while undoubtedly aggravated by the ethnic conflict, would continue even in a more peaceful environment. Moreover, by asserting their autonomy they are recognizing changes and transformations taking place in Sri Lankan society that require better-educated women to grapple with the future challenges their daughters will encounter.[6] Denied opportunities themselves as a result of poverty, "tradition" and culture, these mothers had ardent aspirations for their daughters and were willing to provide for them to obtain skills. In the chapter on Muslims I quoted the reaction of a female-head who, upon her husband's death, flouted his views on limiting education for their daughters (Chapter Four, page 54). Her outlook reveals the readiness of female-heads to contravene patriarchal authority when the immediate sources of authority are weakened or removed.[7]

However, there are other female heads who invoke patriarchal logic to explain their decisions to keep their

---

[6] Among lower-income female-heads there is an interesting generation gap on the issue of educating girls. "Traditional" views on women's education are challenged by women who have themselves had limited education. This echoes Uma Narayan's (1997) point that "it is impossible to describe 'our traditional life' without seeing change as a constitutive element affecting transformations..." (1997: 26).

[7] Such ruptures disclose the fluidity of "tradition" and "culture", which should be seized upon by feminists to espouse necessarily policies that are not only gender-sensitive but also come from within communities. Gender-sensitive development policies that evolve from this research will be discussed in greater detail in Chapter Ten.

daughters in school. This group argued that because their culture prohibited young girls and women from moving around in public places, it was a much more practical decision to keep their daughters in school.[8] Female heads explained their decisions as a black-and-white choice: either to remove daughters from education or keep them in school, where the former allowed them to help in domestic chores and the latter implied limited movement between home and school. By allowing their daughters to remain in school, female-heads reasoned that they were controlling their movements, which was important in communities that frowned upon unnecessary mobility in public spaces (McGilvray 1989). Such a cultural rationale was often provided by female-heads in the Muslim and Tamil communities, but was less frequently an explanation used by Sinhala female-heads.

> I have had a very troubled marriage and all of this of course has made me aware of the need to have independent access to an income. And one possible option open to women to achieve this is through education, and so I have insisted that my daughters be educated. But also Hindu culture is more conducive to keeping daughters in school rather than getting them to work at an early age. Getting them to work at an early age is difficult when the mobility of young girls is frowned upon in my community. So I decided to keep my daughters in school and ensure their educational success.
> (*Vasukhi, a 44-year old Tamil de facto female-head from Batticaloa, and mother of six children*).
>
> In this day it does not make much sense to keep daughters at home, because having educated daughters can only benefit them, their husbands and their families. But also I do not need all my daughters to stay at home and help in domestic chores, and getting them educated is still adhering to cultural norms that permit restricted movements for women in my community. They just move between home and school, and of course even after getting their educational qualifications it is possible for them to find jobs like teaching, secretarial work, etc.

---

[8] This reasoning had an adverse consequence for boys, who were more likely to have their education interrupted. I shall discuss this issue in greater detail in the following section, and here I only draw the reader's attention to this related issue.

These jobs do allow young women their own income, but do not appear to confront values.
(*Zareena, a 52-year old Muslim de jure female-head from Batticaloa, and mother of four children*).

These arguments represent either silent challenges to "authentic" cultural readings or female-heads' creative use of cultural norms to promote the education of their daughters. While female-heads explained their preference for educating daughters in terms of cultural imperatives, it is of course very possible that these female-heads were simply appropriating patriarchal logic to justify what they wanted to do, namely keep their daughters in school. As third-world feminists have rightly pointed out, "there are many ways, of inhabit[ing] nations and cultures critically and creatively", and the possibility of female-heads reading and mobilizing cultural norms differently should not be dismissed (Narayan 1997: 33). The critical point is that daughters can derive benefits from prolonged schooling because of the decisions made by their mothers.

As much as ideological structures affect female-heads so do their material realities, and hence there were female-heads who did have to disrupt their daughters' education for economic reasons. However, although such decisions were made, they were not simple resolutions and usually involved a convergence of negative factors. Poverty coupled with illness, the need for extra help in home-based income generating activities and/or domestic chores, motivated these female-heads to disrupt their daughters' education. The description by Lakshmi, a 41-year old Tamil *de jure* female head, of her agonizing decision best epitomizes the complexity of her dilemma to discontinue the education of her oldest child, who also happened to be a girl. Lakshmi married at 15 and was thrust into headship at 24, when her husband died of a poisonous snakebite. She, however, did not interrupt her oldest daughter's education and, as she mentioned "I knew it would be difficult, but I had all good intentions of continuing my children's education." However, three years after her husband's death Lakshmi had a motorbike accident, which required her to be hospitalized. During this time Lakhsmi's oldest daughter, Logi, started staying at home to look after her siblings. When Lakshmi was discharged from hospital, she made the difficult decision to retain this arrangement, realizing that Logi could help her with domestic chores as well as in self-employment activities. In retelling the variety of factors that led to her decision, Lakshmi kept emphasizing both regret and the difficult choices she faced at this juncture of her life. She stressed that it was not simply poverty that compelled her to make the decision to interrupt her daughter's education. Other female heads similarly identified many adverse factors as forcing regrettable decisions about female children's education.

The low value placed on their daughters' education entered the discussion only in exceptional circumstances. This particular justification for interrupting girls' education was so rare, that further inquiry among Sinhala and Tamil female-heads was undertaken. Female-heads acknowledged the difficulties educated daughters may still have in obtaining employment commensurate with their education, especially given the economic turmoil and protracted ethnic conflict. However, these female-heads were insistent that the particular economic conditions in eastern Sri Lanka would pass, and that education can never be a wasted opportunity. As most female-heads from these communities put it:

> We do not have any guarantees that educating our daughters will make them even get jobs after obtaining the necessary qualifications. There are many educated young girls who do not get decent jobs even though they have been educated up to O/Levels and A/Levels, and it is especially difficult given the political and economic turmoil in the region. But things will change and when this happens being educated women will only mean that the possibility of a *bright* future remains an option for our daughters. Those of us who did have to terminate the education of some of our daughters, will only feel remorse for making this decision. And while a variety of circumstances may have brought this about, for not one minute did we delude ourselves into thinking that this was the best decision from the point

of view of our daughters' welfare.⁹
(*Views of a group of Tamil and Sinhala female-heads from the area*).

An interesting divergence was the stance taken by some Muslim and older female-heads. They reasoned that there were restricted benefits to educating daughters for a variety of reasons, rehearsing the range of negatives from the need to limit the movement of girls, to obeying the wishes of husbands, to difficulties associated with finding suitable employment. Each of these themes needs deliberation since they stress the numerous ways in which patriarchal interests impinge on the welfare of girls, and consequently on adult women. The primary issue that this group of female-heads mentioned involved the limits placed on girls moving in public, and how educating girls after they reached puberty would involve having them chaperoned by elderly/trustworthy adults and/or brothers. With intense pressure on the time and work of most female-heads, the additional burden of escorting their daughters to school was not welcomed by many. Since exposing daughters to unguarded mobility in public spaces diminished their prospects of marriage and a better life, it was a serious threat not only to the family as a whole but also to the daughter. Educated girls who have moved freely in public spaces will have reduced their potential to marry eligible men, and having unmarried daughters is likely to create more economic and emotional stress for female-heads. So in a community where permissible marriage can only take place within the group, girls may be enhancing their capabilities at the cost of marriage. It is not girls getting an education *per se* that is at stake in these circumstances, but rather that this process involves other social sacrifices that need to be weighed by female-heads in the quest

---

[9] Such sentiments are not altogether surprising since there is free education right through to university. However, while education is State-funded, this still does not mitigate the education-related expenses that households have to bear, and in this respect such a strong emphasis on education perhaps indicates shifts in attitude towards it between different generations of female-heads.

to make their daughters' lives better. The choices here are not easy ones. For these girls, it is either a better education with fewer marriage options, or more marriage options and limited education.

Moreover, female heads reasoned that a better education might lead to unnecessary conflict with their potential spouses, who were anyway more interested in dowry[10] than in having educated wives. Educated women usually had opinions on issues, such as children's education, health, work patterns, etc., that might be incompatible with their husbands' views and lead to needless clashes. Furthermore, while education was free (i.e. state-provided) there were still incidental costs, such as books, uniforms, and transportation. Female-heads, noting the need to make savings for dowries and the possible negative implications of education for their daughters, had to weigh the constraints on their limited income when making decisions. A related issue was that even if they had educated their daughters and they had the necessary skills to find employment in the formal labour market, once married they were supposed to abide by the wishes of their husbands. Female-heads here, therefore, reasoned that there was no guarantee that their sons-in-law would permit their daughters to work when married, especially since the men would be risking their own social reputations by allowing their wives to work. These women continued to claim that it was not that they thought a working man's income would necessarily be sufficient to meet household expenses, but rather that when there was a need for women to

---

[10] This is an important social issue facing many young women from the middle-classes in the region—and especially Tamils, where the killings and/or migration of young men has put severe pressure on the supply of suitable boys for families to marry their daughters to. It is reported that "eligible" men residing in foreign countries demand $50,000.00 dowries, which most households—and not just female-headed households—are unlikely to be able to raise, leaving many young girls to be spinsters. (Source: BBC Report by Francine Harrison on "Bride and Groom" presented in the http://bbc.co.uk web page on South Asian issues, dated April 17th 2001).

augment household income, then it would have to be confined within the household. This group of female-heads would typically cite home-based income-generating activities as possible occupations. Married women would be likely to choose such activities because they supplement household income without upsetting the delicate balance of marital relations. So where older and Muslim female-heads encountered economic hardship and/or poverty, they argued that it was necessary to bear in mind other social issues when making decisions regarding their daughters' education. Consequently, there was a limited and/or low value placed on educating their daughters when they factored other considerations into the equation, and dutiful daughters did forfeit their personal welfare in such situations.

Significantly, however, there is a notable shift in attitudes of female-heads that sometimes involves the tactical manipulation of patriarchal structures to protect the interests of their daughters. Female-heads here are clearly prudent in their politics. While they may not overtly challenge restrictive social and patriarchal structures, and may seemingly adhere to traditional ways, they are also guardedly expanding the spaces of social and economic opportunity for their daughters. Dutiful daughters may take on many guises. Some have their personal well-being promoted, while the welfare of others is more likely to be linked to their spouses. "Girl power"? Perhaps not, but certainly there are instances where female-heads turned the logic of patriarchy on its head to protect and promote the interest of daughters. As a Muslim female head aptly reminded me:

> What is important in our community is that we *seem* to observe social norms. Cultures do not simply change. We have to make them change without disrupting existing social relations in one go. It is not an easy task, but it can be done. If men are increasingly unreliable then there should be no reason why we should not equip our daughters with more capabilities to overcome the hardship they may have to face. I always "listen" to my neighbours, relatives, and community but I make

the final decision—and this is usually to ensure the current and future welfare of my daughters. On this, I will not fail them.
(*Sameera, a 54-year old Muslim de jure female head from Ampara, and mother of three daughters*).[11]

Patriarchal Structures that Stump the Boys

Earlier chapters have highlighted the important economic support that sons provide to female-heads (Chapters Four, Five and Six). It was not simply girls who had to forgo improving their personal welfare and capability base. Support from sons is not limited to those who have been educated until the end of their secondary school and/or graduate education. A substantial number of sons have had their education disrupted at their father's desertion and/or death. Usually older sons, whether the eldest or not, were taken from school and expected to provide for the household. Female-heads of households across all communities used this route to replace the loss in income they encountered with the absence of their spouse. In rare instances it was a panic reaction by female-heads, but there was a crucial difference between the rationales given by female-heads in the different communities, with Muslim female-heads emphasizing the ease of mobility of boys who therefore were suitable candidates for work from an early age. Sinhala and Tamil female-heads echoed each other in citing the wages sons were likely to muster, their physical ability to perform agricultural tasks, and security objectives, in that getting sons to work left them less likely to join the military and/or para-

---

[11] Readers, however, should be aware that female-heads' emphasis on educating their daughters is not necessarily consistent with other gender-conscious moves. Later I shall illustrate how improving children's welfare is usually done at the expense of female-heads' self-worth and well-being, and that this is because "good mothers" are willing to make many sacrifices to sustain the households welfare level. So the fervent adherence to maternal ideology contradictorily continues to perpetuate gender roles and norms through the social and patriarchal values female-heads inculcate in their daughters.

military forces.¹² Each of the motivations provided by female-heads, however, did entail sons, like their sisters in certain instances, having to make sacrifices to their individual welfare and not having the opportunity to expand their capability base. They too, more often than not, had to give precedence to the interest of their families, especially where families were large, because "responsible" sons were expected to do so. Equally, Muslim and Tamil female-heads pointed out that sons are valuable only when single. Upon marriage their responsibility shifts to their wives' families. Therefore, extracting the benefits from sons needed to take place before they reached the age of

---

¹² An important distinction between the two communities, however, should be noted. For the Sinhala community, joining the military forces is increasingly becoming an effortless option, given the recruitment drives of the forces as well as the increasingly low educational requirements placed on lower-level military cadres. Joining the military forces, therefore, provides households with an assured monthly income and even the high risk of being killed in the ethnic war is weighed against the monetary compensation that households receive from the State. Furthermore, de Alwis (1998b) notes the ideological and gender images the State, via the media, deploys in calling on both mothers and sons to protect the nation-state. Some Sinhala female-heads, however, expressed ambivalence about their sons joining the military forces, mentioning that protecting their lives was more important than defending the country. While these Sinhala female-heads may be a critical and/or cynical few, their views were important in explaining the motivations for getting their sons to work and boosting household income from an early age. They explained that by getting their sons to work early, they were instilling economic and social responsibility in them. And once this was so, they hoped that their sons joining military forces would be much less likely—and this was probably so, if only because they might not have the stipulated educational qualifications. For Tamil female-heads the threat of their sons being abducted by the LTTE as child soldiers is very real, and this took place frequently when boys were attending school. Where it was not forced abduction, boys were more likely to join the para-military forces voluntarily where men (their fathers) had been indiscriminately killed and/or tortured by the State army. Female-heads reasoned that by getting their sons to work, not only did they contribute to the household income, infusing them with social and economic responsibility, but it also became possible to keep an eye on their movements.

marriage. A Tamil female-head of household mentioned this in the following way: "After marriage a son's responsibility is towards his wife and her family. Only a rare gem would still give precedence to his family—this happens, but is rare. So in the absence of a husband, I have to make sure that my sons do ensure the economic stability of the household, and especially of my daughters."[13] In an attempt to depict the complexity of the social world of female-heads and their children, I discuss some main features that lead boys to stumble because of the different ways in which patriarchal structures operate.

Mobility is a male prerogative in the Muslim community, and especially holds true for middle- and upper- income groups. While women in low-income groups may not have the luxury of being able to limit their activities to the household compound, they do attempt to adhere to the norms with their children, especially young, single and unmarried daughters. Where daughters have not been pulled out of school by Muslim female-heads to help with domestic chores and/or self-employment activities, then it is the boys who are likely to play an active role in supporting the household economically. Boys do not have restrictions on their mobility and this provides the primary grounds for removing them from school to participate in income-generating activities. These tasks ranged from finding wage employment, usually as casual labourers, to taking a prominent role in self-employment activities. Moreover, boys are better able to bargain, thus being a more adept link between household economic activities and the wider market. The use of boys as an essential support in self-employment activities indicates the burdens they faced in the community. Yet again, I quote the sentiments of a few Muslim female-heads to explain the processes that can sometimes place boys in precarious positions.

My main income comes from grounding and packaging flour for sale. The main thrust of the work involved I can do, but I have the choice

---

[13] Such views of female-heads and their relationship to their sons are undoubtedly linked to matrilineal norms, which as pointed out in the previous chapters, are a predominant way of organizing kin structures in the region.

of selling the packaged flour through a middleman, in which case I get a low price. Or I get my son to do the rounds in the town area, negotiate with shopkeepers and get a sound price. While I have studied up to grade 7 and I have the basic knowledge for engaging in such transactions, there are too many pressures on my life. When my husband died my 5 children were young, and I knew that I could not look after them, do self-employment work, and do the buying of raw material and selling the final product without any help. So I decided to get the oldest son involved by getting him to do the main buying and selling—but also getting his help with many of the physical tasks. Of course, this did mean disrupting his schooling even though he was 13 years then, but I feel I had little choice under the circumstances. (*Zahra, a 38-year old Muslim* de jure *female-head from Trincomalee, and mother of five children*).

I had not studied beyond grade 5 and I had never been allowed to move in public spaces. I did have a very protected life as a young girl and then as a married woman. So when my husband died of a heart attack, I felt helpless. My eldest, my son, was 16 years and my youngest was then 8 years old. While a relative put me in touch with a NGO that helped me set up a scheme of buying and selling short-eats, I still needed additional help in buying and selling the goods. I spoke with my older children, as I started treating them as equals, about all this, and we decided that my eldest son would stay back and work with me. So ten years later, I have a fairly successful business and have managed to educate my other seven children as well. We had tough times and hard decisions to make, but the worst is now over.
(*Fathima, a 49-year old Muslim* de jure *female-head from Ampara and mother of five children*).

Muslim female-heads' lack of expenence of public interactions and/or their inability to move in public spaces to some extent determine the decision to interrupt their sons' education. They are hesitant to participate in activities that require asserting their will and making decisions, at least in public interactions. As a result they inevitably turn to their sons to get the necessary help and support, even if this implies taking their sons out of school. In fact many female-heads who had relied on young sons for economic support, considered this an obvious choice in a community where there was restricted movement for women and girls. So while girls were usually able to continue with their education in such situations, boys had to forego the accumulation of human capital through education.

Boys are placed in insecure positions in female-headed households in the Sinhala and Tamil communities too, and since their mothers typically expressed similar sentiments I now consider the core premise of their claims simultaneously. Where female-heads had access to land and were occupied in agricultural and/or home-gardening activities, they noted the need for physical labour in undertaking these tasks. In the absence of husbands, and without extensive support from male kin, mostly because there were fewer men in the area, female-heads decided to withdraw sons from schooling.[14] "When my husband started leaving me for sporadic time periods, I rented some nearby land to begin cultivating vegetables for saleable purposes—and I was mostly doing this on my own. However, when I decided to separate from my husband permanently then I also spoke with my children and expressed the need for physical help to carry out the home gardening scheme profitably. Accordingly, I decided that my two older sons would support me with these tasks and the three of us now work together on the land," was the response of a Tamil *de facto* female-head. Similarly, other female-heads noted the ability of men, even young boys, to earn better wages by hiring themselves out as casual wage and/or agricultural labourers. They argued that by getting their sons to work from an early age, boys were able to acquire the necessary skill and training as future workers, and this was in addition to the important contribution they made towards the household income. While poverty thrusts some female-heads into reliance on their sons, they also argued that getting their sons to work from an early

---

[14] I noted in the literature review chapter similar experiences by female-heads in South Asian and other countries, where there was a lack of consistent support from male kin for agriculture-related tasks (Chapter Two). In that case, however, it was explained by male kin recognizing that reciprocal help from female-headed households was unlikely and, therefore, limiting any help to such households.

age is not necessarily negative.[15] Some female-heads did mention that these outcomes may not be the best for their sons, but their economic situation necessitated painful decisions. Finally, the political threat of their sons joining the military and/ or para-military forces made female-heads remove them from school to work alongside them. In this way, most female-heads felt that they could monitor their sons' movements and activities, and any unnecessary association with others was kept at a minimum. The reality of the political conflict and ethnic war, therefore, enters into the decision-making process of female-heads—not only making their economic insecurity very real but also jeopardizing the chances of having a "normal" childhood for boys in the region. The key point is that not all boys benefit from patriarchal structures.[16] Some boys do have a price to pay, at least in the short run, and feminists should pay attention to these contradictions so as to comprehend the complexity of patriarchy itself.[17]

Maternal Ideology—and the Inter-linked Dynamics to Sacrificing Sons and Dutiful Daughters

Whose education faces disruption varies from household to household according to the circumstances and perceptions of female-heads. But not all female-heads made the choice to interrupt their children's education. Though children still remained an invaluable source of support in such households,

---

[15] When Anker discusses issues related to child labour, he makes a comparable point when he contends that "non-hazardous work might provide children some valuable life skills whereas idleness would not", in discussing the relationship between the quality of schooling and child labour (2000: 23).

[16] An interesting observation about the choices made by female-heads for their sons and daughters is the perpetuation of gender roles. The boys replace their fathers and the girls replace their mothers, allowing the latter to do work that her husband would normally have done.

[17] Additionally, recognizing the contradictions of patriarchal structures in relation to children helps further my feminist methodological argument that diverse outcomes are possible under patriarchy (Chapter Nine).

since they performed tasks ranging from caring for siblings to marketing, there was a conscious decision to attempt to hang on to education for children and to delicately balance schooling with household activities. But the endeavours of female-heads to keep their children in school were in most instances linked to a strong maternal ideology that was articulated by these women. Female-heads were willing to forfeit their "good name" to provide their children with a decent and good upbringing, so maintaining particular patriarchal structures while challenging others. Here, female-heads were not sacrificing their sons' futures and not compelling their daughters to be duty-bound, they were generating an image of the mother who creates, nurtures and preserves life (de Alwis 1998a: 188). I contend that female-heads also sustain their families through personal sacrifices. Yet, by making personal sacrifices and even transgressing the acceptable boundaries of womanhood, these female-heads simultaneously, usually implicitly, subverted other patriarchal structures. Noting such contradictions is critical for feminists, since they may be used to counter seemingly stable patriarchal processes. Maintaining particular pillars of the status quo may sometimes require destabilizing other supports, but where such paradoxes occurred without a conscious decision by female-heads then they were likely to reinforce a maternal ideology that did little to challenge gender and class hierarchies.

There were, however, other moments where female-heads made a conscious decision to challenge patriarchal norms on both womanhood and motherhood, thus asserting their agency and creating moments of possibility for evolving social transformations. I shall begin with a discussion, through anecdotal evidence, where challenging norms happened within the contours of propriety and consequently softened the nature of these challenges because it reinforced the concept of maternal ideology.

The decisions female-heads have to make are sensitive. They have to balance the welfare of the household and children against the perceptions of community and/or kin structures.[18]

Dutiful Daughters, Sacrificing Sons   135

With kin and community support so critical for female-heads, putting families and children before themselves even to the point of threatening their own good name could potentially destroy the supportive network structures. Equally, it could undermine relationships with immediate kin that are critical for the households' welfare. However, some female-heads are willing to risk their personal welfare to promote the well-being of the household, even though this may imply putting into peril their network base. Through the use of a particular case study I attempt to capture the dynamics of this process, where the female-head justified her actions by constantly harping on the rhetoric of motherhood—while her own mother was vociferously critical of the choices made by this female-head on the grounds of womanhood.

Box I: A female-head, her female-head daughter and other social relationships

Kumari is a 41-year old Tamil *de jure* female-head in Ampara, whose husband was killed by the state in 1987. When her husband was alive she lived with him and her two daughters. The elder daughter was prone to severe epileptic fits from childhood. After her husband's abduction and killing, the daughter went into several recurrent epileptic fits that left her severely handicapped.

Around the same time Kumari's younger sister, who was in a bad marriage, was advised by their mother (Vijayai) to leave her spouse, even though she was a mother of two sons. Kumari's older sister-in-law was expecting her first child but was to die in childbirth, leaving an infant in the care of her husband and his family.* Vijayai made the decision to care for her granddaughter, acting as a surrogate mother. Since Kumari's husband was killed at the same time, the decision was made for both Kumari's sister and mother—with the young children—to move into Kumari's house.

---

[18] In the next chapter (Chapter Eight) I develop an account of the relationship between community and kin structures and its importance to female-headed households' well-being levels. It is sufficient to note here that this relationship is an important one, and is usually taken into account when female-heads make decisions regarding their households.

While the three family units live in the same house, they do not share the same kitchen—which was the result of a series of disputes between Kumari and her mother. The tensions in their social relationships epitomize the strength of maternal ideology and notions of "proper" womanhood that were expressed by the two women on separate occasions to me.

Kumari mentioned that as her husband had died, two of her siblings provided economic support—but she knew that this was not a permanent source of such support. Therefore, she began tailoring clothes for people in the neighbourhood—and branched out into several other sources of income generation, including poultry farming. When I met her she was being trained as a carpenter. Carpentry is a non-traditional craft occupation for women and in this case the training was organized by a Canadian-funded NGO. I was curious, therefore, to note Kumari's opinions on the choices she made for herself and to maintain the well-being of her daughters. She mentioned that this latter was her primary concern and she definitely did not want to disrupt her younger daughter's education—even though ensuring her older daughter's mental health placed both her and her younger daughter in a precarious situation. So drawing upon many avenues of income generation was an obvious choice, because "female-heads are vulnerable in the community, since we have neither economic nor social security. And I am not even sure if working female-heads have brought a shift in attitude. But I do know that my daughters' welfare is very important to me, and I will do anything to make their lives better—this even though I know that my own mother does not approve of me working with/through the NGO."

Since Vijayai (a 59-year old) was also a female-head with whom I had extensive conversations, she did speak about the various economic and social issues she had to confront in bringing-up her granddaughter. She had particularly strong views on female-heads and the proper role of women, where she noted "People in the community are waiting for an opportunity to gossip about any wrong turn taken by my two daughters, since neither of them has a husband." Yet at the same time she was recounting various anecdotes of other female-heads who, in her view, were behaving improperly. It was during this dialogue that she went on to mention her disapproval of Kumari's decision to take up the training course offered by the NGO. "She has a lamassi (teenage daughter) who has severe mental disabilities. Is it right that she leaves her daughter with us and goes out to work? Do 'good' mothers and women do such things?" she rhetorically asked me.

* This was occasioned by the prevailing conflict situation cutting off links with her natal family, who were from Trincomalee.

Juxtaposing conflicting views on motherhood and womanhood in this particular case study helps elucidate the inherent tensions between the various patriarchal concepts that female-heads use to shape their behaviour. Younger female-heads were willing to challenge convention so that they could secure better opportunities for their children, and in doing so they justified their actions and behaviour within the rubric of motherhood. Thus, while they may be expanding the capability bases of their children, by sustaining their educational opportunities, their behaviour is likely to inculcate in children patriarchal concepts of appropriate social roles. Aspiring to maternal roles does very little to subvert the accepted contours of gender relations: although female-heads may be increasingly accessing independent sources of income, a seeming challenge to the patriarchal status quo, they do so by resorting to another gendered standard, "motherhood", to validate their transgressions. Implicitly, through their own behaviour and actions, most female-heads socialized their daughters and sons into the prevalent gender status quo.[19]

Thus, older female heads pointed to the "improper" behaviour of younger female-heads when they undertook tasks that did not seem appropriate to their circumstances, were frequently seen in public, and/or were engaged in a multitude of self-employment schemes. The interesting twist in the intrinsic ambiguities of patriarchal structures came in those rare instances when female-heads made the necessary associations,

---

[19] Additionally, those female-heads who choose home-based occupations both implicitly and explicitly reinforce notions of proper womanhood and motherhood simultaneously—and the high frequency of such events among female-heads across all ethnic communities is, of course, a cause for concern.

and acted to assert their rights with a social awareness of these issues. The view of one Muslim female-head conveys this rare insight.

> I do not have people controlling my behaviour and I do not listen to every utterance. This is because every aspect of our behaviour is subject to some criticism or another. If we work, then this is questioned, and if I get our children to work then this is criticized too. I made the decision that my daughter should continue with her studies, because I think good schooling is the passport to a girl's success—she will be able to stand on her own two feet. But also I continue working and being active in the community, helping other vulnerable female-heads. If Chandrika, a widow, can be the President of Sri Lanka, then all other women can aspire to similar heights. It is usually patriarchal structures—that come in many forms and shapes—that prevent women from realizing their capabilities.
> (*Fasmeena, a 32-year old de facto Muslim female-head from Batticaloa, and mother of one daughter*).

Fasmeena was an exception in articulating the relationship between patriarchal structures, womanhood and mothering with such keen awareness. But it is important to note that there were other such women, though limited in number, and that these cut across all ethnic groups. They were conscious of the political, social and economic transformations taking place in the region, and made the connection to how their particular predicament was linked to the dynamics of this process. While their economic insecurity may have been compounded by their being thrust into assuming headship, and in most instances it was this that propelled them to seek employment—whether as wage labourers, white-collar workers and/or home-based workers— many of their other decisions challenged patriarchal structures. And acknowledging the multiple ways in which their lives were circumscribed by these structures was the route adopted by such female-heads. This was most visible on the question of their relationship with their children, where the decision to keep their daughters (and sons) in school was made in conjunction with that of seeking employment, thus reflecting their interests as well as those of the household. Usually, such female-heads began their working-life as home-based workers but through their own initiative made the effort to obtain training in other crafts so that they were able to branch out. Such female-heads recognized the importance of their own well-being as well as that of their families, though at no time did they perceive such an economic route as the only path to flouting structures that usually placed restrictions on them. A young Sinhala *de facto* female-head aptly declared:

> I do not make enough money to consider myself wealthy and I barely live a comfortable life. However, one need not have money to interrogate structures that restrict our behaviour. Yes, we need to be economically sufficient—because otherwise we do have to depend on kin and community relations to a great extent, which may stifle our behaviour. But my consciousness did not come about because of stable employment. This helps, but before, like many others, I was primarily depending on homework, when I realized that this is an exploitative trade to be in—and since I had studied until my O Levels I decided to volunteer part-time with an NGO until I was permanently employed by them. With this exposure, each time a kin and/or community member said this was not right/proper, I began to challenge them—and ask myself—the reasons. Now I think what makes a good woman and mother is what society tells us, and what society tells us can always be changed.
> (*Swarna*, a 27-year old Sinhala de facto female-head from Ampara, and mother of two children).

Such sentiments reveal the willingness of some female-heads to act autonomously and question the various strands of patriarchal ideology, including maternal ideologies and notions of womanhood. These instances are not only inspiring for feminists, but also provide illustrations of the diverse ways in which female-heads may interpret similar experiences. But the general picture of female-heads is one infused by a strong notion of maternal ideology and womanhood, without the space for emancipation and/or realization of their social, political, and economic base.[20] Given this scenario, how then do maternal

---

[20] This is not altogether surprising. Other feminist scholars working on motherhood and womanhood in Sri Lanka have pointed to particular constructions of these concepts in nationalist projects—whether Sinhala or Tamil—that allow little space for creatively contesting patriarchal and

ideological constructions impinge upon daughters and sons who remain in school, as well as on those who get withdrawn from school? Does the former group necessarily end up having the potential to overcome the structures that make their mothers' lives vulnerable? Obviously, the response is contingent upon many factors, including their ability to make the necessary associations between different structures that preclude political, economic, and social security in most female-headed households. However, a more vulnerable group is that of girls who have had their education disrupted during their early years—who, I will argue in the next section, are more likely to suffer in the long term than boys with similar experiences of limited schooling. But I conclude by emphasizing the need to focus on the short-term negative consequences that children, as a group, are likely to suffer by having their education interrupted. This is an important point for feminists in advocating development policy that is politically strategic.

Conclusion: Saving the Children?

Patriarchy is a complex set of social arrangements. However, feminists too often narrate a simple-minded story where patriarchy victimizes girls, especially in poor and female-headed households (Chapter Two). By focusing on children and maternal ideology, I have shown the many varied ways in which patriarchal concepts and thoughts are used. Sometimes, female-heads creatively resorted to patriarchal justification to further the welfare of their daughters, often at a cost to their sons. Moreover, their decision to continue and/or disrupt the schooling of their sons and daughters was not simply and only linked to poverty. Poverty was an important variable, but where female-heads recognized the importance of educating daughters they would then justify their decisions by turning upside down

---

class structures (Maunaguru 1995, de Alwis 1998a, 1998b, and Ismail 2000). Unfortunately, however, similar anthropological and/or historical studies uncovering the relationship between gender and nationalism in the Muslim community have not been done.

the patriarchal logic that usually limits the education of girls. Female-heads' own experiences, coupled with economic exigencies, usually coloured their decisions on educating daughters, while boys carry the economic burden. Where female-heads did take such actions, they ruptured patriarchal structures. This exposes the simple-mindedness of always seeing women and girls as victims and complicates decisions on children's schooling where female-heads are faced with bitter choices. However, by showing how such ruptures were the result of maternal ideology, I stressed the limitations and added caution to my optimism. Where decisions on children were linked to conventional ideas about maternal roles, any enthusiasm for the emancipation of female-heads must be tempered accordingly. Similarly, it is important to analyse in more detail the outcome in the long term for girls and boys who did have their education discontinued. Girls in this group are not simply thwarted from realizing their capabilities for ideological reasons but also may be unable to build upon their social capital base, whereas boys in similar situations only have to overcome a lower educational capability base. Ideologically and institutionally, the array of structures stacked against boys, as adults, will be of a lesser magnitude.

Female-heads' own experiences also influence decisions on their children's education in another important way. Mothers may resist disrupting either girls' or boys' schooling by behaviour that compromises their reputation. But some female heads challenged such constraints to be good mothers by recognizing the patriarchal controls imposed through the ideology of the "good mother". Such female-heads were rare gems who challenge constraints because they are unjust, but nevertheless they effectively articulated the inequities embedded in gender relations by linking them to their own experiences as female-heads, mothers and women. Rajini, a 38-year old Tamil female-head, expressed her extraordinary insight on these issues as follows:

> Most widows have been thrust into female-headship at a very young age, and yet because of cultural factors they continue in this status-

quo throughout their lives... Economic survival and ensuring the welfare of our children is only one aspect of our existence. When you are thrust into female-headship at a tender age, as was my case, our sexual urges and needs remain. Though I am 38 years old, my sexual needs have been repressed since I was 29 years old... If a female-head takes up to religious matters, read prayer books, and so forth then she may be able to repress her needs. And some female-heads do take to religion fervently upon the death of their spouse...For the average female-head, therefore, the emphasis is on being a mother and a widow and not women in their own right. And our culture continues to emphasize this again and again... my decision to continue my daughter's education, therefore, is taken in the hope that she too will critically look at these issues. By being active in the community my hope is that I can help create a space for her and other young women—where cultural norms become lax, there are less restrictions placed on women, and women's needs and rights are recognized in holistic ways.
(*Rajini, a 38-year old Tamil* de jure *female-head from Ampara, and mother of one daughter*).[21]

The decision to examine how the different dimensions of social and cultural practices link to issues of female-headship has been useful to my study. It helps accentuate the level of feminist consciousness some female heads possessed. Their decisions about educating their children, especially daughters, therefore were an implicit challenge to patriarchal relations and maternal ideology.

The main themes I have taken up in this chapter also provide some interesting evidence for the feminist methodological arguments I shall make in the penultimate chapter (Chapter Nine). To conceive the social world as dependent on human agency captures reality as differentiated and interconnected,

---

[21] This female-head was one of the few who touched upon issues that I had originally no intention of pursuing. Discussing issues of female sexuality during my fieldwork, I realized, was taboo. This was not because I subscribe to the view that sexual unions outside of marriage do not take place in rural communities, but rather that open discussion of such issues rarely occurs. Yet, where female heads did broach this issue they convincingly tied it to their desire to make their daughters lives "better" than their own experiences.

and the narration of female-heads and their decisions on children's welfare, I believe, elucidates this particular issue. My chapters on feminist methodology and development policies will return to the themes and evidence I have explored in this chapter (Chapters Nine and Ten, respectively). And in this way I shall connect the evidence of my research on female-headship in eastern Sri Lanka to both its feminist methodological and development policy implications.

EIGHT
Juggling Acts
Political, Economic and Social Realities

Female-heads' Access to Economic and Non-economic[1] Resources

My investigation of the economic circumstances of female-headed households has revealed the importance of kinship and community networks in their survival. These too can be seen to vary by ethnicity, but also to have important similarities. An excellent illustration of the parallels across ethnicity is the gender

---

[1] I use the term "non-economic" to cover the support provided by women. But it should be noted that much of this support is non-financial, such as childcare, giving each other left-over food, doing domestic chores and such rather than strictly "non-economic". Equally, the focus of this chapter does not explicitly pore over issues of sexuality that are likely to bear upon the material and social support female-heads receive, especially for younger female-heads. Patriarchal morality on sexuality and sexual mores—and particularly women's sexuality—did seem to matter for many of the younger female-heads in this study, and thus the applicability of empowerment notions is rendered more problematic in such situations. However, only a very few younger female-heads directly and explicitly spoke about the ways in which they felt their sexuality was constrained and controlled. Therefore, there was not sufficient qualitative fieldwork material for me to examine the ways in which sexual issues bear on the support female-heads did receive. Not withstanding this limitation, it is fair to say that section 8.4 implicitly draws attention to the possible resilience of patriarchal notions of women's sexuality in the discourse of 'good' behaviour that many female-heads constantly mentioned.

dimension to support, with economic support usually coming from men and non-economic support being provided by women. Focusing on the relationship between networks and female-heads' welfare highlights many critical issues that are usually ignored by economists and social scientists, and this is an important component of my study. In this chapter I also, however, focus on contradictions that arise in network support for female-headed households. Examining these incongruities serves to exemplify the means whereby patriarchal values and norms are upheld, and transgressions from accepted roles and behaviours disciplined, through the withdrawal of support and limiting of access to networks.

Using the economic profiles of female-heads as an entry point facilitates a comparative perspective on ethnic, cultural, class, and gender relations, which are all infused by patriarchal structures and ideologies. This comparative perspective aids the main premise of my study that there are diverse ways in which female-heads rely on networks and uncovering these complexities contributes to my depiction of patriarchal structures as manifest in plural forms. While female-heads mediate their economic interests through networks, these structures are neither static nor identical, demonstrating, the variety of patriarchal outcomes. This is most apparent in the fundamentalist pressures, ethno-nationalist ideologies, and attitudes that members of networks entertain towards widows across ethnic communities. Networks, therefore, are historically and culturally located, making them dynamic and overdetermined institutions laden with their own values, hierarchies and particularities (Althusser 1990). As such, networks are also inherently variable and specific to each time-space location.

Access to economic resources links the material and the ideological realms, and female-heads revealed this when they discussed their negotiation of economic strategies within networks (Hirschon 1984: 5). The economic welfare of female-heads depends upon networks that mediate the patriarchal-ideological nexus, although the distinctions and similarities of the ethnically-based experiences of female-heads provide a sound basis for a coherent feminist perspective. Moreover, from a methodological perspective this exercise provides partial support for the view that there is uniformity in the underlying structures—i.e. feminist economists need to pay attention to ontological issues too.[2] So the purpose of this chapter is to argue that, despite noteworthy differences between Muslim, Sinhala and Tamil female-heads, there is an over-arching theme of patriarchal values, relations, and/or structures that pervade their lives. My argument here is that this process takes place via kin and community structures, and though these are important for sustaining the economic well-being of female-headed households, they also shape the decision-making processes of female-heads. Considering the dynamics of this process from a feminist economic perspective also reveals the "non-economic" resources that female-heads have to draw upon for their survival, a process that is gender-laden, and hence, unaccounted for in orthodox economics. Off-loading economic survival issues on to network structures may sustain female-heads in the short run, but over a period of time their quality of life will be affected.[3] Understanding female-heads' reliance on non-economic resources, therefore, necessitates examining the structure of these network systems, which vary according to class, ethnic, and cultural dimensions.

I organize this chapter by starting with an appraisal of the dynamics between kin and female-heads that lead to economic support. I then go on to discuss the most reliable source of support for female-heads: non-economic support and the

---

[2] Issues related to feminist methodology will be explored in depth in Chapter Nine, where I draw upon critical realist and feminist standpoint theory to reconcile the possibility of diversity within a structured social reality.

[3] The human development gains made for/by Sri Lankan women will deteriorate, unless gender-sensitive policies are set in place. The concluding chapter on the development policy implication of female-headship will focus on this and other issues, where the complex evolution of household structures underscores the limitations of relying on a patriarchal model for development planning in Sri Lanka.

gender dimension to these support bases. While networks are important to female-headed households' welfare, they impose constraints on female-heads' behaviour and this is then discussed. The concluding section of this chapter, makes the point that while some generalities can be found in female-heads' experience with networks, there are also contradictions and ethnic variations that should be noted. The intrinsically dynamic nature of these patterns is underscored in the concluding section. This chapter, therefore, is concerned with fleshing out the political and economic dimensions of kin and community structures, which not only have a gender aspect but also have implications for female-headed households.

Kin Relationships and the Political Economy: Reading for the Dynamics

Conventionally, kin structures have been considered a likely source of economic support for distressed households and their members. They are generally stable and resistant to change, and therefore economic support is likely to be forthcoming for vulnerable members, especially female kin (Yalman 1971: 6). While social anthropologists emphasize kin structures as a key source of support, economists have tended to neglect them. But feminist economists have progressively emphasized the importance of "structures of constraint" and cultural systems in explaining women's choices (Folbre 1994, Wyss 1999). Even feminist economists, however, have not paid adequate attention to the economic and non-economic dimensions of kin structures. A central objective of this study is to show both the opportunities and limits of network systems for the survival strategies of female-heads in eastern Sri Lanka. Unlike Folbre and Wyss, for my own understanding of these systems I borrow extensively from anthropological studies that have attempted a unified analysis of gender and kinship.[4] Besides this, of course,

---

[4] This is partly a result of following my own convictions that feminist economics ought to cross over disciplinary boundaries so those holistic interpretations of social realities can be made.

anthropologists' analysis of gender and kinship is extensive, making it a rich source of insight for feminists (Yanagisako and Collier 1992: 14-50). Moreover, such an investigation helps demonstrate that kin relationships are shaped by the political-economic milieu, while wider political and economic structures are predicated on gender relations (Comaroff 1992: 83).

Economic support for female-heads from network members is not an unusual occurrence in eastern Sri Lanka, and the support I refer to does not include the support of resident children. There are variations in the magnitude and frequency of support according to ethnicity, with Muslim female-heads noting the highest proportion of support from kin (Chapter Four, Table 4H). But the support received by Sinhala and Tamil female-heads, while insignificant, cannot be ignored when considering the welfare of the group. The concern here is not the economic welfare of female-heads but the likely sources of support and the political-economic conditions that make kin/community support possible. Using case studies I discuss some probable sources of economic support for female-heads, and then discuss the political economic conditions that make this possible. Many of these examples help elucidate the fluctuating and fluid nature of kin and community structures, as well as the implications for gender relations in Muslim, Sinhala and Tamil ethnic communities.

The most usual source of economic support for female-heads is close family, including fathers, brothers and/or maternal uncles. This shows that while matrilineal kin structures and inheritance patterns shape the three communities, it does not negate the prevalence of patriarchal ideology and structures across ethnic groups. Usually, fathers and brothers come to the economic assistance of female-heads at the death, desertion and/or separation of their spouses, whether or not spouses were killed by the ethnic conflict, died suddenly, and/or abandoned their family. But where economic support is forthcoming there is no guarantee that this will continue indefinitely. Indeed most female-heads, whether from their own experience and/or recognizing the socio-economic realities, do not expect such

Juggling Acts 149

economic support to be permanent. Anecdotal evidence from three female-heads in the Muslim, Sinhala and Tamil communities, respectively, illustrates this point.

> My husband died when I was 32 years old, and I had never worked during my lifetime. So his death left me totally vulnerable, especially because my oldest was a daughter and my younger sons were still in school. Since my husband had been a businessman, I thought my sons were too young to take over the running of the business. My younger brother, who was unmarried but working, took over supporting my household. This is not uncommon in our community, since when my mother was widowed it was our maternal uncles who supported her economically. But of course my younger brother's economic support did not continue indefinitely, and I did not expect it to be permanent either. Once he was married this support came to an end: this is natural, isn't it? When he marries his responsibility shifts towards his wife and her family. But by then my sons had started earning an income towards the household.
> (*Fatima, a 40-year old de jure Muslim female-head in Batticaloa, and a mother of one daughter and two sons*).

> A few months after my daughter was born, I woke up one morning to find that my husband had disappeared. We did have problems in our marriage, but I did not expect him to abandon me so suddenly. While I was educated up to my A/Levels, my daughter was simply a baby and looking for work so suddenly was not possible for me then. Since my parents were working and able to support me they came to my help. My father essentially gave me all the financial help I needed until my daughter was a year old, and by then I had slowly started giving tuition to children in the neighbourhood as a way of earning an income.
> (*Nishanthi, a 28-year old de facto Sinhala female-head in Ampara, and a mother of a three year old daughter*).

> My husband was killed in the 1989 riots, I was 32 years old then. Even though I had studied until my O/Levels, I stopped working after I married—which I did when I was 25 years old. Added to this my daughter was just 5 years old when my husband was killed, and starting to work immediately did not seem like an option for me. Fortunately for me, my brother came to my rescue by paying for my household expenses. As time went I slowly started finding work as a wage labourer, and now I support my daughter and myself with my income. It is difficult, but I still do it.

(*Yasothini, a 41-year old de jure Tamil female-head in Trincomalee, and a mother of a 15-year old daughter*).

So economic support from male kin does take place, but this help is temporary. Consequently, female-heads eventually end-up being self-reliant and/or depending on children, with the latter most likely among Muslim female-heads (see Chapter Seven, and Chapter Four, Table 4H).

But financial support for female-heads is not a male prerogative; it also comes from sisters. Although it is not as frequent, and there are variations according to ethnic groups, with Sinhala female-heads noting many more instances of economic support from female-kin, this support is important. Damyanthi, a 41-year old *de jure* female-head, encapsulates the help she had from her sister as follows:

> There is only my sister and me in our family. So we have to stand by each other. And my sister has faithfully and unhesitatingly done so to my family and me. Until my son started earning an income, my sister contributed a monthly allowance of Rs 1,500.00—and even now she comes to my assistance during unforeseen financial emergencies.
> (*Damayanthi, a 41-year old de jure Sinhala female-head in Trincomalee, and a mother of two children*).

Financial help from female kin, as from male kin, is not permanent. A noteworthy distinction, however, is that female-heads were less hesitant to draw upon their female kin, even later on.

However, such support from both male and female kin, while critical for female-heads' survival, does constrain female-heads' behaviour. The key point is that economic support from kin is forthcoming, but that such support is temporary and is determined by a variety of political and social factors, such as the particular social, economic, and demographic position of the kin. There is, therefore, no reason for economic support from kin to be forthcoming in all circumstances, and paying attention to those conditions where it is more likely is important. It should be noted, however, that I am not making the argument that kin support is only predicated on some political-economic conditions. Such a reading would not only be facile but also subject to the limitations of economic determinism. My point rather is that the ideological practices that construct women's and men's ability to be independent also need a favourable economic state to perpetuate gender inequities and maintain kin-based power structures (Whitehead 1984: 176). So while material realities may be eliminating traditional kin support structures, this does not entail a breakdown in patriarchal ideologies. Network systems remain important sites through which inequities in gender relations are perpetuated, and this point is one issue that will be examined in this chapter.

Financial support is provided more often for younger female-heads simply because they have unmarried and/or married siblings with few encumbrances. Older female-heads are more likely to have working-age children they can rely upon, and relatives see no need to support female-heads with older children.[5] In addition, older female-heads will have similar age brothers who will normally be married, with families and therefore, their own economic problems and burdens. Besides this, female-heads themselves are quite aware of the general economic difficulties their siblings face, particularly in eastern Sri Lanka, and so find it hard to depend on their kin for extended periods of time. A Sinhala female-head summed this up as follows: "It is not right for me to expect financial help from my sisters like that. They have their own families and have small children too. How can I keep depending upon them, when I know that life is not easy for them either?" Furthermore, even where kin have the economic resources to help, the may not feel obliged to help female-head relatives. An older Tamil female-head explains why financial assistance is not available from her wealthier younger siblings: "When we are so poor, our wealthy relatives do not even want to acknowledge us as relatives. How can we then expect any support from them, or

---

[5] In the chapter on Muslims a larger proportion of female-heads were found to depend upon children for income support for the household (Chapter Four). Muslim female-heads also belonged to an older age group relative to Sinhala and Tamil female-heads, and their reliance on children for supporting household income should come as no surprise.

even go to them seeking help?" Such commentaries indicate certain limits to the support provided by kin systems, suggesting support is more likely to work across homogenous and reciprocating households. Where relatives belong to different income groups, then support channels may break down. Class is evidently an important social marker that kin affinities may not overcome, and consequently some relatives may not be a dependable source of support for female-heads. In addition, the ethnic conflict in eastern Sri Lanka has rendered social relationships unstable, with displacement an everyday reality. Equally, an awareness of the economic hardships may prevent female-heads from seeking help from kin in the first instance. If this is the more likely scenario, then what is the most likely setting for resilience of kin support? And indeed, are there sources of help that female-heads take for granted, indicating frequency of support? In the next section I argue that kin and community support are usually guaranteed when it comes to non-economic help, which interestingly is a strongly feminized source of support, provided and mobilized almost exclusively by female kin and community.

Drawing on "Non-economic" Resources: the Gender-Class Dimensions of Networks

Networks for female-heads tend to include both kin and neighbours. I call relations with the latter community structures. Community structures also go beyond the immediate neighbours since they are largely based on informal relationships that female-heads develop with people they feel are sympathetic to their predicament. A gender bias exists here, with a preponderance of women maintaining and sustaining these networks. But men are part of the backbone of these networks, too, and their role is acknowledged. The non-economic support that female-heads receive from men is qualitatively different from that which they receive from women, and this makes most networks particularly gender-based. Moreover, there is a class dimension to network systems as in most instances networks are unlikely to cross class-boundaries. Since most neighbourhoods consist of households with similar income levels, there is little opportunity for support across class boundaries. Also, non-economic help involves intimate and ongoing relations—for example, childcare, allowing sharing of toilet facilities, etc.—so there are reasons why networks emphasize same sex members and are unlikely to involve richer kin. Both class and gender, therefore, determine networks. As this argument unfolds it is worth bearing in mind the political-economic nature of such network structures.

What underlying factors sustain networks for supporting female-headed households and lead their heads to count on this support? The answer is partly found in the socialization process that has inculcated particular social values and norms in female-heads as girls and young women. Similar endowments, rights, responsibilities, norms and preferences result in shared identities and interests based on gender, and lead to gender-based collective action (Folbre 1994: 53-5). An overwhelming proportion of female-heads across ethnicity noted the "obviousness" of supporting each other in situations of difficulty and distress, as well as taking for granted the non-economic help they offer each other. A second significant question is: what makes non-economic support more reliable for female-heads in eastern Sri Lanka? The answer lies partly in the political context, which ranges from a background of a violent ethnic conflict to grinding economic deprivation and hardship. These factors make non-economic support a more likely option for female-heads, and this in turn indicates shifts in the gender dimensions of support. So the response to the two questions raised is like the two sides of coin: economic deprivation and the ethnic conflict both intensify female-heads' dependence on non-economic support from networks and the non-economic nature of the support highlights the role of women's assistance. Although I draw upon theoretical contributions made by feminist scholars in analogous situations, my focus on the gender dimensions of networks is innovative.

Socialization is an effective way of perpetuating the shared values and interests of communities, and feminists have frequently drawn our attention to the measures through which women's interests are circumscribed. These range from dowry systems, marriage arrangements and folk rituals to property and kinship relations (Hirschon 1984: 10, Sharma 1984, Whitehead 1984: 185, Bourdieu 2000: 114). Along with other structures, such as class, ethnicity, age, and religion, they position and shape gender relations. However, since people occupy multiple social positions, diverse social situations are likely to generate competing interests and divided loyalties (Folbre 1994: 53-70). Older female-heads, for example, constantly repeated the need to adhere to, and protect, cultural norms and values, illustrating the power older women can derive from maintaining the patriarchal status quo (Safilios-Rothschild 1982: 119). Younger female-heads were more critical and willing to challenge norms, especially when they thought norms were constraining their ability to maintain the economic welfare of the household. Despite such diversity, female-heads conceptualized a shared identity as female-heads, which was an operative mechanism through which their interests were promoted and protected. Several Tamil female-heads noted their feelings regarding their dependence on, as well as their support towards, other women in similar situations in the following ways:

> We are well aware of the difficulties and obstacles we face as female-heads, and know only too well the particularities other women in similar circumstances must face. When we have this awareness, then not helping others through whatever means, even if this simply means talking to her/them daily, is simply not right. So while we may not be able to economically support other female-heads in the village, we do our best to share and help them cope with their problems. This is simply because in our darkest days many women/female-heads come to our support. Now that our lives are better, we need to return to others in their hour of need.
>
> (*A group of Tamil female-heads in Ampara*).

Muslim female-heads similarly noted "Only we are there for each other. If we don't help each other, who will help us during difficult times?" Reciprocity here is based largely on female-heads empathizing with other women's vulnerability, as well as women recognizing their own susceptibility in the unstable social and economic circumstances of eastern Sri Lanka. Assistance, however, mostly takes a non-economic form and this is explained by the very economic hardship female-heads and women of particular classes tend to face. Investing in the social capital of community and kin structures, then, is an effective strategy adopted by women and female-heads alike, since this increases their chances of having such support reciprocated during their own needy periods.[6] Caring for children and the elderly, attending to domestic chores, going to the market, cooperatives and/or grocery stores, and sharing left-over food are some of the means by which female-heads and women support each other. Another significant feature of these networks is assisting each other in income-generating activities, especially since a substantial number of female-heads opt for home-based work. Childcare is one example of non-economic support critical to female-heads, where the ability of female-heads to engage in self-employed income-generating activities is largely dependent upon the backing they receive from networks, whether regular or intermittent. Pounding-rice, buying raw materials, and selling final goods, exemplifies other widespread forms of support that female-heads and women offer each other. Along with such practical sources of support are the chatting, advising, discussing, and sharing of experiences that take place among female-heads and women within network circles.

I noted earlier that non-economic support is not simply a woman's domain, and that men too participate in these networks. While men's role was not often mentioned when female-heads were discussing their dependence on networks, some female-heads did explicitly draw my attention to the

---

[6] Bourdieu defines social (and/or cultural) capital as capital successfully possessed and managed by members of domestic units (1998: 70-1). In my use of the term, I extend this notion of social capital to community and kin structures as capital owned and managed by networks so as to perpetuate their common interests at a wider community level.

importance of men in network systems. Most female-heads, across ethnicity, noted the role of men in attending to activities that required signing papers, visits to government institutions, and travelling. A Tamil *de facto* female-head noted the need for help from men as follows: "Even though I am educated and I am a teacher, I still do depend on male kin. This is not because I am unable to do these tasks on my own, but that I am able to get things faster when I am accompanied by a man—people tend not to push you around when there is a man present. And I also tend not to get questioned unnecessarily by security forces when travelling." So such support from men was not necessarily linked to low educational levels in female-heads, but is here explained by ideological obstacles as well as the perils of travelling in public spaces. Even educated female-heads noted their reliance on male supporters, whether young nephews, uncles, and/or elderly men. They explained this by the reality of sexual harassment that lone women encounter when travelling into public places—especially, when the threat of sexual harassment and rape from security and para-military forces is very real.[7]

Men were also drawn into conventional roles of helping in tasks that required physical stamina, ploughing agricultural fields, and acting as gurus, especially where female-heads had young sons. It is not just physical strength that is at stake here. The formal manifestation of separate public and private spheres is also of central relevance in the forms of help obtained from men. Female-heads also noted that if the men they depended upon were not kin, they were usually the spouses of women with whom female-heads had close relationships. There is a strategic reason for female-heads leaning on these men. It is

---

[7] Social conditions in eastern Sri Lanka are creating new forms of dependence between men and women—or, so the stories of female-heads appear to reveal. The consequence of such realities is that there is a price female-heads have to pay in terms of their personal autonomy. From a feminist perspective such instances highlight the disquieting new forms of constraint that arise out of the present ethnic conflict in Sri Lanka, which will be discussed in greater detail in the next section.

simply so that they can reciprocate their time, energy and advice to these women, and reciprocate the help obtained from husbands through their wives. Also, these men are generally considered "safe" as they are married and, therefore, unlikely to sexually harass female-heads. But still the help of men is obviously an important resource that female-heads did draw upon, even if the frequency of such support is significantly less than that provided by female-heads. Marketing, cooking and childcare are every-day tasks, while specialized tasks performed by men are less frequent. To accentuate this point is not to downplay the significance of the part of men in network structures, but rather to ensure that the reader bears in mind the fundamental proposition of this chapter. There is an important gender-dimension to network structures, especially when examining the non-economic attributes of these systems.

I have demonstrated in the previous paragraphs that to ensure non-economic support from networks, female-heads need to invest in the social capital of these structures. Even where female-heads rely upon men, ways exist whereby they actively maintained their network structures by reciprocating services to the wives of their male helpers. The renewal of social networks takes many forms since help can be reciprocated and support stored up in many different channels, which in turn helps explain the resilience of such forms of support even in adverse economic and political conditions. My argument does not imply that networks are static structures, which is in any case unlikely given the continuously changing environment in eastern Sri Lanka. Indeed, the absence of female-heads who rely on kin structures reflects the massive displacement and disintegration of extended family units, which has been a prominent characteristic of the ethnic conflict (Samuel 1994: 16, Hyndmann and de Alwis 2000).

Additionally, female-heads themselves acknowledge that network support may break down due to family disputes, quarrels, jealousy and misunderstandings. Such situations may involve building alternative support bases from scratch. Moreover, in rare instances where economic mobility from one class to another takes place, the possibility of non-economic support failing is widely acknowledged. Female-heads reasoned that this was because social relations came under stress when kin and/or community members were moving into other economic classes. A Sinhala female-head sums this up as follows: "Becoming wealthy and marrying wealth usually means losing touch with others' reality. The wealthy easily forget others' poverty and deprivation, or, for that matter, what life was like when they were poor." Undoubtedly people in low-income groups view the capital accumulation process as involving conspicuous consumption patterns and values that lead to their better-off relatives and neighbours distancing themselves from them. Such perceptions clearly shape relationships, with real consequences. For a variety of reasons, therefore, networks are in continual flux.

My argument here has been that the support bases of female-heads have shifted from economic to non-economic forms, and that this has been an outcome of the ethnic conflict and of economic pressures. Both these factors make conventional economic support towards female-heads less likely. With the resource base of support changing from economic to non-economic forms, there is also an alteration in the gender composition of such networks. To a greater extent, women appear to be supporting each other through non-economic but nonetheless important forms. Political-economic conditions have promoted a particular form of non-economic support that is gender-biased, and which is critical for female-heads in devising particular survival strategies and maintaining the well-being of their households. Does this non-economic support from networks come free? Are female-heads able to rely on networks without sacrificing their own-interest? Obviously this is an important issue that feminists should examine in analysing new and evolving forms of non-economic support, since such shifts are creating spaces that female-heads may be able to utilize to exercise autonomy. Exploring this particular issue requires taking into account female-heads' perceptions of themselves and their awareness of expectations placed upon them by their communities. By looking at these two issues, which are inextricably linked, it also becomes possible to locate female-heads' activities between structure and agency. This exercise is pursued in the following section, where the restrictions female-heads encounter as well as their attempts at challenging network norms are examined in more detail.[8]

The Price of Network Structures: Constraints that Female-heads Face

What are the implications for gender relations in this shift from economic to non-economic forms of support? While feminists would no doubt wish to observe a significant shift in attitudes reflecting progressive and accommodating values towards female-heads, this is not taking place on any scale in these communities. Rather, the most noteworthy thing is the perpetuation of restrictive social values and behaviours, particularly on the part of elderly women and those female-heads in the community who have taken on the guardianship of the proper roles, values and behaviours of its female members. While younger female-heads articulate their needs to reflect material factors, there is a price to be paid for depending on networks. So contradictions abound in the social realities that female-heads encounter. This section examines the constraints that female-heads face, along with an analysis of their negotiation of social, material, and cultural spaces.

The centrality of 'respectability' (*lajja-baya* in Sinhala and *lajjam-bayam* in Tamil) to women's lives has been well documented by feminist scholars of Sri Lanka, who have carefully detailed its embodiment in the national psyche through colonial to post-colonial times (de Alwis 1994, 1997). De Alwis

---

[8] This theme is probed separately from the premise of motherhood, which was evaluated in Chapter Seven. However, the ability of female-heads to exercise their agency separately from networks and their roles as mothers are connected. In the discussion that ensues where these issues overlap—and they undoubtedly do—I shall point to the similarities in themes as they arise.

notes how the education system was used to restrict the freedom and mobility of women, thus circumscribing their social spaces (1997: 105). Historical and socio-political contours locate the myriad ways whereby female subject positions are created and recreated within networks. Women are no longer socialized into "respectable" roles simply through the education system; this is also achieved through social, formal and informal organizations (de Alwis 1994: 142-7). Networks as I have described them are another important site for producing and reproducing female respectability. Where female-heads do rely on networks they are also conscious of the associations between the public-private persona these necessarily involve. Female-heads constantly articulated the thought that their ability to depend on networks is symbolic of their "good behaviour", and even younger female-heads expressed their awareness of having to adhere to expected norms. Enoka and Rajini, a Sinhala and Tamil female-head, respectively, convey this as follows:

> I receive their help because I act in ways to win their hearts and not behave improperly...People are always on the watch for women whose husbands are not with them. If anyone sees me talking with another man then it leads to speculation and gossip. So I always remain alert to my environment, with whom I talk, and for how long, because I want to make sure that I maintain the respect of my community.
> (Enoka, a 23-year old de facto female-head in Trincomalee and a mother of two young sons).
>
> In making decisions, I am the final arbiter. My decisions are best, I feel. And although I do not challenge cultural norms head-on, I do make decisions that have at their core the paramount interest of the well-being of my daughter. But I ensure that the decisions are acceptable to the community as well. I live in this community and to disregard the way they perceive me would be foolish for my welfare.
> (Rajini, a 38-year old de jure Tamil female-head in Ampara, and a mother of one daughter).

Two inter-related factors were conveyed by female-heads when discussing their need to keep to proper behaviour and the rules implicitly set by the community. On the one hand, female-heads are alert to the central importance of these structures for their well-being. On the other hand, it shows how female-heads have to shape their behaviour according to the social and cultural constraints they face. A negative corollary of networks, then, is that in most instances there are restrictions placed on the behaviour and roles of female-heads, which do little to widen the space for emancipation and the subversion of acquired gender roles and relationships.[9] Furthermore, female-heads themselves are involved in propagating the social values that bind them to particular gender roles and social relations. A remarkable age-based distinction regarding the perceptions of the "proper" role of female-heads became apparent when talking with women in these communities. Older female-heads are far more likely to uphold values that restrict each other's behaviour. This group of female-heads would recount various incidents and anecdotes of villagers that both upheld patriarchal social norms as well as portraying themselves as paragons of patriarchal virtue. Rapid remarriages of *de jure* female-heads were particularly frowned upon, since such female-heads were ignoring customs and traditions that required periods of mourning and/or seclusion. Frequent mobility of female-heads was equally queried, and this was considered

---

[9] My assertion is not that female-heads have not been querying, challenging and pushing the borders of "acceptable" behaviour for themselves. Indeed, Rajasingham-Senanayake in her anthropological work on displaced Tamil female-heads in Sri Lanka speaks of cultural transformations that have led to "some hidden moments and routes of women's empowerment" (1999: 149). While I agree with her that social upheavals in this community do challenge certain aspects to previous gender roles and relationships, I do not necessarily agree with the view that this has led to their empowerment. In this section, similarly, I too shall identify female-heads across ethnicity criticizing patriarchal structures and a burgeoning awareness of women's rights. But as much as social awareness feeds into women's empowerment—and this is a key variable—very few female-heads whom I came across identified themselves as economically secure. Surely economic security must be a basis for women to realize their capabilities—without this their sustained empowerment seems improbable. Apart from this concern, I agree with her completely that female-heads did have "moments" of consciousness of their rights, roles, and relationships.

particularly inappropriate where there were teenage daughters (Chapter Seven, Box 1). An older *de jure* Muslim female-head routinely emphasized "I and my daughters are respectable women and therefore, there are ways in which we are allowed to act—and this is so even when our financial circumstances keep rapidly deteriorating. So when women go out into public spaces their behaviour will obviously be watched."[10]

Thus, female-heads have to be cautious and aware of their decisions and actions, especially when they depend on network structures to sustain their welfare. But even where there may not be obvious dependence on networks, female-heads are always influenced by their social context. While some female-heads are willing to challenge and push the structural contours, they do so with the awareness that they may be subject to criticism from the community. Yet there remain female-heads willing to confront patriarchal structures and respectable values head on, if only because they recognize that political, social, and material conditions are rapidly changing. The sort of contradictory situation that a female-head can encounter is well encapsulated by Jeeva, a 39-year old Tamil *de facto* head.

> People in the community think of me in two distinct ways. Some people look at me with respect because I look after my family well. Others do not, because I do not live with my husband. People think that I am arrogant because now that I earn a living I do not want to take my husband back. But I feel that I don't need a husband who spends everything I earn... Those days I used to think that a husband was very important for my existence. I do not any longer subscribe to

---

[10] Paradoxically, this female-head did have two of her daughters a typist and a teacher), working and supporting the household's income. I came across other instances of similarly incongruous situations where there were discrepancies between rhetoric and reality, and this I deem to be a consequence of "respectable" female-heads attempts at clouding the reality of their circumstances. Indeed appearing to be respectable and adhering to patriarchal norms it seemed was a more effective mechanism for the community's acceptance of these households, and this is especially so where the ethnic conflict alone is fracturing "traditional" social realities.

this view...If a husband is irresponsible, then a woman should not feel obliged to keep him. This has been my experience.
(*Jeeva, a 39-year old de facto Tamil female-head in Trincomalee, and a mother of two young sons*).

Similarly, a Muslim *de facto* female-head asserted: "Society is always reluctant to accept women as equals. Because we face many obstacles our voices rarely get heard, and this is so even though we are working hard to improve our social and economic positions. When I feel that I am being pushed aside, I am resolute in my thinking that we should not give in to 'accepted' social roles." In this and other ways, some female-heads confront the patriarchal status quo, dogged in its prescription of particular gender roles, and assert their social rights and their independence. However, such female-heads· are a rare minority. The more common scenario is limited assertiveness within accepted boundaries for each class-ethnic social group. Female-heads would draw my attention to their altering material conditions, and the economic difficulties and deprivations they faced, but still emphasize the importance of considering the views and perceptions of the community.

Female-heads, consequently, exercise their agency within the accepted norms set by social structures within each ethnic-class community. But as Rajasingham-Senanayake (1999) justly argues, the apparent fissures in the material basis of these structures, brought about by economic pressures and the ethnic conflict, are paving the way for moments of potential cultural transformation with respect to legitimate gender roles. This is unsurprising at one level, since crisis may provide a necessary condition, though not a sufficient condition, for questioning the established status quo. With the social world losing its "natural order", a questioning of social norms constantly re-occurs (Bourdieu 2000: 169). Such moments highlight social structures as evolving and dynamic, a social reality with which female-heads constantly engage and negotiate their social, political, and economic place. That female-heads exercise their agency at many levels, therefore, should come as no surprise. When social reality is analysed for its contradictions and diversity, it allows historically specific readings of social relations. Such an investigation permits the ways in which distinct and complementary social units can both challenge and yet perpetuate gender and class inequities. Female-headship offers the potential for transforming gender relations and realizing women's capabilities, yet the contours of this process are socially determined through network systems, whether kin or community structures. So long as this remains the case, most female-heads continue to be trapped within kin/community structures, with their economic vulnerability being very real.[11] It is not simply their economic security that is at risk, but in most instances their social autonomy too.

The discussion so far has focused on the similarities across ethnic groups of female-heads' negotiation with network structures. Such experiences are indeed common to female-heads across ethnicity, class and age, but there is a variety of experience that is worth noting. The nature of support provided by kin and community does vary according to ethnic and class location. Explaining social reality, however, necessitates acknowledging the diversity and inconsistency that social scientists find. From a feminist economic perspective, this is a critical part of social exploration. A feminist methodological argument for differences and diversity requires an explanation for such variations in social reality (Chapter Nine). Before I undertake this it is important to describe and discuss such moments as we encounter them in our examinations of social situations. This is not to deny the pervasiveness of the social structures that we have seen to cut across female-heads from different ethnic, class and social groups. Rather, the hope is that it will help support my premise that political and economic reality form and reform kin and community structures, while at

---

[11] And it is not just female-heads' economic risks that are a reason for disquiet; the socio-economic well-being of their children is at stake here too. As the previous chapter argued, the "non-economic" role played by children in female-headed households is critical for many households, but at the same time it demonstrates the potential inability of children to realize their human capabilities.

the same time political economy predicates itself upon gender inequities and relations. In order to achieve this objective, I conclude this chapter by capturing some dimensions of these variations as I came across them in my fieldwork.

Conclusion: Contradictions and Diversity

Methodological perspectives incorporating a structured social reality are well developed in the social sciences (Bourdieu 2000). This research contributes in important ways to the attempt of feminist economics' attempts at understand the diversity and contradictions in social situations. I focused on explaining differences based on ethnicity in Chapters Four, Five, and Six with the purpose of acknowledging possible variations in female-headed households' survival strategies. My data analysis looked at ethnic and regional differences, even though it did not look specifically at the class-ethnic dimension to differences, which is likely to exist too. But my in-depth case studies were spread across female-heads from different social and economic groups. And this, together with the ethnic and regional difference, helps explain the qualitative and quantitative issues that female-heads face. Such an analysis helps us bear in mind that social situations offer several outcomes and it is only one such difference that I am attempting to capture in this study. While I use ethnic categories as demarcation points for this study, as noted previously in the introductory chapter, the intention is to highlight diversity of outcomes rather than to consider such differences as fixed and stable. Social structures are historically, politically, and culturally mediated, and human needs potentially manifest themselves in many ways (Lawson 1999: 47). This holds true for female-heads in eastern Sri Lanka, too, and it is worthwhile explaining some gaps in the story. This chapter, therefore, clarifies the importance of gender relationships for particular political economic conditions, which are enmeshed within inequities.

Chapter Four highlighted the importance of kin structures for Muslim female-heads. As a social group, Muslim female-heads were more likely to rely on relatives than Sinhala and Tamil female-heads. Sinhalese female-heads mostly noted their dependence on the community, while Tamil female-heads rely on both kin and community members. This is an outcome of economic and cultural norms: where "correct", the former makes possible latter practices. Nonetheless, where women's mobility is severely restricted and their cultural value is inexorably coupled with men, then there is more pressure on male kin to support female-heads economically. Among middle-class Muslim female-heads the task of economic support passed on from maternal-uncles to sons. Generally, the rationale varied from low educational and employment skills to cultural restrictions on mobility, which was compounded by security issues in the region. Moreover, with ethno-nationalist discourses continuing to redefine the "religious traditions, ideologies and customs" that impinge on women's lives, there is a "legitimate" basis for female-heads' economic dependence on men from their community (Rajasingham-Senanayake 1995: 234). This, however, only keeps Muslim female-heads trapped within their community structures, with very little economic autonomy. Additionally, there is very little economic security for Muslim female-heads in such situations, since they realize the temporary nature of the support, as indefinite support from the same male kin is unlikely. The more likely scenario is financial assistance to begin from a maternal uncle and/or a female-heads' brother, and then from her sons and/or sons in-law. Shifting economic backing from one male relative to another accentuates the economic vulnerability of Muslim female-headed households, since the amount of support received is also likely to vary, with female-heads having to alter their survival strategies accordingly.

Low-income and poverty-stricken Muslim female-heads rarely have the luxury of guaranteed support from their male relatives. Such groups acknowledge that, though maternal male kin are supposed to provide financial help, their own economic difficulties may make this unlikely. At best, financial support for Muslim female-heads is sporadic. Lack of pecuniary help is not necessarily concomitant with meagre non-monetary help, since female-heads take for granted their sisters' help in domestic and child care activities, which women willingly extend despite pressures on their own households. Deteriorating economic conditions have transformed the nature of networks and support structures, with the economic/financial dimensions giving way to social support. Needless to say, such changeovers do have a gender dimension, with non-economic/ social support usually being provided by women. Discernible distinctions in the non-economic support received by Muslim female-heads were particularly apparent, with women giving domestic and caring help, and men assisting in documentation, banking, and administration.[12]

The more significant matter for explaining the relationship between political economy and gender is that Muslim female-heads find themselves in occupations of a restricted range. This outcome is easily explained through the strength of ideological practices coupled with social insecurity that led Muslim female-heads to choose particular low-skilled and low-paid occupations. Muslim female-heads frequently explained their limited occupational choices in terms of low educational levels, lack of social mobility and/or the need to supplement household incomes. This was usually linked to patriarchal practices that relegated them to such limited choices. For example, low-income Muslim female-heads would explain their involvement in home-based work on the grounds that they had not received the necessary education, either because their own parents were too poor and/or they were taken out of school to perform domestic duties. Their particular life paths were intelligible to them, since educating girls beyond a certain level was seen as countering (patriarchal) custom and tradition.[13] With a limited

---

[12] Among middle-class Muslim female-heads, however, grocery shopping (conventionally perceived as a female task) was undertaken by male members since "respectable" women should restrict their social movements in public. This, however, is a class-based phenomenon, since low-income and poverty-stricken female-heads did overturn such norms by working as wage labourers and the like.

[13] As I noted in the preceding chapter, however, there were notable generation-based distinctions that emerged from female-heads across

capability base, they would reason that their occupational choices were "natural", though very few female-heads linked this to patriarchal constraints. Female-heads in low-income groups frequently put the choices made by their parents down to poverty, while female-heads from other income levels explained their disrupted education as following the social conventions in the community. Low educational levels of the social group together with younger age of marriage are additional reasons for preferring home-based employment (Chapter Four, Table 4D). These factors accentuate the importance of gender inequities for maintaining particular political economic relations, where social structures are permeated by class inequalities. Gender then becomes an important indicator of social systems, where social practices are conditioned both by political, economic and class structures; the latter do, however, makes variations probable, given the specificity of cultural, historical, social and political conditions.

Compared to Muslim female-heads, Sinhala and Tamil female-heads depend less upon male kin for financial support (Chapters Five and Six, Tables 5H and 6H, respectively). The reasons are obvious for each ethnic group. Sinhala female-heads generally have fewer social restrictions placed on their mobility, and therefore they take it upon themselves to find employment. Indeed, most Sinhala female-heads prefer to have access to their own independent income since in this way they do not have to abide by restrictive social norms such as those faced by female-heads from the Muslim community. Further, having access to their own income is a sensible option, since it is their duty to look after their parents.[14] Here too, while sisters were an assured

---

ethnic groups. Muslim female-heads, in particular, tended to stress the importance of educating their daughters as long as their finances allowed them to do so. One Muslim female-head echoed the thoughts of the group: "Our daughters must get the opportunities that we never had, because this may provide them with a basis to socially and economically uplift themselves."

[14] Interestingly, unlike Muslim female-heads, their Sinhala counterparts never spoke about getting help from their brothers and/or uncles. For them the most apparent source of financial support was parents and then

source of non-pecuniary and social support, their financial support was intermittent, as, in most instances, they were only marginally better off. The very few Sinhala female-heads who depended upon their fathers for economic support were usually very young, and had fully able and working fathers. Here the support female-heads receive is temporary. Working fathers grow old and young female-heads may remarry. In the absence of remarriage, female-heads will consider entering the labour market and having their own independent income. Where female-heads were dependent on fathers not only were they usually young, but they frequently mentioned that it was because they had infants that they did not seek employment. However, they also revealed that indefinite dependence on their working fathers was not possible. So planning for contingencies in terms of self-employment schemes and/or entering the formal labour market is never out of the question for these groups of women.

Regardless of the economic support some Sinhala female-heads received from their fathers, and the non-economic support, most of the group received from kin and community systems, there was a greater variation in the occupational patterns of Sinhala female-heads (Chapter Five, Table 5G). The question is, why? Firstly, these women saw themselves as having more skills and better educational achievements. Normally, the Sinhala community sees education as an important asset base for both girls and boys. Such a favourable attitude towards educating girl children does not occur because the Sinhala community is devoid of patriarchal values and norms. It is rather because there is a recognition that educated family members can contribute towards household income (Chapter Seven). So unless severe poverty had hit the parental households of female-heads, in which case they (or, their sisters) were most likely to have had a disrupted and/or limited education, this group of female-heads generally had better access to education.

---

their sisters. Of course, this is not surprising given the different kinship patterns for the two ethnic communities. Still, economic support was generally supposed to come from men in both communities.

Secondly, greater mobility was possible, both from a security point of view and from a social one. These were Sinhala women and they were less likely to be subject to the extent of sexual harassment that Tamil female-heads usually face from the Sri Lankan (read: Sinhala) forces conducting security operations. Furthermore, anthropologists have cited the prevalence of an accommodating attitude towards women in Sinhala community, which makes possible female-heads' access to an independent income (Yalman 1971).[15] Thirdly, where Sinhala female-heads are found in home-based occupations this is connected to the young age of their children, which makes it necessary to combine productive and reproductive work. Thus, in the Sinhala community, a variety of reasons led to diverse outcomes in female-heads' survival strategies. The root causes, however, were in one way or another linked to patriarchal relations, although less severely so than in the Muslim community, and had particular outcomes because of more accommodating historical, political, cultural, social and class locations. This same point was summarized by a Sinhala female-head:

> We women in certain ways are better placed than Tamil and Muslim female-heads. There are fewer social restrictions on our movements and if we try hard enough we can find some form of work. But this does not mean that our behaviour is not under scrutiny, and we can do as we like. Even in our community everyone is watching each other's behaviour, and should we take a step out of line, a barrage of criticism is likely. Still the small spaces we have are a tremendous boon, and this means a lot when there so much instability and fighting in the area.
>
> (Jayanthi, a 38-year old de jure female-head in Trincomaalee and mother of three children).

Conversely, the narratives of Tamil female-heads highlight social transformations taking place, with these women silently

---

[15] The flip side of this, however, is that implicitly kin and community members may feel less social compulsion towards helping female-heads, since accessing employment is a viable option. But such assumptions ignore the gender-based occupational segregation of the labour market, since only a very few Sinhala female-heads were found in the service sector (leaving aside the upper/better-skilled end of this sector).

or stridently asserting their agency. Tamil female-heads, unlike their Muslim and Sinhala counterparts, are mostly unable to rely on (maternal) male kin, for reasons directly related to the ethnic conflict. One female-head said, "There are no men here. Most of them have been killed, have disappeared, and/or have gone to war. So we simply have to depend on each other." While her statement on the absence of men in the community may be an exaggeration, Tamil female-heads have certainly witnessed a reversal in the proportion of men in their communities. Demographic shifts also affect women's perceptions of their own roles. The abrupt loss of men together with most female-heads' exposure to violence and trauma has in some instances led to more self-assurance, social movement and assertiveness (Rajasingham-Senanayake 1999). And even *de facto* female-heads expressed opinions conveying a sense of change and transformation. Such changes are new in a community that has customarily viewed widows as an ominous symbol (Thiruchandran 1997). A Tamil female-head reminded me that, "By targeting Tamil female-heads, NGO activities in the region have made possible our access to self-employment. This has not only enabled an independent source of income, but it also brought us into the forefront of the community. Such experiences are new to most of us, because customarily widows have been pushed into the background as a sign of ill luck." With this community's social and political security under siege, the variations in employment patterns reflect transformations taking place, especially from the perspective of female-heads. While networks may impose restrictions on Tamil female-heads, there are also anomalous situations indicating both diversity and contradiction. Across class distinctions, households concede that reproduction and change of prior structures is taking place, with a notable number of female-heads emphasizing the economic necessities that make them venture into different income-generating activities, one "unheard" of in the past.[16]

---

[16] There was general consensus within the community of Tamil female-heads on areas of change and on the stagnancy of social values and norms, and this was generally true across class groups. Such consistency is partly

While Tamil female-heads may not have had their education disrupted to the same degree as Muslim female-heads, most of these women did not work unless pushed into the unexpected situation of assuming headship. As a group of women they have basic educational abilities but not the skills acquired through working. The rapid changes brought by the ethnic conflict created the necessary conditions to utilize their endowments and realize their own capabilities as well as those of the households. Essentially, this jarred with other factors that worked against an overhaul in attitude towards female-heads in the community. Networks were used as an entry point in this chapter to discussing their importance as a site through which gender inequalities and power relations are maintained and transformed. Others have similarly discussed the importance of ethno-nationalist discourse in effecting similar results (Coomaraswamy 1996, Maunaguru 1995, de Alwis 1998a, 1998b, Ismail 2000). Yet again, impositions on and expectations about the gender roles of women have been important mechanisms through which inequalities in the political economy are maintained.

There is a two-fold purpose in accentuating the contradictions that are apparent in this social context. Firstly, from a feminist economic perspective, providing a nuanced analysis of social situations helps reinforce the argument that development policies that deny room for manoeuvre and assume uniformity of purpose and response are not likely to be effective. This particular issue will be further developed in the final chapter. Secondly, as anthropologists have rightly emphasized, access to resources is historically and culturally located, where the material and ideological features of the social order are intricately linked (Hirschon 1984: 5). For female-heads in every ethnic community there is a common thread to their

---

unexpected, given the distinct class-based views of Muslim female-heads, the other matrilineal community in the region. It is feasible, however, that the ethnic conflict has paved the way for some critical re-thinking of social structures within those groups most exposed to political, social and economic risks.

experiences, and this despite the particularities of social location. But feminist economists, as social scientists, should record these distinctive attributes for the very reason that social reality is structured around a variety of possible outcomes. A feminist methodology needs to recognize uniformity and distinctiveness as co-existing. The subsequent chapter will make the links with the possibility of a structured ontology that allows for specific and diverse outcomes. As Hartmann argues, "patriarchy, like capital, can be surprisingly flexible and adaptable" (1981: 27). I go on to claim that this flexibility also brings with it contradictions that should not be ignored, and this is best summarized by Comaroff:

> For the very fact of hierarchical centralization implants a contradiction at the core of any social order, a tension that primes human action and, through it, shapes the surface contours of economy and society (1992: 84).

NINE
Nearing Limits or Pushing Boundaries?

A Narration of Household Structures
and Women's Well-being

My objective in this chapter is to contribute to the theorizing of female-headship. The dominant perspective in modern economics treats the household as an undifferentiated unit. In contrast, many empirical studies, including my own on female-headship in Sri Lanka, indicate that the household is anything but an undifferentiated unit (Chant 1997, Chen 1998). An adequate social theory of the household must be able to accommodate and explain the degree of differentiation that is repeatedly found. My aim in this chapter is to develop such a theory in the light of my findings in the previous chapters.

Becker's (1965) contributions on time allocation within the household, the basis of the neo-classical approach to the household, serve as an illustration of how the household is treated as an undifferentiated unit. The basic thrust is two-fold. Familial relationships are determined by self-interest. It is argued that marriage, like any other contract, takes place only if there are gains to both partners: people marry if the relationship is expected to deliver each partner a higher level of happiness. Once self-interested individuals have entered a marital relationship, their behaviour is concerned with maximizing the joint utility of the household, that is, the behaviour patterns of "self-interested" individuals take an altruistic turn. Both economists and feminists have criticized this approach (Sen 1984b, Folbre 1986a and 1986b).[1] Furthermore, problems with aggregating individual tastes to obtain a joint utility function have been noted in neo-classical theory, and are side-stepped rather than resolved by assuming that the head of household acts like a benevolent dictator.[2]

The contradiction between assumptions of self-interest in the marketplace and assumptions of altruism in the household are evident. Further, the power relations between spouses that usually lead husbands into the market sphere and relegate wives to the domestic sphere are not considered. The social/political/economic basis of the gender dimension of skills and opportunities is unaccounted for (Sen 1984b: 372–3, Folbre 1986a: 10–11).

It is not neo-classical theory alone that has failed to provide an adequate theorization of the household. Early Marxist literature on the domestic labour debate manifests the same limitations (Engels 1978). Thus Folbre (1986a) sees Marxist analyses as suffering several deficiencies. First, the role of

---

[1] Arguments against the neo-classical conceptualization of the household also reveal the methodological limits of the theory. Among others, Lawson (1997) argues that because mainstream economics is formalistic, it requires the positing of event regularities or relations of the event regularity form. In order to facilitate the latter, social theory in turn can consider only entities treated as isolated atoms. Applying this analysis to the household shows that the household (and anything else) must be treated in the same atomistic fashion, with Becker's contributions illustrative of such methodological practices in mainstream theory. Hence, methodological evidence undermining theoretical contributions that treat the household as an undifferentiated unit also reveals something about the nature of the social material and the nature of modern mainstream economics. While this particular line of reasoning will not be followed in toto, the contributions below demonstrate the importance of not assuming a given method *a priori*, but of fashioning a method after also giving explicit attention to the ontological structures of social reality. The nature of the household depends fundamentally on its constituents and on the context in which it is situated.

[2] Feminist economists have commented on this as well (Folbre 1986a, 1986b, Evans 1991, Kabeer 1994).

domestic labour in lowering the value of labour power is explained only through its relationship to the logic of the capitalist system. Second, the non-applicability of socially necessary labour time to domestic labour is claimed on the basis that household producers are non-optimizers, unlike labourers in the capitalist system. Finally, the sexual division of labour within the household is explained by household members' differential access to the means of production (ibid: 10–12).

Feminist Re-readings of the Household

Studies by Sen (1984b) and Folbre (1986a) contributed to feminist social theory by uncovering the economic basis of women's subordination within the household. However, the analysis of patriarchal institutions, domestic labour, household dynamics, and the complex web of relationships between class, ethnicity and gender, entered the discussion only in the 1980s. The re-reading by Beneria and Sen (1981) of Boserup's influential work on the marginalization of women in capitalist economic development addressed these very issues. They show how women's "unproductive" labour within and outside the household distorted policy planning and its implementation in economic development. Anthropologists have noted that the biases and misconceptions of policy-planners regarding the role of women in the private/public sphere have resulted in the absence of women's participation in irrigation projects (Casey 1993, Gardner and Lewis 1996).

In discussions of household and domestic labour, later Marxists-/Socialist-feminists' contributions focused on the interaction between patriarchy, class and gender, which placed women in vulnerable positions. For no group is women's vulnerability clearer than for that of female-heads: their vulnerability demonstrates the independence of patriarchal structures from the exercise of authority by individual men. The previous chapters have underscored how most female-heads risk abrupt decline in their economic status through the death or desertion of their male partners and/or separation from them.

Because of the variety of ways in which patriarchal norms operate, female-heads are more susceptible to poverty and economic decline.

A concrete example of this is the dependence of female-heads on patriarchal kin-networks: middle-class Muslim widows in eastern Sri Lanka are dependent upon the goodwill of their maternal uncles, brothers and/or sons to maintain the economic well-being of their families. For low-class Muslim widows in particular, their seclusion for three months on the death of their husbands means that ready access to income-generating activities is severely limited.[3] Most Tamil female-heads, while beginning to challenge patriarchal attitudes and values, remain susceptible to poverty. The realization of their economic capabilities is still a dream for a great number of these female-heads. Distinct cultural and religious practices are played out in diverse ways in the perceived status of women. But ideological representations of widows and female-heads as "unlucky women" affect the well-being of female-heads in all three communities. Such representations influence not only the abilities of female-heads to access economic resources independently, but also the extent to which alternative household structures can transform existing patriarchal relations. Where there are more social constraints on female-heads, they are more likely to become dependent on wider kin and community structures—with continued economic vulnerability combined with an inability to challenge the patriarchal status quo without threatening their conditional assistance.

To recapitulate: traditional economic approaches to the household, whether Marxist or neo-classical, are, in a narrow sense, economically determined. My study on female-heads in eastern Sri Lanka has shown that while the material basis of household structures has an impact on well-being, it is not the only factor. I have shown how children, broader kin and

---

[3] For these women, however, the practice of purdah is a luxury since their options are between survival and adhering to cultural norms, with the former usually outweighing the latter.

community structures, in a specific historical and political context, mediate gender and material relations.

Do feminist economists, then, have a theoretical framework that will allow female-headship as I have found and described it, and indeed, other alternative household structures, to be understood? Two leading proponents of more realistic, but also more complex, models of the decision-making process of household structures have been Sen and Agarwal (Sen 1990, Agarwal 1997). I begin by drawing upon the works of Sen and Agarwal, which have been inspirational to many feminist economists seeking to theorize household structures. Let me reconsider their contributions at this point.

Perspectives of Bargaining Relations and Co-operative Conflicts for Female-headship

Intra-household analyses have traditionally sought to focus on gender relationships by looking at the bargaining power of men and women. Exit options available to men and women would determine negotiations over resources within the household. Since men have an advantage over women in gaining access to employment and income-generating activities, the bargaining position of men within the household, is strengthened by their economic position, while that of women is weakened. The economic basis of unequal power relations between men and women is depicted in these ways. However, recent contributions by Sen (1990) and Agarwal (1997) provide the framework for a more complex analysis by emphasizing the qualitative dimensions of bargaining relations. Such economic relations have not only economic features but are also tied up with cultural, religious, ideological and material factors.[4]

---

[4] In my study, too, many female-heads from each ethnic community frequently justified their survival strategies by drawing attention to the particular social and cultural norms that bear upon their lives. Certainly, the nuances provided by Sen and Agarwal are pertinent to understanding the modes through which female-heads go about realizing their economic capabilities. I shall discuss this further later in the chapter.

The literature on co-operative conflicts (Sen 1990) and that on bargaining/gender relations (Agarwal 1997) has not necessarily been read together. However, I treat them as mutually related in this section. Agarwal's work (1997) is concerned with incorporating the qualitative dimensions of bargaining over social norms and perceptions into household relations. Her assessment is similar to Sen's in that, for her, endowments, entitlements, and entitlement relations are related to cultural factors, which have an impact on co-operative conflicts in intra-household dynamics. Likewise, Agarwal is concerned with two qualitative dimensions of bargaining relations. First, she investigates how social perceptions influence intra-household dynamics (echoing Sen in his co-operative conflict model). And second, she asks how these social factors are themselves bargained over, which can be considered an extension of earlier work on bargaining relations as well as of the gender co-operative conflict literature.

Sen's key point in formulating co-operative conflicts is to extend entitlements in order to incorporate notions of perceived legitimacy in intra-household divisions (Sen 1990: 125). Entitlements, as Sen defines them, can be broadly thought of as the social, economic, and political structures that allow individuals access to resources.[5] It is these that enable an individual's capabilities to be fully realized. Sen acknowledges that in the case of women, entitlements *per se* do not necessarily translate into minimum standards of well-being. His view is that qualitative relations, the cultural and social dimensions, influence the informational base of the "legitimate" status of women vis-à-vis men. These are factors that define views on propriety and norms, which in turn characterize acceptable gender roles in communities (ibid: 125). Therefore, it is not merely entitlements that matter in determining the well-being of women, but also the informational base. My interpretation of Sen is that the "informational base" is a framework through

---

[5] Entitlement in Sen's (1999) framework is defined as an appropriate space in which individuals have "substantive freedoms—the capabilities—to choose a life one has reason to value" (1999: 74).

which women's entitlements are filtered and determined, and the usual standards demanded of women as mothers and moral beings. An illustration from my study is when Sinhala female-heads had to deal with *opa-dupa* (gossip) when accessing resources. The "informational base" Sen speaks of is *opa-dupa* in this scenario (ibid: 126).[6] Hence there is a need to discuss women's well-being in terms of "extended entitlements". By incorporating extended entitlements, gender issues and political awareness are brought into intra-household analysis. If the basis for determining women's perceived legitimacy is intricately linked to an informational base, there remains a case for development policy to make concerted efforts to change this informational base. As Sen argues:

> There are considerable variations in the perception of individuality, even within [..] traditional society, and the lack of a perception of personal welfare, where that holds, is neither immutable nor particularly resistant to social development (ibid: 126).

Sen goes on to develop the consequences of existing gender-bias in the informational base, the perceived legitimacy of gender relations and the impact these factors have on co-operative conflicts in intra-household relations.

Agarwal's concerns are twofold. As mentioned before, her first is similar to Sen's. What is the role of social norms and perceptions in the bargaining process? Her view is that social norms affect the strength of a person's fallback position in bargaining relations. Secondly, she examines how social norms and expectations are themselves bargained over. This is an extension of Sen's analysis of co-operative conflicts. Sen's concern with the informational base is similar to Agarwal's premise of social norms and perceptions determining the fallback position of individuals. However, Agarwal goes further by conjecturing that social norms, expectations, and perceptions can themselves be bargained over (1997: 1–11). Sen's informational base becomes endogenous. For gender issues in

---

[6] The "informational base" can operate in many ways and the discussion in Chapters Seven and Eight elucidates other instances from my fieldwork.

household relationships, the implication is that factors such as State intervention, feminist political activity and awareness building, institutional reform and the like can lead to positive shifts in the informational base.

There are possibilities for progressive transformation in social norms that can affect the well-being of women. However, the process of bargaining for social legitimacy need not be uni-dimensional. The complex twist to the analysis lies here. Social legitimacy has a variety of facets to it. While certain factors influence gender issues positively, others could be working to the detriment of progressive gender relations. Disentangling particular effects may be hard. An illustration from the experience of female-heads may help. Extended network and community structures strengthen women's fallback position (ibid: 7). These very important support networks, however, may also perpetuate traditional gender roles and norms. Evidence from my study shows that many female-heads face bitter contradictions in seeking the support of these networks. Similarly, female-heads make hard choices about disrupting their children's education to obtain another helping hand in the household and to avoid dependence on networks. Hence the complexity of the narrative.

I draw attention to all this, however, not to make a case for a simpler framework, but rather to acknowledge the complexity of household relations. The important point of Agarwal's theme, however, is that there is an explicit role for the State in influencing bargaining relations within the context of social norms and legitimacy.[7]

Nearing Limits or Pushing the Boundaries?

So what value do these theoretical contributions have for understanding issues of female-headship in eastern Sri Lanka?

---

[7] While Agarwal does not expand on her notion of the State, there is little doubt that her reading of this institution is not a simplistic one either. It has been a site through which oppressive gender, class, ethnic relations have been perpetuated in the past (Chatterjee 1993: 116–34, Jayawardena and de Alwis 1996: ix–xxiv).

Undeniably, there are many ways of pushing the borders of Sen and Agarwal's framework for my own project on female-headship. Here I sketch some possibilities. But I conclude that we come to the limits of the usefulness of gender and co-operative conflict models when speaking about female-headship. So an open-ended theorizing of household structures, that is, a form of theorizing that is not bounded, unitary and homogenous, is promoted in this chapter, supporting feminist advocacy of methodological shifts away from mainstream economics. Here, I begin with some possible ways in which co-operative conflict models can provide a backdrop for female-headship.

The co-operative conflict literature makes links between extended entitlements, the perceived legitimacy of female-headship and their households' levels of well-being. Can we study how female-heads transform these links into claims on the community and State resources in order to expand their entitlement base? Have matrilineal practices for Muslim and Tamil communities legitimated the status of female-heads and widows so as to establish entitlement relations and sharpen extended entitlements? The evidence is moot, since matrilineal practice does not mean the absence of patriarchal values and/or structures. Do matrilineal practices override other cultural constraints? Even though there are ethnic and class-based variations, the response here is less controversial. The discussion, so far, seems to indicate that, generally, repressive cultural practices are not a pervasive feature. But this does not negate the existence of patriarchal structures and patriarchal institutional laws that run counter to matrilineal inheritance, and are likely to work against the interests of women, and of female-heads in particular. Such divergences will not positively affect/inform the informational base of female-heads, since they only serve to perpetuate patriarchal interests from which female-heads have no legal recourse.

The basic thrust of co-operative conflict theories is that women subsume their perceived self-interest in order to work together with their men in negotiation over resources, and that

Nearing Limits or Pushing Boundaries? 183

this helps maintain the well-being of families. So even where women's own interest is in conflict with the larger familial interest, they are more likely to co-operate with men to avoid a breakdown in marital relations. Can a case be made that female-heads subordinate their own social, economic, and emotional interests so as to obtain the support of their kin and/or community in maintaining the welfare of their households? Evidence from Chapter Seven and Eight supports this, demonstrating how female-heads make difficult choices and forego their own individual interests to ensure the welfare of their families. Indra, a Sinhala female-head, describes this as follows:

> My (younger) sister said that if I remarry she will stop helping me and my family. I had two reasons to heed her advice. My relationship with her was solid and important to me, and it was more assuring than a relationship I may build with another man. Secondly, my sister was economically supporting me at that point, so I had to overlook the option of remarriage. Even now, I will always take my sister's advice into account—and I never dismiss it because she has been an important source of support to me.
> (Indra, a 41-year old de jure Sinhala female-head from Trincomalee, and mother of two children).

Where economic support available to women is crucially dependent upon the community's benevolence and support systems for female-heads, one is likely to witness the repression of women's own self-interest. In the absence of targeted welfare policies and institutional structures supporting female-heads there is likely to be a multiplication of such incidents. But does this mean, in turn, that the community will provide resources indefinitely to "honourable" female-heads? This does not seem to be the case, since community and kin support for most female-heads is intermittent and/or temporary. The lack of a patriarchal figure in their household may mean that female-heads are not subject to the bargaining over resources characteristic of two-person households. But nonetheless they may remain trapped in community and kin structures that perpetuate patriarchal values, and where women's individual self-interest continues to be pushed aside. Two issues are at stake here. First, where benevolent community and/or kin support is available female-heads may be able to extend their entitlement base, thus sustaining the well-being of their households. But, second, such extensions of entitlement relations may do nothing to expand their capability base. Without an expansion in capabilities, female-heads' economic vulnerability and susceptibility to poverty remains very real.

But even the conditional support of kin and community is not offered to all. Most female-heads do not get continuous economic support from their kin and neighbours. For most female-heads, the support received is largely non-economic in nature, which brings to the debate the gender dimension of network structures, and the theoretical implications for feminist methodology.

The Specific versus the General: the need for Undifferentiated Households

It is possible to extend Sen and Agarwal's analysis of co-operative conflicts in households to the community. However, this renders the limitations of their discourse more apparent. There are many points at which I show these limitations. First, the focus is on women suppressing their own interest. My study has shown that female-heads do not simply deal with men, but have to negotiate with patriarchal structures in the shape of networks, labour markets, and other institutions. These structures, whether represented by men or women, are imbued with patriarchal values.[8] Female-heads may have to repress their own interest to ensure community and/or kin support. Second, these structures in turn depend upon women to sustain, maintain and reciprocate them. Since most women take it for granted that it is their "duty" to help each other, they rarely step back to analyse their symbolic value in perpetuating particular gender roles. Even where female-heads are strongly aware of

---

[8] While Agarwal (1997) does incorporate the processes through which social norms and perceptions are bargained over, her analysis still implicitly focuses on patriarchal households.

the material and social changes that make them adopt a critical standpoint towards their new realities, they still constantly have to bargain with other women in the community to ensure that they do not face their wrath.

From a feminist perspective, the point here is that the very absence of any consideration of community structures in modern economics is revealing of the discipline's limitations. But does an incorporation of the relationship between the market, state and household suffice to comprehend social realities? The answer is in the negative, as social reality is more complex. The basic co-operative conflict model assumes a patriarchal household, leaving little room for those alternative household structures within which women devise survival strategies. The female-headed household is one example of an alternative household structure that reproduces children into their social and reproductive roles.[9] Such alternative household structures, of course, show up the need for feminist economists to move beyond frameworks that simply focus on patriarchal household structures. So for all the strong points of the co-operative conflict framework, the latter has limitations when applied to understanding alternative household formations.

Important links between the perceptions, well-being, and agency of women in co-operative conflict situations bring into the household debate social and personal parameters that lead to particular outcomes for household relations. My assessment departs from Sen's and is closer to Agarwal's view that "what is needed is less making women realize they deserve better, than having them believe they can do better" (1997: 25). The ethnic conflict in eastern Sri Lanka is opening up spaces for female-heads to question accepted patriarchal values and norms. The extent of their willingness to challenge the status quo has links to ethnicity and/or class. Tamil female-heads are, in most instances, openly critical of the legitimacy and authority of social norms and values in their community that devalue their interests.

---

[9] Indeed there are other household structures, including that of extended families, homosexual families, etc., that require similar analysis, though these will not be discussed here.

Most Muslim female-heads reserved their criticism of social and patriarchal norms for those that restrict their movements and interests. And although Sinhala female-heads are aware of patriarchal values pervading their lives and options, they see no real reason to challenge such structures overtly. The rationale is that as long as there was ease of movement and access to economic resources, there was little reason to confront the status quo.[10] Female-heads facing poverty or belonging to low-income classes across ethnic communities, however, are vociferous critics of those structures that make their economic survival difficult. Either way, however, female-heads in each ethnic group face barriers that prevent them from realizing their capabilities. Impediments translated through community and/or kin networks espouse the values of each ethnic community, and perpetuate patriarchal interests. Female-heads in eastern Sri Lanka, therefore, are placed in particularly contradictory positions. Matrilineal inheritance patterns and community structures place female-heads in a favourable position, but this positioning was only relatively so.

I have shown that female-heads within this particular context in eastern Sri Lanka nevertheless have lives that remain shaped and influenced by patriarchal relations. Patriarchal restraints sit together with structures that have traditionally favoured women, and manage to survive and mutate according to historically specific circumstances. For example, at the current juncture in Sri Lanka, ethno-nationalist discourse has become an effective medium through which patriarchal interests are promoted (Jayawardena and de Alwis 1996, de Alwis 1999). My discussion has revealed how these patriarchal interests also find their way through network structures in numerous ways. Since these structures are the very basis through which female-heads realize their economic interests, such women are particularly affected.

---

[10] The subtle workings of patriarchal interests in the Sinhala community are well hidden, the lack of transparent mechanisms helps in sustaining a status quo that limits the women in realizing their capabilities.

While most feminists working in development economics discuss the gradual erosion of traditional kin support to female-heads, I have shown that kin and networks continue to support them although increasingly in non-monetary forms. Rather than waning, kin and/or community support has shifted from monetary support to non-monetary activities, with obvious gender implications. Women mainly carry out care-giving tasks, which are both unpaid and unaccounted for in development activities. Earlier chapters analysing this dimension of network support, a support that is important to female-heads for economic and social reasons, also illustrate women's roles in maintaining, reciprocating and sustaining these network structures. Women rarely look at their symbolic value in perpetuating gender roles and relationships, and almost always take as given the necessity of maintaining these structures. Since their very economic survival depends on these networks, the common sense in upholding them is apparent. More importantly from a feminist methodological standpoint, a pushing aside of community structures in economic analysis serves to underscore the gender biases in the discipline.[11] Both Sen and Agarwal, while cognizant of the social parameters that determine particular outcomes for women's entitlements and their capabilities, limit their analysis to male-headed households.[12] The network institutions and their gender composition are not given enough consideration.

Gender outcomes, I have found, are not linked simply to bargaining relations within patriarchal households but also to a gender-biased community that generally espouses patriarchal

---

[11] Even Agarwal (1997) who analyses the importance of the community for intra-household bargaining relations overlooks the gender composition of communities, and indeed what this reveals about the field of economics.

[12] Analysing this bias is important not merely from a feminist perspective. From a policy position, also, its central import should not be missed: if women are at the core of network structures, then shaping and influencing gender aware policies has to be directed at many levels and at many groups. Social capital of networks, therefore, should not be ignored either in formulating or in promoting gender-sensitive policies.

values. Analysing communities in development economics, therefore, is necessary not simply to show the methodological limitations of the mainstream framework but also because a feminist reading could make for better policy prescriptions as well (Chapter Ten).

The neglect of network and community structures within co-operative conflict models arises because of the assumption of a household structure that is headed by a patriarch, where women actively negotiate their interests and agency. While there is great validity in this particular reading, since after all, a fair proportion of households are headed by men,[13] it also implicitly assumes a particular type of household. But households are not everywhere the same, simply because their structure is dependant upon social context and they are a sub-system of wider social relations and realities. Understanding households requires us to study the varied contexts in which households are situated as well as the social relations of individuals within these institutions. There is a need, therefore, to study female-headship by locating these women in their ethnic and class backgrounds, and it is a specific reading of female-headed households that is provided in this study. This analysis calls for considering of the wider social structures in economic readings of female-headed households, since the well-being of these households is over-determined by an interplay of factors that are ignored when an uniform patriarchal household is assumed. Furthermore, the implied economically deterministic readings of households are another limitation, since female-heads' participation in economic activity has not necessarily increased the perception of the 'naturalness' of these women's households and/or their roles as primary income earners. Shaping values that are beneficial for women will require more than their having access to income, economic activity and/or land. While these may be crucial for female-heads' survival and the well-being of their households, their autonomy and emancipation are not guaranteed through improvements in economically determined

---

[13] And indeed this point of view captures dimensions of social reality that are simply left out of orthodox household readings in economics.

fallback positions. To ensure the autonomy of female-heads requires considering the wider social structures which shape the parameters of their agency. The argument for incorporating social structures into the conceptualization of households, therefore, is also about broadening the methodological boundaries of household analysis. Put simply, accommodating the differentiated nature of households requires moving out of the *doxa*[14] of development economics, since it is within this *doxa* that the cooperative conflicts framework is located. To move out of the *doxa* requires borrowing from feminist and social theoretical contributions on economic methodology, and this will be done in the next section.

Understanding Universal Households?

Realist social theory contributes in important ways to understanding the social structures within which humans participate. Critical realism,[15] on which I draw here, shows in particular that event regularities, the backbone of mainstream economic theory, are a special case that occurs when stable structures are isolated under experimental conditions (Lawson

---

[14] *Doxa* is a particular perspective that is generally accepted as a self-evident consensus. This consensus is in many ways arguably a mere principle of construction that we socialize into our *habitus*, which has often been struggled over in the past (Bourdieu 1998: 56–7, 67).

[15] Realist social theory is acknowledged for its relevance in the social sciences (Bourdieu 1998, 1999, 2000), but is rarely is used in economics (Lawson 1997, 1999). Through the use of theoretical contributions, I have illustrated the interdependence of social structures and social relations in my work on female-headship. Unfortunately, most economic methodology ignores social relations and structures in its analysis of the social world. Lawson's use of realism, particularly critical realism, serves as an example of the relevance of this methodology to economics (Lawson 1997). His use of realism finds inspiration specifically from critical realism (à la Bhaskar). I find areas of overlap between Bourdieu and Lawson useful to feminist economic methodology, and my feminist economic project utilizes theoretical contributions from these scholars I find useful for this study.

1997).¹⁶ Social structures cannot be isolated in the real world. Narratives of female-headed households accentuate again and again the inter-connections of social structures, which reveal that they cannot be isolated in the social world. Moreover, the case studies of female-heads' interactions with these social structures show that the latter are constantly being shaped and reshaped.

Chapter Seven illustrates many instances where female-heads make difficult decisions about their children's future. Social theorists argue that this happens because of the social realm's "dependency upon human intentional agency" (ibid: 157, Bourdieu 1998: 25). Here, social structures depend on human agency, and are intrinsically dynamic and internally related to each other. Two aspects are said to be internally related when they are what they are and can do what they do in virtue of the relation in which they stand to one another. For example, internally related social positions produce the relationship networks that we enter in our daily lives. Illustrations from my study on female-headship provide many instances of internally related social positions and interactions, including those of mothers and daughters, sisters and sisters-in-law, mothers and children, women and maternal uncles, women and their in-laws, and so on. The emphasis on social position rather than on people is an essential feature of this particular perspective. Focusing on social position also opens up the possibility of each individual occupying a multitude of positions simultaneously. According to this conception, then, social reality

---

¹⁶ While I am in sympathy with Lawson (1997, 1999) in this particular reading of economics, I am not in total agreement with his rationale for economics' proclivity to formalistic modelling. Yes, mainstream economic theory does rely upon formalistic models, but why it does is left out of his discussion on the relationship between feminism and realism (Lawson 1999). Here I am more in agreement with feminists who perceive that this practice is linked to gender values embedded in scientific thought, that economists constantly attempt to emulate (Ferber and Nelson 1993: 10, Harding 1995). However, there are many insights that Lawson offers feminists, which I employ, but when in disagreement with him I point this out accordingly.

is a network of positioned practices, where social structures are not reducible to people but consist of relations, rules and positions which are dynamically linked and facilitate the possibility of complexly structured human practices (Lawson 1997: 159).

Indeed, the position of female-heads in eastern Sri Lanka was shown to be linked to rules and relations emerging from ethnic, religious, class, and gender structures that interact with each other in dynamically multifaceted ways. Such a conception of social reality helps highlight the fact that neither these structures nor the positions of female-heads are static or unchanging, but are constantly being reconstituted in the very interactions they facilitate. However, routine and regular behaviour patterns do follow from the generalized procedures of actions, which are an outcome of the relational practices and positions of people (ibid: 160–3). But disparities across individuals regarding these practices are obvious and likely, since social positions themselves usually imply hierarchy and segmentation. It is also the case that such differentiated ascription of rule-governed practices is inter-connected to class, gender, ethnic and other such relations: social positions exist only in relation to these institutional modes.[17] Female-heads, therefore, occupy a particular position, one which, though in most instances they are thrust into, is shaped and constituted by their relations with other social positions as well as by other relations and structures. The analysis of these facets of social reality is important for understanding household structures. It paves the way for considering households as open, dynamic, and heterogeneous entities that are related to other social institutions, and at the same time may be constituted by each other.

---

[17] Lawson's reading of social positions asserts that agents are slotted into these numerous positions (1997: 165). I complicate this particular reading by claiming that agents do not simply slot themselves into positions but actively exercise their agency in choosing particular social positions, although shaped by social structures and relations, over others. Since their individual agency may be limited by social conditions, the need for social action is thus incorporated into this perspective.

We traced above the ability of people to exercise their agency and how it is interconnected with social position, relations and structures. Like social positions and relations, social structures too are constituted and connected to each other. My study of the experiences of female-heads showed the interconnections between ethnicity, the economy, religion, culture, and gender identities and how these are linked to each other in a myriad, layered ways. And this, of course, includes the household and network structures too. The household always exists as a subsystem, a structured process of interaction, which is internally related to other sub-systems: the local and wider culture, religion, the education system, the economic system, the market, the State, etc. Consequently, variations in household structures are inevitable, and certainly systematic differences between social groups, that is, Muslims, Sinhalese, and Tamils, reveal patterns and tendencies towards one particular formation of the household rather than another. This reading of structures allows leeway for identifying the particularities of the ways in which structures operate in different contexts. Put differently, from this perspective it would indeed be surprising if culture, education, the market, and other structures were everywhere the same. Similarly, households, too, are unlikely to be the same everywhere. Conventional (read, patriarchal) households, female-headed households, nuclear households, extended households, and so on, are all likely to exist and co-exist, with some household formations more likely to have a greater presence in certain contexts than others. In this perspective, female-headship need not be perceived as an aberration, but rather one way of forming kin relationships among many possibilities, one which, needless to say, is context-dependent.

Shifting Theories: Partial Perspectives on the Household

To consider female-headed households as an alternative form of kin relationship, of course, implies that economic theory needs to shift its focus from bounded readings of the household. And development policies, in particular, should recognize that even the more progressive readings of household structures and relations, e.g. Sen and Agarwal, provide only partial perspectives on the social reality of these structures. Similarly, community and kin structures are shaped by individual interactions with other institutions: Muslim female-heads noted more support from older children and kin, which is an expression of their links to ethnic, religious, and kin formations. Sinhala female-heads, on the other hand, noted their dependence upon community members since there is less emphasis placed on kin structures to support vulnerable households. Likewise, most households in all ethnic groups noted a shifting from monetary to non-monetary support from community and kin as a consequence of altering material realities and the ethnic conflict in these communities. Such cases illustrate the inter-connections between different structures, and how both household and network structures exists as subsystems related to other structures. In addition, variations in community and/or kin support in each ethnic group also typify the specificity of structures in different situations. For instance, even within a similar economic environment, community and kin agents organize and reorganize themselves very differently because of their inter-relationships with other structures, such as ethnic, class and/or gender identities.

Additionally, there are two related points relevant to households and networks that warrant deliberation in this study of structures. Firstly, human intentional agency presupposes the existence of social structures, so that the latter cannot simply be viewed as a creation of individuals. Secondly, since social structures depend upon humans, and there is wilful intention on the part of all individuals to exercise their agency, these structures cannot be regarded as static (ibid: 167). So the emphasis is on reproduction and transformation rather than on creation or determination: by drawing upon social structure as a condition of acting, and through the sum total of their actions, social structures are either reproduced or transformed (ibid: 168–9). Household structures and networks here maintain the social order as well as reproduce and/or transform the structure of social space and social relations (Bourdieu 1998: 69). Household structures, then, whether patriarchal, female-headed, or of any other formation, essentially serve very similar functions in the social system.

But the ability of agents within these household structures to realize their social and economic capabilities will depend very much upon the interconnections with other social structures. The analysis of structure and agency, then, allows us to note their distinct yet interdependent nature so that space for conflict of interests between agents—whether based on class, age, gender, or ethnicity—as well as for collective action, is made possible. So individual female-heads may have conflicting interests in relation to their mothers, older female kin, and/or sisters that will bear upon the ways in which their households are created and recreated. Yet, at the same time female-headed households as a group may have similar interests that need championing so that they are able to realize their capabilities through cooperative efforts, which in turn of course may lead to changing perceptions and/or formations of households. Equally, individuals, mostly women, configure networks by exercising their agency; and yet the ability of women/(agents) to transform network structures is shaped by the prevalent social order. This dual feature of social structure, where it is both a condition and consequence of action, is termed the *duality of structure*, while the dual feature of action, where motivated and unmotivated reproduction takes place, is called the *duality of praxis*. Interpreting action and structure as a duality allows structure and its action to be viewed from two distinct perspectives. Firstly, it ensures that neither is reduced to the other. Secondly, it makes certain that as social scientists we do not ignore the fact that structure and human action presuppose each other (Lawson 1997: 169–70). Certainly, much of this study has accentuated the multitude of ways in which such a perspective is relevant for understanding the economic well-being of female-headed households. Female-heads, in most cases, try to achieve economic self-reliance but this is critically contingent upon their interaction, as agents, with other social structures and relations. Obviously, this standpoint also sees the social sciences, and specifically economics, as intrinsically dynamic areas of study, with human action leading to social reproduction and transformation (ibid: 170).[18] While some structures may be more enduring than others, there is nothing normal or natural about either endurability or change. Equally, this continued existence of structures does not imply stagnation, since in this study the existence of matrilineal kinship and inheritance systems for Muslims and Tamils shows how they have taken very new shapes and forms at this particular political-historical juncture.[19] Social structures are, therefore, fluid and dynamic entities, and household and network structures are no exception. This contributes to an understanding of the household and networks in a particular and changing context, and thus to the recognition of the opportunities its participants have in transforming relations.

Moving Forward: Feminism and Social Reality

What exactly is the part played by feminist theory in understanding social reality and theory? How does Lawson's (1999) focus on ontology help feminists to look at the interaction between realist theory and feminism? While I think the focus on social structures provides an important entry point for

---

[18] While social transformation is likely here, there is little clarification of whether such change will be rapid and/or inevitable. My view is that, though social change is constantly taking place, it is not inevitable that such change will be for the benefit of marginalized social groups, here female-heads. And so I find a role for policies that will promote and secure the interests of such groups. But I should quickly add that this is not the same as saying that female-heads' interests are everywhere the same, since clearly this methodological analysis also calls for the particularities that are determined by specific backgrounds.

[19] The point I am making here has similarities to that raised by Bourdieu. "The deepest logic of the social world can be grasped only if one plunges into the particularity of an empirical reality, historically located and dated, but with the objective of constructing it as..an exemplary case in a finite world of possible configurations" (1998: 2).

feminists, especially to avoid sliding into cultural relativism, I do not start from the same place as Lawson. Rather than looking at the use of formal modelling in economics as a good place to start a study for a feminist standpoint, I believe the feminist' focus should remain on the deeply embedded gender biases in economic thought (England 1993, Ferber and Nelson 1993, Folbre 1993). But this focus need not mean ignoring ontological issues, which can help us recognize how a multiplicity of actualities can remain consistent with a degree of uniformity at the level of underlying structures (Lawson 1999: 49). The encapsulation of social reality and space at the level of structures should, therefore, provide feminists with a voice of difference as well as some commonality of structures. I begin with a sketch of the main points of interaction between realism and feminist theory, and subsequently move to arguing that this methodological analysis allows for a general understanding of households that are nevertheless diverse, context-specific and dynamic.

The attempt to incorporate feminist concerns into the social sciences can be traced back to the 1960–70's feminist movement, where a need to recognize women's role was argued for by many feminists. Early contributions by feminists in economics focused on women's differential access to the labour market, on informal sector activities, and on 'unproductive' work in the household (Humphries 1977, Hartmann 1981, Ferguson and Folbre 1981). While such feminist contributions brought into focus women's secondary status as workers in the economy, there was very little challenge to the discourse of economics itself. In other words, the patriarchal, androcentric and/or ethnocentric ideologies informing the economics paradigm were not touched by this first wave of critiques by feminist economists.

The next stage of feminist economics has concerned itself with the patriarchal biases in orthodox economics, whether it is Marxist or neo-classical (England 1993, Folbre 1993). An underlying purpose of this feminist critique has been to bring out the social and historical context of economic knowledge-construction, so that male biases in selecting, making operational and interpreting research programmes are unravelled. These phases together lead us to ask how the ideologies of gender, knowledge and economics are mutually constructed at a particular social and historical juncture. Knowledge, here, is partial, transient, and fallible, and is imbued with social and cultural interests and biases. Objectivity, from this perspective, then, is socially constructed, and like all social constructs is also instilled with dimensions of power.[20] Feminist calls from other social science disciplines for the construction of alternative forms of perceiving reality and objectivity have also increasingly influenced the economics discipline (Harding 1986, 1995, Hartsock 1987, Smith 1987, Longino 1990, Haraway 1991). These methodological readings are important for my study as well, since they facilitate my reading of the gender and co-operative models as partial and limited.[21]

An epistemology of standpoint is about recognizing that material reality structures and limits the understanding of social relations. The access that groups and/or classes have to material resources determines the vision, and hence if the structure of material life is fundamentally different for diverse groups then each group's version of reality will be deeply different.[22] So knowledge systems are limited and constructed by a division of labour, shaped by class, gender, race, and ethnic dimensions

---

[20] This particular conceptualization of knowledge is similar to that championed by Lawson (1997, 1999). But from a feminist perspective it differs in one important respect: Lawson is curiously silent about the power dimensions embedded in knowledge structures. Having made this observation, however, it should be noted that Lawson's structured ontology easily allows for issues of power to be incorporated.

[21] No doubt, similarly, my study too is partial and limited to this particular historical, political and social juncture in eastern Sri Lanka.

[22] While versions of 'reality' may be different for different social groups, this still does not mean that social structures do not exist. And it is precisely the very existence of social structures that makes our experience of reality so diverse. So here I am more in agreement with Lawson that ontology does matter, and from my perspective it matters primarily for political reasons.

(Hartsock 1987: 159–64). Political struggles against exploitative social and economic relations help reveal the patriarchal and sexist attitudes that shape social, economic, and political ideologies (Harding 1986: 156). Such struggles prove that the resilience and strength of ideology and knowledge systems reveal the extent to which material life shapes and defines knowledge production. Women's lives are for the most part "institutionally defined by their production of use values in the home". Their distinct experiences, therefore, result in a different set of relational issues (Hartsock 1987: 164–8). A woman's construction of the self and her experiences lead to the valuation of the concrete, a sense of continuity, connection, and structuring of consciousness through material life very different from men's experiences (ibid: 170). A feminist perspective provides a counter-balance to male perspectives on epistemology and social theory. Possibilities for challenging the androcentric nature of knowledge are, then, brought to the forefront by focusing on power relations between men and women in the material world. Material structures limit human understanding, and this gives excluded social groups the potential to reveal the realities of social relations and experiences not available to the dominant classes. Social situations of 'objective' knowledge claims necessitate conceding that certain values and interests are imparted through the production of knowledge (Harding 1986: 185). And this enables a search for 'strong objectivity', where the continuous social, political, feminist, class, and ethnic struggles of diverse social groups reveal the partial and limited nature of knowledge claims.

Does this description of a feminist standpoint preclude a concern for a structured ontology? Moreover, is it possible to appraise ontological concerns as an extension of feminist epistemological issues? For feminist economists interested in grappling with reality and making sense of it in development economics, what potential does Lawson's analysis offer? For me, like Harding (1999), epistemological and ontological arguments are closely intertwined (1999: 132). Unlike Harding, however, I do not deem sticking to naïve realism to be a good epistemic strategy. The recognition that reality is structured, transient, relational and dynamic is a good starting point for feminists, and in my view is not widely different from feminist calls for recognizing the structured basis of material conditions. Since material conditions are structured, a feminist standpoint that begins its analysis from this implicitly acknowledges the existence of an ontological basis, i.e. that the layered aspects to structure lead to diverse material realities. The question then, is, how does one link ontological issues to a feminist standpoint primarily concerned with epistemology?

Our social space is structured and not reducible to events, and still it exists independently of being identified as this or that. The acknowledgement that experimental results are made intelligible only by evoking an ontology of structures that govern a flux of events in an effectively open world is crucial to this analysis (Lawson 1999: 31). Reality then is open and structured. Furthermore, as discussed above, reality is also internally connected and intrinsically dynamic. The suggestion here is that of "formulating interesting contrastive explanations at the level of actual phenomena" (ibid: 38). Here, differences that are systematically at odds with conventional expectations are recognized as such, so that observed relationships between features of different groups other than those expected are a real possibility. An emphasis on contrastive explanations is relevant to situated knowledge. "Outsiders" in social sciences reflect upon themes that are shaped by their perspectives, understandings and political-social histories: i.e. the 'situations' of social investigators' matter. While there is a multiplicity of causes, the interests of researchers shape the way we pay attention to some issues rather than others, thus reflecting our own social and/or political positions. Here, marginal social groups are better able to appreciate the effect of dominant structures, processes and/or inequities because they understand divergent situations from their insider-outsider perspective (ibid: 40).

Factoring Social Reality into Development Studies

Development studies are concerned at one level about giving voice to marginal social groups. Listening to socially excluded communities and groups allows us to identify the causes responsible for different outcomes, which may run counter to conventional wisdom. A focus on contrastive explanations can helps development economics and studies to explain phenomena better, and facilitate the democratic participation of diverse social groups. My study demonstrates many instances of such contrasts, where I have provided explanations for these new situations. In this study I have established that the prevalence of female-headship is not only linked to the ethnic conflict in the region, but is also rising on account of non-conflict-related factors such as desertion, separation, alcoholism, etc. (Chapters Four, Five and Six; see also Ruwanpura 2003, Ruwanpura and Humphries 2004).[23] This observation goes against the conventional wisdom in Sri Lanka that sees female-headship in the Eastern Provinces as a product merely of the ethnic conflict. It is undoubtedly my training as a feminist and economist that prompted me to look at other factors that may lead to female-headship, especially since most studies on female-headship in eastern Sri Lanka have focused solely on war widows (Rajasingham-Senanayake 1999, Thiruchandran 1999). My assertion here has been that, though war widowhood is an important factor pushing women into assuming headship, there are other underlying mechanisms that also lead to female-headship. Similarly, listening to female-heads describe their decisions about their children's education and welfare made me realize the need to complicate the simple feminist story

---

[23] The prevalence of uncertainty and volatility in the region could be a triggering factor in certain cases of female-headship, for example where women are abandoned. It is difficult to disentangle the dynamics of such factors, but the important point I make is that female-headship is not simply linked to war widowhood. Moreover, Sri Lankan studies for "non-conflict" areas reviewed in Chapter Three showed the prevalence of female-headship as precipitated by a variety of factors, and a partial purpose of this study is to highlight this possibility for eastern Sri Lanka too.

about girls as victims of patriarchy. In some circumstances, boys are more likely to be withdrawn from school and sacrificed to the family's need for income.

These examples capture the complexity of social reality. From a feminist perspective, we discover that household structures and their decision-making processes are increasingly complex. This is an issue that development policy, infused by mainstream economic theory, refuses to face. My study also supports feminist assertions on the situated nature of knowing, where reflecting on the multiple causation of phenomena reinforces this particular connection between realism and feminist standpoint theory.

In what other ways do contrastive explanations aid feminist standpoint theory make situated knowledge vital to the explanatory process? People excluded from the orthodox discourse may thereby be enabled to identify relevant discrepancies from the norm, and consider such findings interesting, and pursue them accordingly. Marginal voices occupy both outsider and insider positions, facilitating awareness of significant contrasts. As persons from the community they are conscious of the traditions, values, and practices of the dominant group, but still they live within their own specific structures. This allows marginal groups to become aware of contrasts between inner and outer structures, and the bearing of these structures on people's lives, their inter-links, and the functioning of the social whole (Lawson 1999: 41–2). Contrastive explanations that outside perspectives bring into the discourse, therefore, are likely to be significant in particular contexts, and, equally importantly, this reading allows the input of a diverse community of economists, which is both democratic and good methodological practice (ibid: 41). For feminists, it is important to admit a diverse group of voices into the discourse. The notion of *contrastive explanations* ensures that we need not assume that "marginal voices provide truer accounts". It also avoids the result necessarily being "(a) a plethora of contradictory voices (b) possibly backed up by a judgmental relativism (i.e. a relativism in which any discrimination amongst contending claims is impossible or arbitrary)" (ibid: 42). Thus, the advantage of being situated differently to the majority is in revealing different contrasts and pursuing alternative lines of inquiry.

In this study, uncovering the limits of the cooperative conflict model in understanding female-headship can be read as an illustration of a similar exercise, where studying alternative household formations and relations exposes contrastive explanations which are central to feminists' engagement in household bargaining relations (Chapters Seven and Eight). Reflecting upon the different dimensions of household formation and relations within the household reveals a variety of causes, and these varying perspectives need not necessarily be incompatible and/or contradictory. Certainly, the previous sections outlining the cooperative conflict model and its application to female-headship can be read in this way, with points of relevance to agreement with the particularities of female-headship being noted. However, my analysis went further in noting the limitations of the cooperative conflict models in its relevance to theorizing female-headship, and did so in the spirit of drawing upon comparative issues that feminist economists should bear in mind when discussing household formations and bargaining relations.

Conclusion: Making Decisions on "Social Reality"

The question that emerges is of how one decides between competing claims on social reality. The response is simply its greater explanatory power in appraising social reality, where a wide range of empirical phenomena are explained, which largely depends upon the context of the conditions upon which they bear (Lawson 1997: 213–5). In the specific instance of elucidating household formations and relations, cooperative conflict models have much ability in explaining social reality. But because such models implicitly assume a homogenous, unitary and static household unit, their explanatory power is inadequate when theorizing female-headship. Hence, a tracing of the social structures, social positions and agency of female-headship better encapsulates their realities than do cooperative conflict models. This particular account has more explanatory power, which is not the same thing as saying that cooperative conflict models are inaccurate, but rather to contend that they only provide a partial perspective. Therefore, extending the analysis in different directions as well as focusing on diverse aspects can only help explain the diversity of social reality in household formations and relations, which is a key point in the agenda of feminist economists.

Returning to the main thrust of a feminist realist perspective, then, it is essential to recognize that a diversity of outcomes remains consistent with a degree of uniformity at the level of underlying structures. This is the importance of ontology for a feminist economic methodology. Thus, while social structures depend upon the intentions and agency of humans, they are also rooted in distinctive historical, political and cultural junctures. Household formations and relations are simply not the same everywhere, and contending claims on the theorizing of household bargaining relations provide a partial perspective on these manifest differences. Consequently, cooperative conflict models reflect particular dimensions of social reality. But by not giving explicit consideration to ontological issues, their applications are limited in explaining alternative household formations. From a feminist economics perspective, then, paying attention to ontology helps describe the social realities of female-headship, while still recognizing that diversity within these household structures is also very real. Certainly, paying particular attention to distinct ethnic groups of female-heads in Sri Lanka is an attempt to illustrate differences that get played out according to social, cultural, political, and economic spaces. Yet regardless of this diversity there is a sameness of structured ontology, where social structures, positions, and spaces are structured similarly. By recognizing this particular emphasis, it is feasible to examine these themes of kin relationships and motherhood that female-heads stressed. Such a methodological perspective allows feminist economists the possibility of recognizing diversity and yet at the same time of advocating gender-sensitive development policies.

TEN

Conclusion

Interested Engagement—Feminist Issues in Development Economics

Introduction

Feminist economists frequently call for a broadening of economics (Ferber and Nelson 1993, MacDonald 1995, Pujol 1997). The task is to identify the cultural values embedded in economics and to acknowledge the social situation of knowledge production (Harding 1995). Feminist economists' calls are receiving an airing even among orthodox economists (Solow 1993). But work by feminists on the differential impact of economic issues on women's lives is not new (Boserup 1970). Feminists were engaged in uncovering the limitations of orthodox economic analysis three decades ago (Humphries 1977, Ferguson and Folbre 1981, Hartmann 1981). Making economics "more objective" requires capturing the complexity and nuances of social reality (Harding 1995).

My project contributes to the feminist economic literature by theorizing the complexity of alternative household structures and by calling for consciously feminist development policies. The relevance of the latter is particularly apparent in Sri Lanka, which has been considered an archetype of sound social and human development, egalitarian gender-based HDI achievements and of the favourable positioning of women (Sen 1981, 1984a, 1988, Agarwal 1990, 1996).

The arguments I have developed through this project have sought to establish the diverse dynamics that lead to female-headship in eastern Sri Lanka. The sources leading to female-headship reflect the different social, economic and political realities of the region. Tracing the origins of female-headed households across ethnicity is important for two reasons. First, it has implications for feminist methodological readings of the household. Second, this helps determine the shape and type of development and social policies most appropriate to the group. The point I make is that there is a real need for targeted social and development policies for female-heads in eastern Sri Lanka. The reality is that even where female-heads belong to matrilineal communities they still have to negotiate patriarchal institutions and realities. Here, I summarize the implications of my findings on female-headship in eastern Sri Lanka. I focus on a) for theorizing feminist-conscious household structures and b) for gender-sensitive development policy-making on female-headship.

Social Diversity, Varied Realities and Household Structures

The orthodox economic concept of the household is that of an undifferentiated and isolated unit. In this particular formulation there is no interest in looking at the inter-connections between different social structures, with the methodological individualistic underpinnings of the economic discourse limiting a social analysis of the household that reflects reality (Folbre 1986a, 1986b, Humphries 1998b).

Others have proposed better and more realistic frameworks (Sen 1990, Agarwal 1997). Indeed, they have introduced various complexities missing from the mainstream approach. In particular, while the mainstream method treats the household as a single unit, Sen (1990) and Agarwal (1997) recognize the patriarchal nature of the household and focus on the gender divisions and negotiation patterns within the household. In Chapter Nine I discussed in detail the drawbacks to this particular systematization of household structure and relations and its inability to deal with the multiplicity of factors affecting households. Therefore, utilizing a feminist and realist methodology I reasoned the need to move beyond surface phenomena in evaluating social issues, in order to uncover deeper structures embedded in social reality.

My study shows that it is necessary to acknowledge the social diversity and varied realities of female-heads across ethnic groups. Yet the underlying and enduring aspects of the patriarchal social structures that female-heads experience should not be ignored. The key is to reveal the workings of household structure that are embedded in a structured ontology capable of encompassing multiple levels of reality. While Muslim, Sinhalese and Tamil female-heads' experiences are unique, their identities and interests are shaped within patriarchal and social structures that have a degree of space-time durability. The important aspect to this feminist interpretation is to acknowledge the multiple aspects of patriarchal structures and relations, which themselves are structured by the inter-dynamics of ethnic, class, religious, political, historical and social factors.

Therefore, by using the work of feminist standpoint theorists and realists, I advanced the idea that the household is a structured process of interaction. It is a system embedded in and internally related to the sum total of all other social structures. Therefore, its precise form and nature in a given context depends on a web of ethnic, religious, social and gender relations. I suggest that this reading allows us to view household structures as context dependent and multi-faceted social systems, which gives my observations a coherent theoretical base for explaining the variety of social experiences that female-heads face within an underlying patriarchal structure. Patriarchy, therefore, is not everywhere one and the same, though this does not negate the enduring aspects of patriarchal structures. Consequently, the welfare of female-heads and of individual household members depends on the prevailing relations in the community, which is itself imbued with relations of hierarchy, production, co-operation and conflict—and, therefore, is subject to continuous transformation.

Theorizing households in this particularly specific manner feeds into the need for engendering development planning for female-heads. In the following two sections I develop this aspect of my project in greater detail, with the concluding section arguing the need for gender-sensitive policies capable of tackling the varied aspects of female-heads' lives.

Gendering Development Planning

With female-headship occurring for different reasons in eastern Sri Lanka, there is an obvious need to advocate policies that meet these women's practical and strategic needs (Moser 1989). Because of the continued neglect of gender-sensitive policy planning, feminists continue to reiterate this need for gender-sensitive policies (Moser 1989, Pearson and Jackson 1998, Kabeer 1999). The key feminist issues relevant to gendering the planning discourse are spelled out in the works of Moser (1989) and Kabeer (1999). A partial aim of my project has been to incorporate these factors into the realization of women's capabilities within a particular type of household structure— households headed by women. I shall, therefore, begin with a short summary of the key features applicable to the gendering of the development discourse, promoted by feminists working in the development sphere.[1]

Moser (1989) makes an important distinction between the practical and strategic needs of women, which she bases on the triple roles of women (1989: 1801). Women in most low-income households are involved in reproductive, productive, and community management work, which they frequently cope with as routine. Managing these three inter-related tasks entails various responsibilities, which are usually not recognized by policy-makers (ibid: 1801). There were numerous examples in my study where female-heads were involved in these three activities simultaneously. The best illustration is when a young female-head looks after her young children as well as those of

---

[1] My purpose in highlighting the main points is to draw out their relevance for my project, which I do through appropriate illustrations.

another woman/female-head and at the same time is also involved in an income-generating activity. In such a scenario these different layers of her multiple roles can easily be deciphered to substantiate the point made by Moser. By caring for her own children, the female-head is carrying out her reproductive role, and by extending her childcare time to include the children of another community/kin member she is engaged in a community management task. She is also occupied in her productive role by earning an income through a home-based economic activity. Moreover, in Chapter Eight I showed other instances in which female-heads were constantly engaged in maintaining and renewing network contacts, as a crucial aspect of their households' well-being.

By distinguishing the multiple positions women occupy into three particular roles, Moser is able to identify the needs and interests of women in the practical and strategic spheres (ibid: 1802). This is an important exercise, since she simplifies the complexities of social reality into easy-to-relate procedural tools necessary for gendering development planning.[2] When the prioritized interests and concerns of women are translated into planning terms, these are noted as practical and strategic gender needs capable of accomplishing the desired goals of the development planning process (ibid: 1802–3). Practical gender needs are formulated to meet the immediate wants of women within a particular context, and these may range from income-earning activities to housing and basic services (ibid: 1803–4). My investigation has pointed to several options available to female-heads in securing their practical needs, and this even though most female-heads were primarily engaged in self-employment activities.[3] Transforming existing gender inequities

---

[2] Bringing down abstract methodological standpoints to concrete realities is important, because it helps link theory with practice—which should be an ultimate purpose of all social science analysis.

[3] NGOs in the eastern region played an active role in targeting the practical gender needs of female-heads. As pointed in the introductory chapter, space constraints did not permit my analysis to examine the role of NGOs in maintaining, reinforcing and/or subverting existing gender roles.

requires the incorporation of the strategic gender needs of women. These are needs that are devised "from the analysis of women's subordination to men", and depend on the particular social, cultural, and political situation. These needs are "identified as 'feminist' as there is a level of consciousness required to struggle effectively for them" (ibid: 1803). Meeting the strategic needs of women is, not surprisingly, difficult, since it requires a feminist awareness-building. The "moments" of consciousness, noted especially by Tamil female-heads, on their rights, roles and relationships are one illustration of women being aware of their strategic needs (Chapter Eight). Such occurrences were, however, few and far between.

The analysis provided by Moser is important because it lays the basis for understanding the conditions and consequences of seeking to empower women at multiple levels (Kabeer 1999). I have shown throughout this research that patriarchal realities operate at a multitude of levels, with female-heads having to confront patriarchal ideologies, institutions and structures. At a very basic level, seeking to empower women will require development planners to move from realizing practical gender needs to strategic gender needs. For women, the latter entail the ability to make choices and realize their capabilities, which will need a widening of the resource base, providing the ground for exercising their agency and for obtaining the necessary outcomes (ibid: 2–3). Issues of power and identity are invariably linked to this conceptualization of gender realities, with no linear model of change being applicable to tackle feminist-consciousness raising and for moving towards egalitarian gender relations through development (ibid: 47). Conditions of social upheaval may provide fertile ground for social movements and development agencies to take a dynamic role in achieving these feminist goals (ibid: 48). In the following section, I discuss some of the missed opportunities I have found in this study when dealing with female-headed households in eastern Sri Lanka. I also discuss the need to integrate these issues from a development, gender and feminist perspective.

Infusing Feminist Consciousness into Gender Development Discourse

The diversity of household structures was outlined in the previous chapters. The central importance of recognizing the variety of household formation is to help us understand the survival strategies adopted by low-income social groups (Moser 1989: 1801). Female-headed households are no exception to the rule. They too adopt multiple sources of income-generation, reflecting the range of their needs and interests. In my data chapters, a critical issue is the need to distinguish between the ability of female-heads to separate their practical needs from their strategic needs. This differentiation is important since female-heads' ability to achieve the former indicates the strength of the patriarchal structures that thwart any real transformation in gender relations. This hampers the realizing of the gender strategic needs of female-heads.

The occupational choices of female-heads exemplify the schism between practical and strategic gender needs that re-occurs across ethnic groups and age composition. Younger female-heads have very different needs from older female-heads. Women in the former social group have younger children and a higher dependency ratio, thus needing to balance their time between childcare and income-generating activities. Older female-heads, on the other hand, are able to rely on their older children to take an active role in securing income for the household. In both scenarios, however, female-heads opted for home-based work, being motivated by their age, social roles and/or cultural norms.

While home-based/self-employment schemes allow female-heads to earn an income by remaining in their homes, the flip side of such trends is the possible insecurity of home-based workers (Chen, Sebstad and O'Connell 1999, Ruwanpura 2004b, Carr, Chen and Tate 2000). Moreover, where female-heads abide by cultural norms the need to maintain "respectability" as well as earn an income may imply greater economic insecurity. Overcoming economic vulnerability in such circumstance will, therefore, require policy-makers to recognize the difference between meeting the immediate survival needs of female-heads and enhancing their capability base. The latter will require creating appropriate institutional conditions for economic security, ones where meeting gender strategic needs is an option for female-heads.

Female-heads choose particular occupations not simply because of cultural restrictions but also because of their low human capital skills. Making connections between restrictive cultural practices and the low human capital of women, and the consequences for women's capabilities, is an argument made before and will not be repeated here (Klasen 1993, Kabeer 1994). Suffice to note, that in addition to cultural limits on their mobility, female-heads often have low educational skills that compound difficulties in finding suitable employment. Female-heads willingly acknowledge the constraints that low educational achievements place on their well-being levels, and the negative consequences of this handicap for their household's economic security. Awareness, however, also implies the possibility of positive change, with more female-heads stressing the importance of educating their daughters. Translating this awareness into practice, which has the potential to achieve gender-strategic needs, will require concerted efforts by State agencies to implement gender-conscious education and training programmes. Without the appropriate interventions, this awareness of female-heads may otherwise become another missed opportunity.

This focus on girl's education brings us to another outcome for female-headed households, the role and well-being of the children. Without the necessary support structures, younger female-heads will be more susceptible to poverty, with their children likely to face poor nutrition and limited access to education. Similarly, children of older female-heads may have their education abruptly disrupted to support their mothers and households. Both groups of children are prone to deterioration in their human capital formation. Furthermore, female-heads living below the poverty line, irrespective of age group, will also project poverty inter-generationally through the low human capital of their children. This is commonly perpetuated in such low-income households, where the educational and nutritional patterns of the children are likely to have had a negative impact during their formative years. The particular concern for gender-sensitive policy planning is the burden borne by all children, irrespective of their gender, as well as the long-term consequences that girls and boys will face in their later years. Focusing on children as a social group may be an effective way of meeting the short-term practical gender needs of girls, demarcating the strategic gender needs of girls as young women as a separate feminist goal.

Finally, another issue worthy of consideration is the formation, shape, and composition of networks. Economic support from kin wanes with economic pressure (Youssef and Hetler 1984). But I have demonstrated how the sources of support have shifted from the economic to the non-economic, with a movement from support from men to support from women. In eastern Sri Lanka, it is not simply socio-economics that has led to changes in network support but also the dislocation and displacement faced by some female-heads. The interesting lesson here is that women come to each other's assistance in meeting their practical gender needs. Additionally, in rare instances some women show a feminist consciousness that can be used to meet their strategic gender needs. The impetus for change here comes from within rather than from outside, but to sustain this awareness will require changes in institutional structures too. So this is an area that social movements, development agencies and legal institutions can improve through gender planning.

Conclusion: Interested Engagement—Feminist Issues in Development Discourse

Feminists in the field of development economics have been implicitly concerned with methodological issues when promoting a feminist standpoint that focuses on social structures.

Kabeer (1994, 1995, 1996, 1999) illuminates the best of such work. She calls for making sense of social reality when advocating women's interests, by considering these in the light of the social structures that hamper the realization of their capabilities. Social structures in much of her work are context-specific: they are rooted in class, ethnic, religious and gender norms. However, underlying social structures do persist and endure, thwarting women's attempts to realize their economic, political, and/or social capabilities. Embedded in this perspective is an ontological preconception that should be clarified and made explicit, which involves locating feminist methodology within the contours of realism. This allows those feminists working in development economics to account for the structure and agency of women's well-being at the same time. Such a reading, therefore, fits neatly with calls for recognizing that structured ontologies with varied outcomes determine each specific location (Bourdieu 1998, Lawson 1999).

Similarly, although my project on female-headship underscores the numerous instances where there is diversity in female-headed households, it has also revealed the enduring nature of patriarchal structures that female-heads in each class and ethnic group have to negotiate in order to sustain the well-being of their households. Undeniably, the previous chapters have also shown the dynamic attributes of social structures: female-heads' experience with patriarchy is not always and everywhere the same. Nevertheless, there is a social space where these structures hinder any real possibilities for empowerment. Such a context, therefore, necessitates developing further a methodology that can incorporate feminist concerns and relate to enduring, yet different and diverse, social space. This translates into concrete development planning as a recognition of the underlying premise of my study: that patriarchal authority reasserts itself in diverse circumstances, with different sources, problems and outcomes for female-headship. This critical analysis, therefore, underscores the need for different policies to grapple with multiple layers of social reality.

APPENDIX A
Map of Sri Lanka

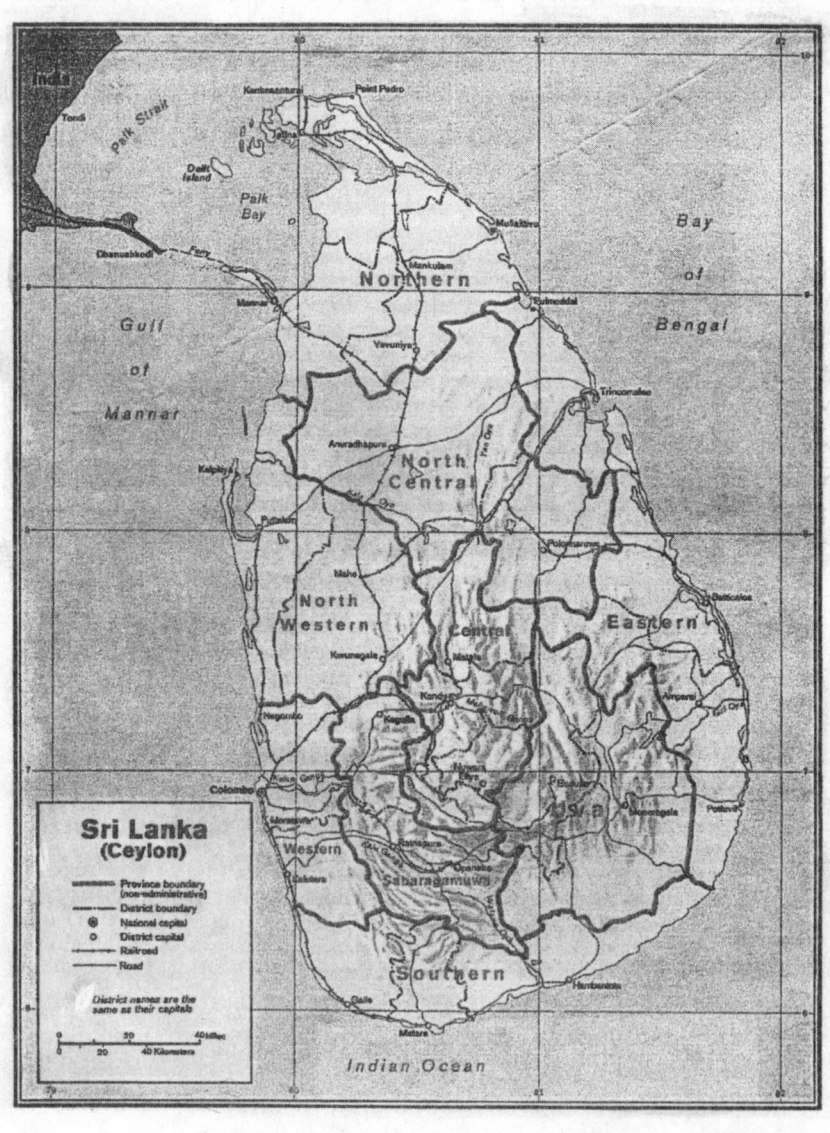

APPENDIX B
Sample Questionnaire for Female-headed Households

A. Demographic Profile

1) i) Name of the person interviewed (optional): _____
   ii) Is the respondent: a) Male   b) Female

2) i) Location: a) Area _____   b) District _____
   ii) Location of household: a) Rural   b) Town   c) Estate

3) i) What is your ethnic group?
   a) Mixed (specify) _____   b) Tamil   c) Muslim
   d) Sinhala   e) Burgher
   ii) What is your religion?
   a) Hindu   b) Islam   c) Buddhist
   d) Catholic   e) Christian (Anglican, Methodist, etc)
   f) Other (i.e. Assembly of God, Born Again Christian, etc.)
   iii) Did you convert recently?   a) Yes   b) No
   iv) Reasons for conversion (CIRCLE all applicable)
   a) Spiritual salvation/reasons
   b) Challenge to established gender and caste hierarchies in form religion
   c) Economic aid and benefits
   d) Other

4) Marital status: a) Married   b) Divorced   c) Deserted
                   d) Separated e) Widow   f) Single
                   g) Other (specify) _____

5) If your husband is dead, the reason for his death:
   a) Natural causes   b) Suicide
   c) Killed (State-sponsored)   d) Killed (para-military)
   e) Killed (non-conflict related) f) Missing
   g) Other (specify) _____

6) i) The household is headed by: a) Male   b) Female
                                    c) Male not present

7) If your husband is present, is he:
   a) Employed (Full-time)   b) Employed (Part-time)
   c) Unemployed   d) Physically disabled
   e) Mentally unfit to work   f) Alcoholic
   g) Terminally/Majorly Ill   h) Other (specify) _____

8) Composition of Household:

Name	Relationship to house-hold head	Sex	Age	Marital Status	Education Level	Occupation

9) Data on children:

Number of children in the household	Sex of your children		
Age group	Male	Female	TOTAL
0-5 years			
6-10 years			
11-18 years			
Over 18 years			
TOTAL			

10) What was your age at marriage? _____ (Appx. at least)

11) What was your age:
   i) at the death, divorce, separation and/or desertion of your husband/partner?_____OR
   ii) when you assumed economic responsibilities because of illness, incapacity, etc. of your husband?_____

B. Economic Profile

1) Who (of members in your household) provides the main source of economic support?
   a) You
   b) Your husband/wife
   c) Another family member (i.e. relative – brother/sister, mother/father, in-laws, etc)
   d) Children

2) What is your occupation?
   a) Wage labourer   b) Service/Clerical/Government worker
   c) Domestic worker   d) Agricultural labourer
   e) Poultry-worker/Goat-rearing/Cattle-herding
   f) Home-gardener (small-scale farming)
   g) Other (specify)

3) i) Does this occupation provide you with your main source of income?
   a) Yes   b) No

4) i) Are you self-employed/engaged in home-based or income-generating activities?
   a) Yes   b) No
   ii) If yes, is it because:
   a) Your education level is low and you are unable to find employment
   b) Insufficient demand for wage labour
   c) Wages are low in the formal sector
   d) Unable to find suitable employment commensurate with your educational qualifications
   e) Self-employment/home-based income activities provide an additional income

5) What are your other sources of income (PRIORITIZE from 1-7)
   a) Wage labourer   b) Service/Clerical/Government worker
   c) Domestic worker   d) Agricultural labourer
   e) Poultry-worker/Goat-rearing/Cattle-herding
   f) Home-gardener (small-scale farming)
   g) Other (specify)

6) Of the people/children in your household, which of them provides economic support towards the household? (CIRCLE all applicable)
   a) Children (M/F)   b) Siblings (M/F)
   c) Friends (M/F)   d) Relatives (M/F)
   e) Parents (M/F)   f) Parents-in-law (M/F)

7) Are your sources of earned income:
   a) Continuous (without disruption)
   b) Regular
   c) Irregular

8) i) What is the total family income (exclude remittances) per month?
      Rs._____
   ii) What is your contribution towards this income (per month)?
      Rs._____
   iii) What is your spouse's (husband or wife) income (per month)?
      Rs._____

9) Is your earned income sufficient towards meeting your (monthly) consumption needs?
   a) Yes   b) No

10) How many rupees per month do you spend on:
   i) Food_____   ii) Kerosene_____
   iii) Clothes_____   iv) Children's needs_____
   v) Electricity_____   vi) Other (specify)_____

11) i) Number of meals consumed per day:
   a) Husband_____   b) Wife_____
   c) Girl-children_____ d) Boy-children_____
   e) Female relatives_____ f) Male relatives_____
   ii) If you (your girl-children or female relatives) do not consume three-meals per day, is it because of (CIRCLE all applicable):
   a) Economic inability   b) Cultural practices   c) Both

12) i) Do you receive an income (i.e. remittances) from outside sources?
   a) Yes   b) No
   ii) If yes, amount of income: Rs._____
   iii) How regular is this income?
   a) Very regular   b) Sporadic
   iv) Is the sources of our income (CIRCLE and SPECIFY Male or Female):
   a) Children (M/F)   b) Siblings (M/F)
   c) Relatives (M/F)   d) Friends (M/F)
   v) What do you spend remitted income on (CIRCLE all applicable)?
   a) Daily needs
   b) Children's needs
   c) For renovation of house, purchase of land, etc.
   d) Marriage purposes (dowry, wedding, ceremonies, etc.)
   e) Other (specify)_____

13) i) Do you have any close relative in a foreign country?
   a) Yes   b) No
   ii) If yes, do they provide regular:
   a) Non-monetary support   b) Monetary support
   c) No support at all

14) In the above case, in your experience who have you found more dependable:
   a) Male relatives   b) Female relatives

15) i) Is the house and/or land-owned by the head of the household?
   a) Yes   b) No
   ii) If no, is the house owned by:
   a) State   b) Rented
   c) Belongs to a relative   d) On Lease
   e) Official residence   f) Other_____

16) i) Does the household head own any other:
   a) Land   b) Property   c) Houses?
   ii) Did you ever own land or property, which you had to forego because it was socially more appropriate that your male relatives (brothers, cousins, in-laws, etc.) claim such property?
   a) Yes   b) No
   iii) Did you forego legal claims to land or property, in the hope that your male relatives would provide economic protection in case of economic hardship or vulnerability?
   a) Yes   b) No
   iv) If yes (and you are a female-head), have these male relatives reciprocated with (consistent) economic support?
   a) Yes   b) No

17) If the household head owns any land, what is the extent of acreage owned?_____acres

18) Livestock (numbers) owned by the household head:
   a) Cows-milking_____   b) Cows-draught_____
   c) Buffaloes_____   d) Goats_____
   e) Poultry_____

19) i) Other assets owned by the household (CIRCLE all applicable):
   a) Jewellry   b) Household furniture
   c) Savings   d) Insurance
   e) Radio and/or televisions   f) Other (specify)_____
   ii) Farm implements owned by the household (specify numbers):
   a) Mammoties_____   b) Tractor (2-wheel)_____
   c) Tractor (4-wheel)_____   d) Bullock Cart_____

20) i) Do you keep relatives or friends to support your household income?
   ii) If yes, are they? (CIRCLE all applicable):
   a) Female relatives   b) Female friends
   c) Male relatives   d) Male friends
   iii) If females do they provide income support to the household?
   a) Yes   b) No
   iv) If females, do they provide non-income (i.e. domestic chores, childcare, etc.) support?
   a) Yes   b) No
   v) If males do they provide income support to the household?
   a) Yes   b) No
   vi) If males, do they provide non-income (i.e. domestic chores, childcare, etc.) support?
   a) Yes   b) No
   vii) Is the monetary support: a) Boarding fees b) Other (specify)_____

C. Socio-economic Profile

1) How many hours of the day are you engaged in your main occupation?
   _____number of hours

2) How many hours of the day are you engaged in work that provides you with a supplementary income?._____number of hours

3) i) Do you work at home?   a) Yes   b) No
   ii) If yes, do any members of the household help in these economic activities?
      a) Yes   b) No
   iii) Are these helpers: a) Male members   b) Female members

4) i) In addition to economic-related activities, do you perform domestic chores?
      a) Yes   b) No
   ii) If yes, how many hours a day do you spend on domestic chores?
      _____hrs
   iii) Do any members of the household help in these economic activities?
      a) Yes   b) No
   iv) Are these helpers:
      a) Males (sons, brothers, etc.)   b) Females (daughters, sisters, etc.)
   v) What form of help do they provide?
      a) Child-care
      b) Cooking/cleaning
      c) Gardening/Sweeping-cleaning the garden

5) i) Do you have leisure time (on a daily basis)?   a) Yes   b) No
   ii) If yes, what do you do for leisure?
      a) Watch television   b) Listen to the radio
      c) Read the newspaper   d) Chat with friends, relatives, neighbours
      e) Other (specify)_____

6) Who makes decisions in the household regarding (CIRCLE and SPECIFY male or female):
   a) Daily activities (M/F)
   b) Children's education (M/F)
   c) Purchase of consumption goods (M/F)
   d) Purchase of furniture/durable goods (M/F)
   e) Purchase of jewellery (M/F)
   f) Investment/savings (M/F)
   g) Monetary transactions (M/F)
   h) Marriage of children (M/F)

7) i) Do your kin/friends extend their support to you?   a) Yes   b) No
   ii) Is it: a) Regular   b) Irregular
   iii) Is this support dependable?   a) Yes   b) No

iv) Is it reciprocated in any way?   a) Yes   b) No
v) What would cause it to stop?
   a) Unconventional behaviour
   b) Family disputes
   c) Economic difficulties faced by kin
   d) You securing employment in the public sphere
   e) Other (Specify)_____
vi) Is this support more likely to come from:
   a) Male kin/relatives   b) Female kin/relatives

8) If you do depend on monetary help, do you feel:
   a) your dignity and self-worth more at risk
   b) relatively constrained in your behavior patterns
   c) concerned about what "they" think of you

9) i) Do your children help you in finding alternative avenues of income?
   a) Yes   b) No
   ii) If yes, are they your:
      a) Male children   OR   b) Female children
   iii) What kind-of income-generating activities are they involved in:
      a) Domestic worker
      b) Selling gram, vegetables, fruit, etc.
      c) Clerical worker
      d) Employed in the city (Colombo, Kandy, Badulla, Galle, etc.)
      e) Labourer

10) What kind-of (non-monetary) support do your:
    i) Male-children provide – e.g. gardening, child-care, etc. (specify)_____
    ii) Female-children provide (specify)_____

11) How important is this support,
    i) to your well-being (specify)_____
    ii) to the well-being of your household (specify)_____

12) Have you gained more respect from family members after starting work?
    a) Yes   b) No
13) Have you saved from your earnings?   a) Yes   b) No
14) Has your involvement in income-generating activities increased your:
    i) Self-confidence   a) Yes   b) No
    ii) Self-esteem   a) Yes   b) No
    iii) Status in the community   a) Yes   b) No

15) Do you feel that female-heads are better accepted by society as workers?
    a) Yes   b) No

16) Have you visited (CIRCLE all applicable):
    a) Colombo   b) Sri-Pada
    c) Kandy   d) Jaffna, Trincomalee, Batticaloa, Amparai

e) Foreign country   f) Other (specify)_____

17) i) Do you consider educating your children important?
   a) Yes   b) No
   ii) If a) are you able to afford it?
   a) Yes   b) No
   iii) If you are not able to afford to educate your children, do you see this as impeding their future economic well-being?
   a) Yes   b) No

18) i) In educating girl-children are you more likely to discontinue her/their education because of (PRIORITIZE):
   a) Economic hardship and pressure_____
   b) Cultural perceptions that perceive the education of girl-children as not critical to their well-being_____
   c) Social pressures (i.e. the need for helping hands in the house, early marriage, etc)____
   ii) Because of economic hardships, are you more likely to discontinue the education of:
   a) Boy-children   b) Girl-children
   iii) If you discontinue the education of boy-children, is it because of: (PRIORITZE)
   a) Economic hardship and pressure_____
   b) Cultural perceptions that perceive the education of boy-children as not critical to their well-being_____
   c) Social pressures (i.e. the need for helping hands in the house, early marriage, etc)____

19) i) In case your children are ill, are you financially capable of seeking medical attention?
   a) Yes   b) No
   ii) If yes, which of your children do you give priority to in case of ill-health or sickness (PRIORITIZE):
   a) Boy-children   b) Girl-children

20) Do you have access to (TICK appropriately):
   a) Water—piped (private)_____   b) Water—piped (common)_____
   c) Well (private)_____   d) Well (common)_____
   e) Tube well_____   f) Toilet (household)_____
   g) Toilet (common)_____   h) Lighting_____

D. Historical analysis of female-headship

1) Have your own mothers headed their household because of the:
   a) Early death of your father
   b) Illness and/or physical injury of your father

c) Father worked in the city and/or town-areas of Sri Lanka
d) Father was an alcoholic
e) Father was unemployed
f) Desertion, separation and/or divorce by your father

2) If yes to question 1, at what age do you think your mother headed her household?_____

3) Do you recall any economic hardship because of the absence of your father in the household?
    a) Yes   b) No

4) If no, was it because:
   i) Your mother owned land and property?
      a) Yes   b) No
   ii) Your kin relatives provided your mother economic support?
      a) Yes   b) No
   iii) If kin relatives provided economic support, was it because of (CIRCLE all applicable):
      a) Tradition and custom
      b) Cultural reasons
      c) Financial ability

5) i) Do you think kin-relatives are less likely to support female-relatives in need at this present juncture?
      a) Yes   b) No
   ii) If yes, is it because of:
      a) Changing economic circumstances and hardships
      b) Eroding traditions and customs
      c) Changing family structures (i.e. loosening extended family structures)

E. Perceptions of female-headed households

1) i) Are you aware of other households headed by women in your community and/or amongst your kin relatives?
      a) Yes   b) No

2) At the death, desertion, divorce, etc., of your husband, did your husbands or your own family provide economic security and help?
    a) Yes   b) No

3) In finding (i.e. productive) "work", how supportive was your family, friend, kin, etc?
    a) Very helpful
    b) Helpful
    c) Not helpful
    d) None of the above

4) In your definition of "work", do you include (CIRCLE all applicable):
   a) Domestic chores   b) Childcare activities
   c) Income-generating activities   d) Gardening

5) i) In non-monetary forms of support, do your relatives, friends, and/or the community provide any support?
      a) Yes   b) No
   ii) If yes, are they:
      a) Male relatives/friends   b) Female relatives/friends   c) Both
   iii) What forms of support do they provide (CIRCLE all applicable):
      a) Childcare (M/F)
      b) Cooking/cleaning (M/F)
      c) Gardening and/or sweeping-cleaning the garden (M/F)
      d) Going to the market (M/F)
      e) Plowing the agricultural field (M/F)
      f) Assisting in filing documents, etc (M/F)
      g) Other

6) i) If female relatives and/or friends provide support, do you think it is because women are more likely to perform traditional rights, duties and obligations?
      a) Yes   b) No
   ii) If yes, is it because women are more dependent upon norms of reciprocity within community structures because of potential vulnerability?
      a) Yes   b) No

7) i) Do you think perceptions held by kin, relatives, etc. influence their support towards you?
      a) Yes   b) No
   ii) If yes, who is more likely to expect you to abide by cultural/social norms of "good" behaviour?
      a) Males   b) Females
   iii) If a) do you see this in terms of controlling women's behaviour?
      a) Yes   b) No

8) i) Do you control your income so that it best suits your interest?
      a) Yes   b) No
   ii) Is your interest separable from the well being of the family?
      a) Yes   b) No

9) Do you think being a female-head had brought about:
   i) Positive social/cultural changes (i.e. where there have been transformations in traditional gender roles)?
      a) Yes   b) No
   ii) Positive economic changes?
      a) Yes   b) No

iii) Has there been an improvement in the well being of the family?
   a) Yes   b) No

10) i) Do you prefer traditional male-headed households?
    a) Yes   b) No
    ii) If yes, is it for: a) Economic reasons   b) Social reasons
                             c) Cultural reasons   d) All of the above

11) Has the change to female-headship brought a drastic change to your economic status?
    a) Yes   b) No

12) i) Do you feel economically vulnerable?
    a) Yes   b) No
    ii) Socially and/or culturally do you feel that female-headship has brought about much change?
    a) Yes   b) No

13) Do you consider single motherhood an aberration to the norm?
    a) Yes   b) No

14) i) Is it the conflict-ridden situation that has brought about this trend?
    a) Yes   b) No
    ii) If no, have there been instances in which you were aware of female-heads in the past (i.e. pre-conflict)?   a) Yes   b) No

15) i) Have you ever considered remarrying?   a) Yes   b) No
    ii) If no, is it related to your (CIRCLE all applicable):
        a) Religion, tradition and customs
        b) Community, kin, or relative's perceptions
        c) Children's disapproval of remarriage
        d) Your own choice

16) If you juggle between competing needs, do you depend on (informal) network connections?
    a) Yes   b) No

17) i) Are you a member of community-level organizations?
    a) Yes   b) No
    ii) If yes, do you think participating in these organizations is important for your well being?
    a) Yes   b) No
    iii) Are you interested and/or involved in political activity?
    a) Yes   b) No

APPENDIX C
Data Analysis: Methods, Motivations and Outcomes

Appendix C1: Methods of Data Analysis

Using SPSS (Statistical Package for the Social Sciences, version 9.0) there were three main techniques used for analysing data. The techniques used were determined by the usefulness of the method in obtaining particular outcomes, and they consisted of:
a) Descriptive Statistics
b) Chi-Square Tests
c) ANOVA (Analysis of Variance) Tests

Appendix C2: Motivations for Data Analysis

- Descriptive Statistics

Frequencies measure the proportion of sub-samples within each sample group. It is measured by:
  Sub-sample/Sample

- Chi-Square Tests

In SPSS a Chi-Square test forms the basis for association between two or more variables. A Chi-Square test is also known as Cross-Tab test, and is performed by carrying out the following steps.
a) Setting the hypothesis → Ho: no association
   → H1: there is an association
b) It calculates statistics by using a standardized measure of actual cell frequencies compared to expected cell frequencies. This statistic is distributed as a Chi-Square with degree of freedom, $n-1$, where n is the number of categories in the sample.
c) The next step involves comparing the computed statistic with the critical values from the Chi-Square tables.
d) If the computed value is greater than the critical value, then we can reject the null hypothesis (Ho) at the significant level of 0.05. In such instances, there is a significant association between the variables, and I have noted such instances as statistically significant.
e) Alternatively, it is possible to assess the probability value level is less than the significance level, then Ho is rejected.

- ANOVA (Analysis of Variance) Test

ANOVA tests assess the statistical significance between different groups.

a) Here the null hypothesis (Ho) is the equality of dependent variable means across groups against the alternative hypothesis (H1), which states that there is a difference between groups.
b) The test is carried out by using the F-statistic, which is calculated by → F = between groups mean square/within groups mean square
c) It calculates statistics by using a standardized measure of actual cell frequencies compared to expected cell frequencies. This statistic is distributed as an ANOVA test with a degree of freedom, $n - 1$, where n is the number of categories in the sample.
d) If the computed value is greater than the critical value, then we can reject the null hypothesis (Ho) at the significant level of 0.05. In such instances, there is a significant association between the variables, and I have noted such instances as statistically significant.
e) Alternatively, it is possible to assess the probability value level is less than the significance level, then Ho is rejected.

Appendix C3: Outcomes of Data Analysis

- Comparing Groups within Districts – The Results of Chi-Square Test
i) Ampara

	Value	Degrees of Freedom	Asymptotic Significance
a) De Facto headship			
Muslims and Tamils	4.786	3	0.188
Muslims and Sinhala	10.962	5	0.052
Sinhala and Tamil	8.806	4	0.066
b) Marital Status			
Muslims and Tamils	11.216	4	0.024
Muslims and Sinhala	5.796	4	0.215
Sinhala and Tamil	13.103	4	0.011
c) Occupations			
Muslims and Tamils	19.880	7	0.006
Muslims and Sinhala	20.390	4	0.000
Sinhala and Tamil	21.584	6	0.001
d) Spousal Death			
Muslims and Tamils	23.729	5	0.000
Muslims and Sinhala	10.781	4	0.029
Sinhala and Tamil	17.337	4	0.002

228 Matrilineal Communities, Patriarchal Realities

ii) Batticaloa

	Value	Degrees of Freedom	Asymptotic Significance
a) De Facto headship			
Muslims and Tamils	9.390	5	0.094
b) Marital Status			
Muslims and Tamils	6.991	4	0.136
c) Occupations			
Muslims and Tamils	33.638	5	0.000
d) Spousal Death			
Muslims and Tamils	17.906	7	0.012

iii) Trincomalee

	Value	Degrees of Freedom	Asymptotic Significance
a) De Facto headship			
Muslims and Tamils	6.465	4	0.167
Muslims and Sinhala	2.534	4	0.639
Sinhala and Tamil	4.684	5	0.456
b) Marital Status			
Muslims and Tamils	1.891	4	0.756
Muslims and Sinhala	4.865	4	0.301
Sinhala and Tamil	5.576	3	0.134
c) Occupations			
Muslims and Tamils	6.963	7	0.433
Muslims and Sinhala	6.942	4	0.139
Sinhala and Tamil	17.726	7	0.013
d) Spousal Death			
Muslims and Tamils	23.579	6	0.001
Muslims and Sinhala	10.969	5	0.050
Sinhala and Tamil	22.571	5	0.000

- Comparing Ethnic Groups across Districts – Results of Chi-Square Test

i) Muslims

	Value	Degrees of Freedom	Asymptotic Significance
a) De Facto headship			
Ampara and Batticaloa	4.277	4	0.370

Appendixes 229

Ampara and Trincomalee	2.544	4	0.637
Batticaloa and Trincomalee	6.360	5	0.273
b) Marital Status			
Ampara and Batticaloa	5.207	4	0.267
Ampara and Trincomalee	3.487	4	0.744
Batticaloa and Trincomalee	1.953	4	0.480
c) Occupations			
Ampara and Batticaloa	22.791	5	0.000
Ampara and Trincomalee	2.668	4	0.615
Batticaloa and Trincomalee	12.606	5	0.027
d) Spousal Death			
Ampara and Batticaloa	8.818	4	0.066
Ampara and Trincomalee	10.578	4	0.032
Batticaloa and Trincomalee	7.725	5	0.172

ii) Sinhala

	Value	Degrees of Freedom	Asymptotic Significance
a) De Facto headship			
Ampara and Trincomalee	8.141	6	0.228
b) Marital Status			
Ampara and Trincomalee	10.640	4	0.031
c) Occupations			
Ampara and Trincomalee	1.438	3	0.697
d) Spousal Death			
Ampara and Trincomalee	2.285	4	0.582

iii) Tamils

	Value	Degrees of Freedom	Asymptotic Significance
a) De Facto headship			
Ampara and Batticaloa	5.394	4	0.249
Ampara and Trincomalee	0.882	4	0.927
Batticaloa and Trincomalee	4.643	3	0.200
b) Marital Status			
Ampara and Batticaloa	12.239	4	0.016
Ampara and Trincomalee	0.386	3	0.943
Batticaloa and Trincomalee	9.320	4	0.054
c) Occupations			
Ampara and Batticaloa	4.716	7	0.695
Ampara and Trincomalee	2.980	7	0.887

Batticaloa and Trincomalee	4.543	7	0.716
d) Spousal Death			
Ampara and Batticaloa	1.873	5	0.866
Ampara and Trincomalee	0.720	5	0.982
Batticaloa and Trincomalee	1.354	5	0.929

Comparing Groups within Districts – Results of ANOVA Test for Income

i) Ampara

	Sum of Squares	df	Mean Square	F	Sig.
Between Groups	6894751.406	2	3447375.703	1.158	.319
Within Groups	285845564.251	96	2977557.961		
Total	292740315.657	98			

ii) Batticaloa

	Sum of Squares	df	Mean Square	F	Sig.
Between Groups	3162701.391	1	3162701.391	1.423	.236
Within Groups	215528662.245	97	2221944.972		
Total	218691363.636	98			

iii) Trincomalee

	Sum of Squares	df	Mean Square	F	Sig.
Between Groups	65479812.643	2	32739906.321	8.365	.000
Within Groups	379666876.317	97	3914091.508		
Total	445146688.960	99			

Comparing Ethnic Groups across Districts – ANOVA Test Results for Income

i) Muslims

	Sum of Squares	df	Mean Square	F	Sig.
Between Groups	55995834.711	2	27997917.356	6.699	.002
Within Groups	459722194.386	110	4179292.676		
Total	515718029.097	112			

ii) Sinhala

	Sum of Squares	df	Mean Square	F	Sig.
Between Groups	14391822.857	1	14391822.857	17.905	.000
Within Groups	54658011.429	68	803794.286		
Total	69049834.286	69			

iii) Tamils

	Sum of Squares	df	Mean Square	F	Sig.
Between Groups	3817030.616	2	1908515.308	.594	.554
Within Groups	359608154.167	112	3210787.091		
Total	363425184.783	114			

References

Agarwal, Bina. 1990. *Gender and Land Rights in Sri Lanka*. World Employment Program Research: Working Paper 49—Rural Employment Policy Research Programme Policy Series. Geneva: ILO.
———. 1996. *A Field of One's Own: Gender and Land Rights in South Asia*. New Delhi: Cambridge University Press (First edition, 1994).
———. 1997. "'Bargaining' and Gender Relations: Within and Beyond the Household." *Feminist Economics*. 3(1): 1–51.
Althusser, Louis. 1990. *For Marx*. Trans. Ben Brewster. London and New York: Verso (First edition, 1969).
Amnesty International (AI) 2000. *Annual Report 2000—Sri Lanka*. On-line. Available http://www.web.amnesty.org/web/ar2000web.nsf/countries
Anand, Sudhir and Ravi Kanbur. 1995. "Public Policy and Basic Needs Provision: Intervention and Achievement in Sri Lanka," in Jean Drèze, Amartya Sen and Athar Hussein (eds.) *The Political Economy of Hunger: Selected Essays*, pp. 59–92. Oxford, Clarendon Press.
Anker, Richard. 2000. *Conceptual and Research Frameworks for the Economics of Child Labour and its Elimination*. ILO/International Programme on the Elimination of Child Labour: Working Paper. Geneva: ILO.
Aturopane, Harsha, Chandra Rodrigo and Sasanka Perera. 1997. *Poverty Among Female-Headed Households in Sri Lanka*. Report prepared for the World Bank, Washington D.C. and the Regional Development Division, Ministry of Plan Implementation, Ethnic Affairs and National Integration. Colombo.
Basu, Kaushik. 1995. "The Elimination of Endemic Poverty in South Asia: Some Policy Options," in Jean Drèze, Amartya Sen, and Athar Hussain (eds.) *The Political Economy of Hunger: Selected Essays*, pp. 372–400. Oxford: Clarendon Press.
Becker, Gary. 1965. "A Theory of the Allocation of Time." *Economic Journal*. LXXV(299): 493–517.

Beneria, Lourdes and Gita Sen. 1981. "Accumulation, Reproduction, and Women's Role in Economic Development: Boserup Revisited." *Signs: Journal of Women in Culture and Society.* 7(2): 279–98.

Berik, Gunseli. 1997. "The Need for Crossing the Method Boundaries in Economics Research." *Feminist Economics.* 3(2): 121–25.

Bhasin, Kamla. 1993. *What is Patriarchy?* New Delhi: Kali for Women.

Bhatt, Ela. 1988. "They Run the Family and an Industry Too." *Social Welfare.* 35(6): 8–9.

Biyanwila, Janaka. 1997. "Suicide—The Question of Agency," in Jayadeva Uyangoda and Janaka Biyanwila (eds.) *Matters of Violence: Reflections on Social and Political Violence in Sri Lanka*, pp. 141–52. Colombo: Social Scientist Association.

Boserup, Ester. 1970. *Women's Role in Economic Development.* London: George Allen and Unwin.

Bourdieu, Pierre. 1998. *Practical Reason.* California: Stanford University Press.

———. 1999. *The Logic of Practice.* Trans. Richard Nice. California: Stanford University Press.

———. 2000. *Outline of a Theory of Practice.* Trans. Richard Nice. Cambridge: Cambridge University Press (First English edition, 1977).

Buvinic, Mayra, Nadia Youssef and Barbara Von Elm. 1978. *Women-Headed Households: The Ignored Factor in Development Planning.* Washington, D.C.: International Center for Research on Women.

——— and Geeta Rao Gupta. 1997. "Female-Headed Households and Female-Maintained Families: Are They Worth Targeting to Reduce Poverty in Developing Countries?" *Economic Development and Cultural Change.* 45(2): 259–80.

Cain, Mead, Syeda Rokeya Khanam and Shamsun Nahar. 1979. "Class, Patriarchy, and Women's Work in Bangladesh." *Population and Development Review.* 5(3): 405–38.

Casey, Margaret. 1993. "Development in Madura: An Anthropological Approach," in J. Pottier (ed.) *Practising Development: Social Science Perspectives*, 100–37. London: Routledge.

Center for Women's Research (CENWOR) 1993. *The Girl Child in Sri Lanka.* Report of a Workshop Held on October 20, 1993. Document Series No. 46. Colombo: CENWOR and UNICEF.

Chant, Sylvia. 1997. *Women-Headed Households: Diversity and Dynamics in the Developing World.* New York and London: McMillan Press.

Chatterjee, Partha. 1989. "The Nationalist Resolution of the Women's Question," in Kumkum Sangari and Sudesh Vaid (eds.) *Recasting Women: Essays in Colonial History*, pp. 233–53. New Delhi: Kali for Women.

———. 1993. "The Nations and Its Women," in Partha Chatterjee *The Nation and Its Fragments: Colonial and Post-Colonial Histories*, 116–34. Princeton: Princeton University Press.

Chen, Martha (ed). 1998. *Widows in India: Social Neglect and Public Action.* New Delhi: Sage Publications Ltd.

——— and Jean Drèze. 1992. "Widows and Health in Rural North India." *Economic and Political Weekly.* October 24–31: 81–92.

———, Jennefer Sebstad and Lesley O'Connell. 1999. "Counting the Invisible Workforce: The Case of Home-Based Workers." *World Development.* 27(3): 603–10.

———, Marilyn Carr and Jane Tate. 2000. "Globalization and Home-Based Workers." *Feminist Economics.* 6(3): 123–42.

Comaroff, John L. 1992. "*Sui genderis*: Feminism, Kinship Theory, and Structural 'Domains'" in Jane Fishburne Collier and Sylvia Junko Yanagisako (eds.) *Gender and Kinship: Essays Toward a Unified Analysis,* pp. 53–85. Stanford, Stanford University Press.

Coomaraswamy, Radhika. 1996. "Tiger Women and The Question of Women's Emancipation." *Pravada* 4(9): 8–10.

de Alwis, Malathi. 1994. "Towards a Feminist Historiography: Reading Gender in the Text of the Nation," in Radhika Coomaraswamy and Nira Wickramasinghe (eds.) *Introduction to Social Theory,* pp. 86–107. Colombo and Delhi: Konark Publishers Pvt Ltd., and International Center for Ethnic Studies.

———. 1997. "The Production and Embodiment of Respectability: Gendered Demeanors in Colonial Ceylon" in Michael Roberts (ed.) *Sri Lanka. Collective Identities Revisited: Volume I,* pp. 105–44. Colombo: Marga Institute.

———. 1998a. "Motherhood as a Space of Protest," in Patricia Jeffery and Amrita Basu (eds.) *Appropriating Gender: Women's Activism and Politicized Religion in South Asia,* pp. 185–201. London and New York: Routledge.

———. 1998b. "Moral Mothers and Stalwart Sons," in Lois Ann Lorentzen and Jennifer Turpin (eds.) *The Women and War Reader,* pp. 254–71. New York and London: New York University Press.

———. 1999. "Changing Role of Women in Sri Lankan Society." Presented at the Symposia on *The Context of the Sri Lankan Societal Conflict.* Held at the Marga Institute, Colombo on February 25th–26th 1999.

———. 2000. "Gender and Ethnicity," *Identity, Culture and Politics.* 1(1): 48–56.

de Beauvoir, Simone. 2000. *Memoirs of a Dutiful Daughter.* Trans. James Kirkup. London: Penguin. (First edition, 1963).

Department of Census and Statistics. 1981. *1971–81 Census of Sri Lanka.* Colombo.

———. 1995. *Women and Development in Sri Lanka.* Colombo.

England, Paula. 1993. "The Separative Self: Androcentric Bias in Neoclassical Assumptions," in Marianne Ferber and Julie Nelson (eds.) *Beyond*

Economic Man: Feminist Theory and Economics, pp. 37–53. Chicago: Chicago University Press.
Engels, Friedrich. 1978. "The Origin of the Family, Private Property, and the State," in Robert C. Tucker (ed.) *The Marx-Engels Reader*, pp. 734–59. New York and London: W. W. Norton & Company. (First edition, 1884).
Escobar, Arturo. 1995. *Encountering Development: The Making and Unmaking of the Third World.* New Jersey: Princeton University Press.
Esim, Simel. 1997. "Can Feminist Methodology Reduce Power Hierarchies in Research Settings." *Feminist Economics.* 3(2): 137–9.
Evans, Alison. 1991. "Gender Issues in Rural Household Economics," *IDS Bulletin.* 22(1): 51–9.
Ferguson, Ann and Nancy Folbre. 1981. "The Unhappy Marriage of Patriarchy and Capitalism," in Lydia Sargent (ed.) *Women and Revolution: A Discussion of the Unhappy Marriage of Marxism and Feminism*, pp. 313–41. Montreal: Black Rose Books.
Ferber, Marianne and Julie Nelson. 1993. "Introduction: The Social Construction of Economics and the Social Construction of Gender," in Marianne Ferber and Julie Nelson (eds.) *Beyond Economic Man: Feminist Theory and Economics*, pp. 1–22. Chicago: Chicago University Press.
Folbre, Nancy. 1986a. "Cleaning House: New Perspectives on Households and Economic Development." *Journal of Development Economics.* 22(1986): 5–40.
———. 1986b. "Hearts and Spades: Paradigms of Household Economics." *World Development.* 14(2): 245–55.
———. 1993. "Socialism, Feminist and Scientific," in Marianne Ferber and Julie Nelson (eds.) *Beyond Economic Man: Feminist Theory and Economics*, pp. 94–110. Chicago: Chicago University Press.
———. 1994. *Who Pays for the Kids?: Gender and the Structures of Constraints.* London: Routledge.
Gardner, Katy and David Lewis. 1996. *Anthropology, Development and the Post-Modern Challenge.* London and Chicago, Illinois: Pluto Press.
Goonasekera, Savitri. 1990. "Status of Women in the Family Law of Sri Lanka," in Sirima Kiribamune and Vidyamali Samarasinghe (eds.) *Women at the Crossroads: A Sri Lankan Perspective*, pp. 153–81. New Delhi: Vikas.
———. 1996. "Gender Relations in the Family: Law and Public Policy in Post-Colonial Sri Lanka," in Rajni Palriwala and Carla Risseeuw (eds.) *Shifting Circles of Support: Contextualizing Kinship and Gender in South Asia and Sub-Saharan Africa*, pp. 302–30. New Delhi, Thousand Oaks and London: Sage Publications.
Gunasinghe, Newton. 1996. "Caste, Kinship and Marriage in Ceylon and South India: A Critical Evaluation of Yalman's Thesis," in Sasanka Perera (ed.) *Newton Gunasinghe: Selected Essays*, pp. 161–70. Colombo: Social Scientist Assocation.

Guneratne, Arjun. 2001 (Forthcoming). "What's in a Name? Aryans and Dravidians in the Making of Sri Lankan Identities," in Neluka Silva (ed.) *The Hybrid Island: Culture Crossing in the Inversion of Identity in Sri Lanka*, pp. 20–40. Colombo: Social Scientist Association and London, Zed Books.

Hamid, Shamim. 1995. "Female-Headed Households," in Hossain Zillur Rahman and Mahabub Hussain (eds.) *Rethinking Rural Poverty: Bangladesh as a Case Study*, pp. 177–90. New Delhi, California, London: Sage Publications.

Haraway, Donna J. 1991. *Simians, Cyborgs, and Women: The Reinvention of Nature*. New York and London: Routledge.

Harding, Sandra. 1986. *The Science Question in Feminism*. Milton Keynes: Open University Press.

———. 1995. "Can Feminist Thought Make Economics More Objective?" *Feminist Economics*. 1(1): 7–32.

———. 1999. "The Case for Strategic Realism: A Response to Lawson." *Feminist Economics*. 5(3): 127–33.

Harrison, Francine. 2001. *Bride and Groom*. On-line. Available http://news.bbc.co.uk/hi/english/world/south_asia/default.stm (April 17th 2001)

Hartsock, Nancy. 1987. "The Feminist Standpoint: Developing the Ground for a Specifically Feminist Historical Materialism," in Sandra Harding (ed.) *Feminism and Methodology: Social Science Issues*, pp. 109–34. Bloomington: Indiana University Press.

Hartmann, Heidi. 1981. "The Unhappy Marriage of Marxism and Feminism: Towards a More Progressive Union," in Lydia Sargent (ed.) *Women and Revolution: A Discussion of the Unhappy Marriage of Marxism and Feminism*, pp. 1–41. Montreal: Black Rose Books.

Hirschon, Renee. 1984. "Introduction: Property, Power and Gender Relations," in Renee Hirschon (ed.) *Women and Property—Women as Property*, pp. 1–22. New York: St. Martin's Press.

Hoole, Rajan, Daya Somasundaram, K. Sritharan, and Rajani Thiranagama. 1990. *The Broken Palmyra: The Tamil Crisis in Sri Lanka—An Inside Account*. California: The Sri Lanka Studies Institute.

Humphries, Jane. 1977. "Class Struggle and the Persistence of the Working-Class Family." *Cambridge Journal of Economics*. 1(1): 241–58.

———. 1993. "Gender Inequality and Economic Development," in Dieter Bos (ed) *Economics in a Changing World, Volume 3: Public Policy and Economic Organization*, pp. 218–33. New York: St.Martin's Press.

———. 1995. "Economics, Gender and Equal Opportunities," in Jane Humphries and Jill Rubery (eds.) *The Economics of Equal Opportunities*, pp. 55–86. Manchester: Equal Opportunities Commission.

———. 1998a. "Female-Headed Households in Early Industrial Britain: The Vanguard of the Proletariat?" *Labour History Review*. 63(1): 31–65.

―――. 1998b. "Towards a Family-Friendly Economics." *New Political Economy* 3(2): 223–40.
Hyndman, Jennifer and Malathi de Alwis. 2000. "Capacity-Building, Accountability and Humanitarianism in Sri Lanka." *Forced Migration Review.* August 8, 16–17.
Institute of Social Studies Trust. 1984. *India's Female Headed Households.* Geneva: ILO.
Islam, Mahmuda. 1991. *Women Headed Households in Rural Bangladesh: Strategies for Survival.* Bangladesh: Narigrantha Prabartana.
Ismail, Qadri. 1995. "Unmooring Identity: The Antinomies of Elite Muslim Self-Representation in Modern Sri Lanka," in Pradeep Jeganathan and Qadri Ismail (eds.) *Unmaking the Nation: The Politics of Identity and History in Modern Sri Lanka,* pp. 55–105. Colombo: Social Scientist Association.
―――. 2000. "Constituting Nation, Contesting Nationalism: The Southern Tamil (Woman) and Separatist Tamil Nationalism in Sri Lanka," in Partha Chatterjee and Pradeep Jeganathan (eds.) *Subaltern Studies XI: Community, Gender, Violence,* pp. 212–82. New Delhi: Permanent Black.
Jackson, Cecile. 1998. "Rescuing Gender from the Poverty Trap," in Cecile Jackson and Ruth Pearson (eds.) *Feminist Visions of Development: Gender Analysis and Policy,* pp. 39–64. London and New York: Routledge.
――― and Ruth Pearson. 1998. "Introduction: Interrogating Development: Feminism, Gender and Policy." in Cecile Jackson and Ruth Pearson (eds.) *Feminist Visions of Development: Gender Analysis and Policy,* pp. 1–16. London and New York: Routledge.
Jayawardena, Kumari. 1986. "Emancipation and Subordination of Women in Sri Lanka," in Kumari Jayawardena *Feminism and Nationalism in the Third World,* pp. 109–36. London: Zed Books.
―――. 1992. "Some Aspects of Religious and Cultural Identity and the Construction of Sinhala Buddhist Womanhood," in Douglas Allen (ed.) *Religion and Political Conflict in South Asia: India, Pakistan, and Sri Lanka,* pp. 161–81. London: Greenwood Press.
―――. 2000. *Nobodies to Somebodies: The Rise of the Colonial Bourgeoisie in Sri Lanka.* Colombo: Social Scientist Association and Sanjiva Books.
――― and Malathi de Alwis. 1996. "Introduction," in Kumari Jayawardena and Malathi de Alwis (eds.) *Embodied Violence: Communalizing Women's Sexuality in South Asia,* pp. ix–xxiv. New Delhi, Kali for Women, London and New Jersey: Zed Books.
Kabeer, Naila. 1994. *Reversed Realities: Gender Hierarchies in Development Thought.* New York and London: Verso and New Delhi, Kali for Women.
―――. 1995. *Necessary, Sufficient or Irrelevant? Women, Wages and Intra-Household Power Relations in Urban Bangladesh.* Institute of Development Studies—Working Paper 25. Sussex: IDS.

———. 1996. *Gender, Demographic Transition and the Economics of Family Size: Population Policy for a Human-Centered Development.* United Nations Research Institute for Social Development: Occasional Paper 7. Geneva: UNRISD.
———. 1999. *The Conditions and Consequences of Choice—Reflections on the Measurement of Women's Empowerment.* United Nations Research Institute for Social Development: Discussion Paper 108. Geneva: UNRISD.
Klasen, Stephan. 1993. *Gender Inequality and Development Strategies: Lessons from the Past and Policy Issues for the Future.* World Employment Programme Research—International Employment Policies. Working Paper 41. Geneva: ILO.
Kodikara, Chulani. 1999. *Muslim Family Law in Sri Lanka: Theory, Practice and Issues of Concern to Women.* Colombo: Muslim Women's Research and Action Forum.
Kottegoda, Sepali. 1996. "Female Headed Housheolds in Situations of Armed Conflict." *Nivedini.* 4(2): 10–19.
Kumari, Ranjana. 1989. *Women-Headed Households in Rural India.* New Delhi: Radiant Publishers.
Lawson, Tony. 1997. *Economics and Reality.* London and New York: Routledge.
———. 1999. "Feminism, Realism and Universalism." *Feminist Economics.* 5(2): 25–59.
Leach, E. R. 1967. "An Anthropologist's Reflections on a Social Survey," in D. G. Jongmans and P.C.W. Gutkind (eds.) *Anthropologists in the Field,* pp. 75–88. Netherlands: Van Gorcum & Co.
Lehmann, David. 1999. *"Female-Headed Households in Latin America and the Caribbean: Problems of Analysis and Conceptualization."* Unpublished Mimeograph.
Lewis, David. 1993. "Going it Alone: Female-Headed Households, Rights and Resources in Rural Bangladesh," *European Journal of Development Research.* 5(2): 23–42.
Lingam, Lakshmi. 1994. "Women-Headed Households: Coping with Caste, Class and Gender Hierarchies." *Economic and Political Weekly.* March 19: 699–704.
Longino, Helen E. 1990. *Science as Social Knowledge: Values and Objectivity in Scientific Inquiry.* New Jersey: Princeton University Press.
Maunaguru, Sitralega. 1995. "Gendering Tamil Nationalism: The Construction of 'Woman' in Projects of Protest and Control," in Pradeep Jeganathan and Qadri Ismail (eds.) *Unmaking the Nation: The Politics of Identity and History in Modern Sri Lanka,* pp. 158–75. Colombo: Social Scientist Association.
MacDonald, Martha. 1995. "The Empirical Challenges of Feminist Economics: The Example of Economic Restructuring," in Edith Kuiper and Jolande Sap with Susan Feiner, Notburga Ott and Zafiris Tzannotos (eds.) *Out of*

the Margin: Feminist Perspectives on Economics, pp. 175–97. London: Routledge.

McGilvray, Dennis. 1982. "Mukkuvar Vannimai: Tamil Caste and Matriclan Ideology in Batticaloa, Sri Lanka," in Dennis McGilvray (ed.) Caste Ideology and Interaction, pp. 34–97. Cambridge: Cambridge University Press.

———. 1989. "Households in Akkaraipattu: Dowry and Domestic Organization among Matrilineal Tamils and Moors of Sri Lanka," in J. N. Gray and D. J. Mearns (eds.) Society From the Inside Out: Anthropological Perspectives on the South Asian Household, pp. 192–235. London: Sage Publications.

Mencher, Joan P. 1988. "Women's Work and Poverty: Women's Contribution to Household Maintenance in South Asia," in Daisy Dwyer and Judith Bruce (eds.) A Home Divided: Women and Income in the Third World, pp. 99–119. Stanford: Stanford University Press.

Moore, Henrietta L. 1996. "Mothering and Social Responsibilities in a Cross-Cultural Perspective," in Elizabeth Bortolaia Silva (ed.) Good Enough Mothering? Feminist Perspectives on Lone Motherhood, pp. 58–75. London: Routledge.

Moser, Caroline. 1989. "Gender Planning in the Third World: Meeting Practical and Strategic Gender Needs." World Development. 17(11): 1799–1825.

Narayan, Uma. 1997. Dislocating Cultures: Identities, Traditions and Third World Feminism. New York and London: Routledge.

Olmsted, Jennifer C. 1997. "Telling Palestinian Women's Economic Stories." Feminist Economics. l 3(2): 141–51.

Panda, Pradeep Kumar. 1997. Female Headship, Poverty and Child Welfare: A Study of Rural Orissa, India. Working Paper No. 280. Thirunanthapuram: Center for Development Studies.

Perera, Myrtle. 1991. "Female-Headed Households—A Special Poverty Group," in CENWOR (ed.) Women, Poverty and Family Survival, pp. 27–64. Colombo: CENWOR.

Pujol, Michele. 1997. "Introduction: Broadening Economic Data and Methods." Feminist Economics. 3(2): 119–120.

Rajasingham-Senanayake, Dharini. 1995. "On Mediating Multiple Identities: The Shifting Field of Women's Sexualities with the Community, State and Nation," in Margaret Schuler (ed.) From Basic Needs to Basic Rights, pp. 233–47. Washington, D.C.: The Institute of Women, Law and Development.

———. 1999. "Post Victimization: Cultural Transformation and Women's Empowerment in War and Displacement," in Selvy Thiruchandran (ed.) Women, Nation and Narration, pp. 136–51. New Delhi: Vikas.

Risseeuw, Carla. 1992. "Gender, Kinship and State Formation: Case of Sri Lanka under Colonial Rule." Economic and Political Weekly. October 24–31: 46–54.

Ruwanpura, Kanchana N. 2003. *The Survival Strategies of Sinhala Female-Heads in Conflict-Ridden Eastern Sri Lanka*. IFP/Crisis Response and Reconstruction. Working Paper 11. Geneva: ILO.

———. 2004a. "Dutiful Daughters, Sacrificing Sons." *Domains*. 1: 8–37.

———. 2004b. *Quality of Women's Work: A Focus on the South*. International Institute for Labour Studies. Discussion Paper 151. Geneva: ILO.

——— and Jane Humphries. 2004. "Mundane Heroines: Conflict, Ethnicity, Gender, and Female Headship in Eastern Sri Lanka." *Feminist Economics*. July 2004: 173–205.

Safilios-Rothschild, Constantina. 1982. "Female Power, Autonomy, and Demographic Change in the Third World," in Richard Anker, Mayra Buvinic and Nadia H. Youssef (eds.) *Women's Roles and Population Trends in the Third World*, pp. 117–32. London: Routledge.

Samaraweera, Vijaya. 1997. "The Muslim Revivalist Movement, 1880–1915," in Michael Roberts (ed.) *Sri Lanka. Collective Identities Revisited: Volume I*, pp. 293–321. Colombo: Marga Institute.

Samuel, Kumidini. 1994. "War and Survival—Women Heads of Household in the East." *Options*. August 1994: 16–18.

Scott, David. 1995. "Dehistoricising History," in Pradeep Jeganatha and Qadri Imail (eds.) *Unmaking the Nation: The Politics of Identity and History in Modern Sri Lanka*, pp. 10–24. Colombo: Social Scientist Association.

Sen, Amartya. 1981. "Public Action and the Quality of Life in Developing Countries." *Oxford Bulletin of Economics and Statistics*. 43(4): 287–319.

———. 1984a. "Development: Which Way Now?" in Amartya Sen *Resources, Values and Development*, pp. 485–508. Oxford: Basil Blackwell. (First published in 1983 *Economic Journal* 93: 745–62).

———. 1984b. "Economics and the Family," in Amartya Sen *Resources, Values and Development*, pp. 369–385. Oxford: Basil Blackwell. (First published in 1983 *Asian Development Review* 1: 745–62).

———. 1988. "The Concept of Development," in H. Chenery and T. N. Srinivasan (eds.) *Handbook of Development Economics, Volume I*, pp. 9–23.

———. 1990. "Gender and Cooperative Conflicts," in Irene Tinker (ed.) *Persistent Inequalities: Women and World Development*, pp. 123–149. New York and Oxford: Oxford University Press.

———. 1999. *Development as Freedom*. New York: Alfred A. Knopf Inc.

Solow, Robert. 1993. "Feminist Theory, Women's Experience, and Economics," in Marianne Ferber and Julie Nelson (eds.) *Beyond Economic Man: Feminist Theory and Economics*, pp. 153–8. Chicago: Chicago University Press.

Sharma, Ursula. 1984. "Dowry in North India: Its Consequences for Women," in Renee Hirschon (ed.) *Women and Property—Women as Property*, pp. 62–74. New York: St. Martin's Press.

Smith, Dorothy E. 1987. "Women's Perspective as a Radical Critique of Sociology," in Sandra Harding (ed.) *Feminism and Methodology: Social Science Issues*, pp. 84–96. Bloomington: Indiana University Press.

Thiruchandran, Selvy. 1994. "The Social Implications of Tecawalamai and their Relevance to the Status of Women in Jaffna." *Nivedini*. 2(1): 73–91.

———. 1997. *Ideology, Caste, Class and Gender*. Delhi: Vikas Publishing House.

———. 1999. *The Other Victims of War: Emergence of Female Headed Households in Eastern Sri Lanka: Volume II*. New Delhi: Vikas Publishing House.

United Nations Development Programme. 2000. *Human Development Report, 2001*. Oxford: Oxford University Press.

Van der Kemp, Oda. 1988. "Female-Headed Households in India," *Social Welfare*.35(6): 4–7.

Van Staveren, Irene. 1997. "Focus Groups: Contributing to a Gender-Aware Methodology." *Feminist Economics*. 3(2): 131–35.

Visaria, Praveen and Leela Visaria. 1985. "Indian Households with Female Heads: Their Incidence, Characteristics, and Levels of Living," in Devaki Jain and Nirmala Banerjee (eds.) *Tyranny of the Household: Investigative Essays on Women's Work*, pp. 50–83. India: Shakti Books.

Weerasinghe, Rohini. 1987. *Female Headed Households in Two Villages, Sri Lanka*. Colombo: Women's Education Center.

Woolf, Leonardo. 1981. *The Village in the Jungle*. Oxford: Oxford University Press. (First edition, 1913).

Whitehead, Ann. 1984. "Women and Men; Kinship and Property: Some General Issues," in Renee Hirschon (ed.) *Women and Property—Women as Property*, pp. 176–93. New York: St. Martin's Press.

Wyss, Brenda. 1999 "Culture and Gender in Household Economics." *Feminist Economics*. 5(2): 1–24.

Yanagisako, Sylvia Junko and Jane Fishburne Collier. 1992. "Toward a Unified Analysis of Gender and Kinship," in Jane Fishburne Collier and Sylvia Junko Yanagisako (eds.) *Gender and Kinship: Essays Toward a Unified Analysis*, pp. 14–50. Stanford, California: Stanford University Press.

Yalman, Nur. 1971. *Under the Bo Tree: Studies in Caste, Kinship, and Marriage in the Interior of Ceylon*. Berkeley: University of California Press.

Youssef, Nadia and Carol B. Hetler. 1981. *Women-Headed Household and Rural Poverty: What do we know?* Washington, D.C.: International Center for Research on Women.

———. 1983. "Establishing the Economic Condition of Women-Headed Households in the Third World: A New Approach," in Mayra Buvinic, Margaret A. Lycette and William Paul McGreevey (eds.) *Women and Poverty in the Third World*, pp. 216–43. London: The Johns Hopkins University.

———. 1984. *Rural Households Headed by Women: A Priority Concern for Development.* World Employment Programme Research: Working Paper 31—Rural Employment Policy Research Programme Policy Series. Geneva: ILO.